Key Stage Two
Year 4 Maths

Homework Sheets

Photocopiable Worksheets for Differentiated Learning

About the Book

This book has homework sheets for all the topics in Year 4 Maths. It can also be used with the books for Years 3, 5 and 6 to make a complete homework scheme for Key Stage 2 Maths.

Each Sheet in a Topic is More Difficult than the Last

We've split the Framework up into topics such as 'Fractions' or 'Number Patterns'. Each sheet covers objectives from the Framework.

For the first homework on Reading Scales, you'll set your class these sheets:

SUPPORT	Sheet 3
CORE	Sheet 4
EXTENSION	Sheet 5

For the second set of homework on Reading Scales, you set your class these sheets:

SUPPORT	Sheet 4
CORE	Sheet 5
EXTENSION	Sheet 6

Objective Coverage is Shown at the Front of the Book

For each sheet of a topic, we've said what objective or part-objective is being covered.

EXAMPLE TOPIC

Topic name.

Anything greyed out isn't covered on this sheet (but will be covered in another topic).

Reading Scales — Page Number

Sheet 3 .... **101**

Year 3 Objective

Key Objective "Read, to the nearest division and half-division, scales that are numbered or partially numbered; use the information to measure and draw to a suitable degree of accuracy."

Sheet 4 .... **102**

Year 4 Objective

"Interpret intervals and divisions on partially numbered scales and record readings accurately, where appropriate to the nearest tenth of a unit."

Sheet 5 .... **103**

Year 4 Objective

"Interpret intervals and divisions on partially numbered scales and record readings accurately, where appropriate to the nearest tenth of a unit."

Sheet 6 .... **104**

Year 5 Objective

"Interpret a reading that lies between two unnumbered divisions on a scale."

Online Resources

We've made a Resource Finder and Homework Tracker to help you use the Homework Sheets. They both have tutorials and are free. They're at www.cgpbooks.co.uk/ks2maths

Use the Resource Finder to Choose Homework Sheets

1. Select the school year and the strand or block you're teaching
2. Choose the topic or objective you need resources for.
3. It'll show you which Homework Sheets to use. It'll also suggest sheets for support and extension groups.

Don't worry, darling — it's not really black and white.

Oh, Hank, thank you. I was so terribly, terribly afraid.

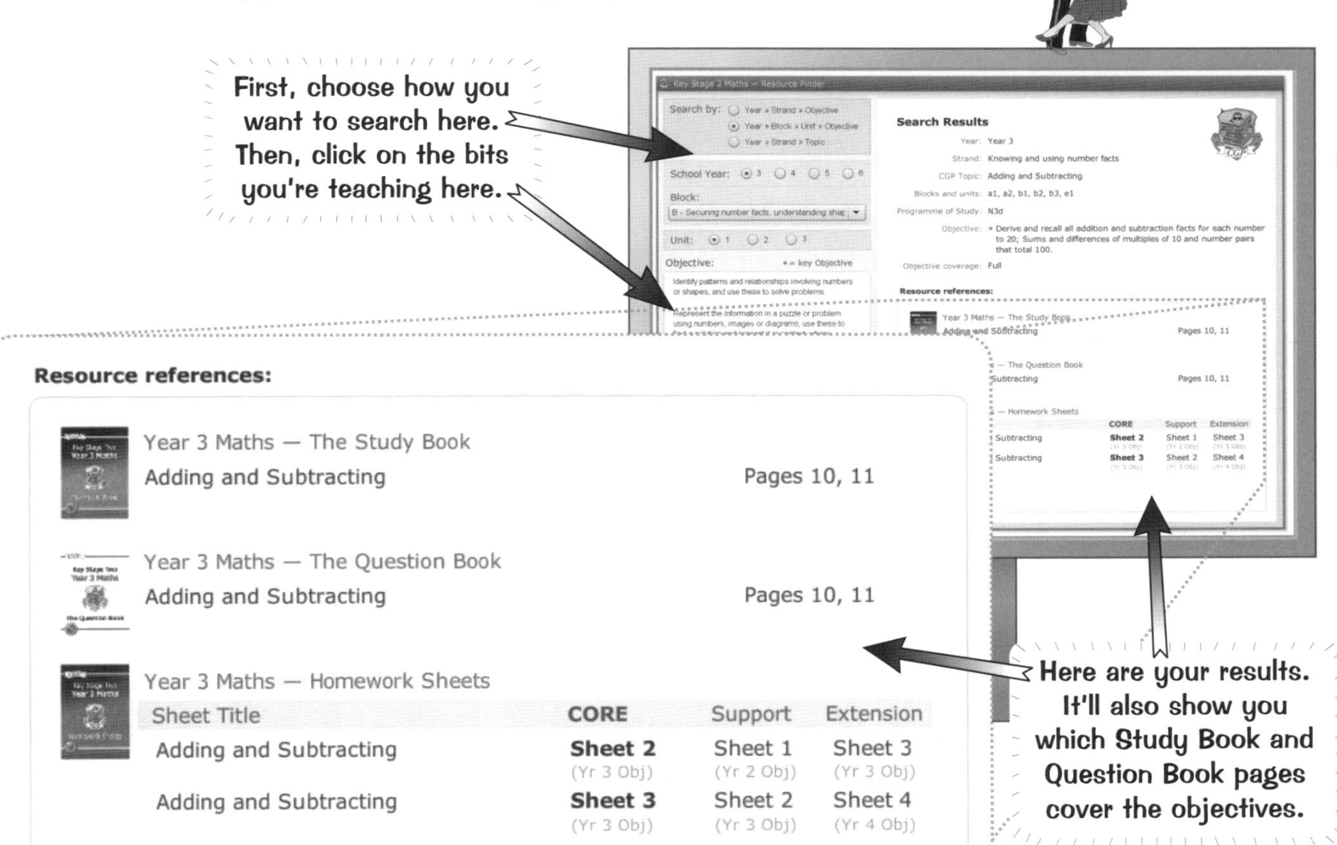

The Homework Tracker Records Each Pupil's Progress

The Homework Tracker is a spreadsheet. It'll help you record which sheets each child has completed, and if they've achieved the objective.

We've used traffic light colour-coding so you can see at a glance how well each child has done on the sheets. You can make sheets for individual pupils for use at parents' evenings.

At the end of the year, you can pass the spreadsheet on to the class's next teacher.

Published by Coordination Group Publications Ltd.

Editors:
Jane Aston, Joe Brazier, Katherine Craig, Charley Darbishire, Heather Gregson, Sarah Hilton, Sharon Keeley, Luke von Kotze, Simon Little, Hannah Louise Nash, Michael Southorn, Julie Wakeling.

Contributors:
Deborah Beattie, Emma Buckley, Stephanie Burton, Barbara Cartwright, Neil Davies, Sue Foord, Adam Higgins, Joanne Kingston, Anita Loughrey, Amanda MacNaughton, Chris Martin, Katy Servanté, Kim Sissons, Alyson Smith.

With thanks to Andrew Meller, Tina Ramsden, Glenn Rogers and Laurence Stamford for the proofreading.

ISBN: 978 1 84762 187 0

Groovy website: www.cgpbooks.co.uk

Printed by Elanders Hindson Ltd, Newcastle upon Tyne.
Jolly bits of clipart from CorelDRAW®
Thumb illustration used throughout the book © iStockphoto.com

Objective Coverage

Section 1 — Using and Applying Mathematics

Explaining Problem Solving

Page Number

Number Patterns

Planning Problem Solving

Objective Coverage

Problem Solving

Page Number

Write and Draw to Solve Problems

Objective Coverage

Section 2 — Counting and Understanding Number

Counting and Sequences

Page Number

Sheet 2 17

Year 3 Objective

"Read, write and order whole numbers to at least 1000 and position them on a number line; count on from and back to zero in single-digit steps or multiples of 10."

Sheet 3 18

Year 4 Objective

"Recognise and continue number sequences formed by counting on or back in steps of constant size."

Sheet 4 19

Year 5 Objective

"Count from any given number in whole-number and decimal steps, extending beyond zero when counting backwards; relate the numbers to their position on a number line."

Decimals

Sheet 1 20

Year 4 Objective

"Use decimal notation for tenths and hundredths and partition decimals; relate the notation to money and measurement; position one-place and two-place decimals on a number line."

Sheet 2 21

Year 4 Objective

"Use decimal notation for tenths and hundredths and partition decimals; relate the notation to money and measurement; position one-place and two-place decimals on a number line."

Sheet 3 22

Year 5 Objective

Key Objective

"Explain what each digit represents in whole number and decimals with up to two places, and partition, round and order these numbers."

Fractions

Sheet 2 23

Year 3 Objective

"Read and write proper fractions (e.g. 3/7, 9/10), interpreting the denominator as the parts of a whole and the numerator as the number of parts; identify and estimate fractions of shapes; use diagrams to compare fractions and establish equivalents."

Sheet 3 24

Year 4 Objective

Key Objective

"Use diagrams to identify equivalent fractions (e.g. 6/8 and 3/4, or 70/100 and 7/10); interpret mixed numbers and position them on a number line (e.g. 3 1/2)."

Sheet 4 25

Year 5 Objective

"Express a smaller whole number as a fraction of a larger one (e.g. recognise the 5 out of 8 is 5/8); find equivalent fractions (e.g. 7/10 = 14/20, or 19/10 = 1 9/10); relate fractions to their decimal representations."

Objective Coverage

Fractions and Decimals

Page Number

Sheet 1 .... **26**

Year 4 Objective

"Recognise the equivalence between decimal and fraction forms of one half, quarters, tenths and hundredths."

Sheet 2 .... **27**

Year 4 Objective

"Recognise the equivalence between decimal and fraction forms of one half, quarters, tenths and hundredths."

Sheet 3 .... **28**

Year 5 Objective

"Express a smaller whole number as a fraction of a larger one (e.g. recognise the 5 out of 8 is 5/8); find equivalent fractions (e.g. 7/10 = 14/20, or 19/10 = 1 9/10); relate fractions to their decimal representations."

Numbers and Number Lines

Sheet 2 .... **29**

Year 3 Objective

"Read, write and order whole numbers to at least 1000 and position them on a number line; count on from and back to zero in single-digit steps or multiples of 10."

Sheet 3 .... **30**

Year 4 Objective

"Partition, round and order four-digit whole numbers; use positive and negative numbers in context and position them on a number line; state inequalities using the symbols < and > (e.g. -3 > -5, -1 < +1)."

Sheet 4 .... **31**

Year 5 Objective

"Count from any given number in whole-number and decimal steps, extending beyond zero when counting backwards; relate the numbers to their position on a number line."

Partitioning

Sheet 2 .... **32**

Year 3 Objective

Key Objective "Partition three-digit numbers into multiples of 100,10 and 1 in different ways.."

Sheet 3 .... **33**

Year 4 Objective

"Partition, round and order four-digit whole numbers; use positive and negative numbers in context and position them on a number line; state inequalities using the symbols < and > (e.g. -3 > -5, -1 < +1)."

Sheet 4 .... **34**

Year 4 Objective

"Partition, round and order four-digit whole numbers; use positive and negative numbers in context and position them on a number line; state inequalities using the symbols < and > (e.g. -3 > -5, -1 < +1)."

Objective Coverage

Objective Coverage

Section 3 — Knowing and Using Number Facts

Adding and Subtracting

Page Number

Sheet 3 41

Year 3 Objective

Key Objective "Derive and recall all addition and subtraction facts for each number to 20; sums and differences of multiples of 10 and number pairs that total 100."

Sheet 4 42

Year 4 Objective

"Use knowledge of addition and subtraction facts and place value to derive sums and differences of pairs of multiples of 10, 100 or 1000."

Sheet 5 43

Year 5 Objective

Key Objective "Use knowledge of place value and addition and subtraction of two-digit numbers to derive sums and differences and doubles and halves of decimals (e.g. 6.5 ± 2.7, half of 5.6, double 0.34)."

Checking Calculations

Sheet 2 44

Year 3 Objective

"Use knowledge of number operations and corresponding inverses, including doubling and halving, to estimate and check calculations."

Sheet 3 45

Year 4 Objective

"Use knowledge of rounding, number operations and inverses to estimate and check calculations."

Sheet 4 46

Year 4 Objective

"Use knowledge of rounding, number operations and inverses to estimate and check calculations."

Sheet 5 47

Year 5 Objective

"Use knowledge of rounding, place value, number facts and inverse operations to estimate and check calculations."

Objective Coverage

Doubling and Halving

Page Number

Year 3 Objective

"Use knowledge of number operations and corresponding inverses, including doubling and halving, to estimate and check calculations."

Year 4 Objective

"Identify the doubles of two-digit numbers; use these to calculate doubles of multiples of 10 and 100 and derive the corresponding halves."

Year 5 Objective

Key Objective

"Use knowledge of place value and addition and subtraction of two-digit numbers to derive sums and differences and doubles and halves of decimals (e.g. 6.5 ± 2.7, half of 5.6, double 0.34)."

Fraction Pairs

Year 4 Objective

"Identify pairs of fractions that total 1."

Year 4 Objective

"Identify pairs of fractions that total 1."

Year 4 Objective

"Identify pairs of fractions that total 1."

Objective Coverage

Objective Coverage

Mental Maths

Page Number

Multiply by 10, 100 and 1000

Using Fractions

Objective Coverage

Written Adding and Subtracting

Page Number

Year 3 Objective

"Develop and use written methods to record, support or explain addition and subtraction of two-digit and three-digit numbers."

Year 4 Objective

"Refine and use efficient written methods to add and subtract two-digit and three-digit whole numbers and £.p."

Year 5 Objective

Key Objective

"Use efficient written methods to add and subtract whole numbers and decimals with up to two places."

Written Multiplying and Dividing

Year 3 Objective

"Use practical and informal written methods to multiply and divide two-digit numbers (e.g. 13 × 3, 50 ÷ 4); round remainders up or down, depending on the context."

Year 4 Objective

Key Objective

"Develop and use written methods to record, support and explain multiplication and division of two-digit numbers by a one-digit number, including division with remainders (e.g. 15 x 9, 98 ÷ 6)."

Year 5 Objective

"Refine and use efficient written methods to multiply and divide HTU x U, TU x TU, U.t x U and HTU ÷ U."

Objective Coverage

Section 5 — Understanding Shape

2D Shapes

Page Number

Sheet 2 77

Year 3 Objective

"Relate 2-D shapes and 3-D solids to drawings of them; describe, visualise, classify, draw and make the shapes."

Sheet 3 78

Year 4 Objective

"Draw polygons and classify them by identifying their properties, including their line symmetry."

Sheet 4 79

Year 5 Objective

"Identify, visualise and describe properties of rectangles, triangles, regular polygons and 3-D solids; use knowledge of properties to draw 2-D shapes, and to identify and draw nets of 3-D shapes."

3D Shapes

Sheet 2 80

Year 3 Objective

"Relate 2-D shapes and 3-D solids to drawings of them; describe, visualise, classify, draw and make the shapes."

Sheet 3 81

Year 4 Objective

"Visualise 3-D objects from 2-D drawings; make nets of common solids."

Sheet 4 82

Year 5 Objective

"Identify, visualise and describe properties of rectangles, triangles, regular polygons and 3-D solids; use knowledge of properties to draw 2-D shapes, and to identify and draw nets of 3-D shapes."

Angles

Sheet 2 83

Year 3 Objective

"Use a set-square to draw right angles and to identify right angles in 2-D shapes; compare angles with a right angle; recognise that a straight line is equivalent to two right angles."

Sheet 3 84

Year 4 Objective

Key Objective

"Know that angles are measured in degrees and that one whole turn is 360°; compare and order angles less than 180°."

Sheet 4 85

Year 5 Objective

"Estimate, draw and measure acute and obtuse angles using an angle measurer or protractor to a suitable degree of accuracy; calculate angles in a straight line."

Objective Coverage

Coordinates

Page Number

Year 3 Objective

"Read and record the vocabulary of position, direction and movement, using the four compass directions to describe movement about a grid."

Year 4 Objective

"Recognise horizontal and vertical lines; use the eight compass points to describe direction; describe and identify the position of a square on a grid of squares."

Year 5 Objective

Key Objective "Read and plot coordinates in the first quadrant; recognise parallel and perpendicular lines in grids and shapes; use a set-square and ruler to draw shapes with perpendicular or parallel sides."

Drawing Shapes

Year 3 Objective

"Use a set-square to draw right angles and to identify right angles in 2-D shapes; compare angles with a right angle; recognise that a straight line is equivalent to two right angles."

Year 4 Objective

"Recognise horizontal and vertical lines; use the eight compass points to describe direction; describe and identify the position of a square on a grid of squares."

Year 5 Objective

Key Objective "Read and plot coordinates in the first quadrant; recognise parallel and perpendicular lines in grids and shapes; use a set-square and ruler to draw shapes with perpendicular or parallel sides."

Symmetry

Year 3 Objective

Key Objective "Draw and complete shapes with reflective symmetry; draw the reflection of a shape in a mirror line along one side."

Year 4 Objective

"Draw polygons and classify them by identifying their properties; identify the line symmetry of polygons."

Year 5 Objective

"Complete patterns with up to two lines of symmetry; draw the position of a shape after reflection or translation."

Objective Coverage

Section 6 — Measuring

Calculating Perimeter and Area

Page Number

Year 4 Objective

"Draw rectangles and measure and calculate their perimeters; find the area of rectilinear shapes drawn on a square grid by counting squares."

Year 4 Objective

"Draw rectangles and measure and calculate their perimeters; find the area of rectilinear shapes drawn on a square grid by counting squares."

Year 5 Objective

Key Objective

"Draw and measure lines to the nearest millimetre; measure and calculate the perimeter of regular and irregular polygons; use the formula for the area of a rectangle to calculate the rectangle's area."

Drawing and Measuring

Year 3 Objective

Key Objective

"Read, to the nearest division and half-division, scales that are numbered or partially numbered; use the information to measure and draw to a suitable degree of accuracy."

Year 4 Objective

"Draw rectangles and measure and calculate their perimeters; find the area of rectilinear shapes drawn on a square grid by counting squares."

Year 5 Objective

Key Objective

"Draw and measure lines to the nearest millimetre; measure and calculate the perimeter of regular and irregular polygons; use the formula for the area of a rectangle to calculate the rectangle's area."

Objective Coverage

Reading Scales

Page Number

Year 3 Objective

Key Objective "Read, to the nearest division and half-division, scales that are numbered or partially numbered; use the information to measure and draw to a suitable degree of accuracy."

Year 4 Objective

"Interpret intervals and divisions on partially numbered scales and record readings accurately, where appropriate to the nearest tenth of a unit."

Year 4 Objective

"Interpret intervals and divisions on partially numbered scales and record readings accurately, where appropriate to the nearest tenth of a unit."

Year 5 Objective

"Interpret a reading that lies between two unnumbered divisions on a scale."

Time

Year 3 Objective

"Read the time on a 12-hour digital clock and to the nearest 5 minutes on an analogue clock; calculate time intervals and find start or end times for a given time interval."

Year 4 Objective

"Read time to the nearest minute; use am, pm and 12-hour clock notation; choose units of time to measure time intervals; calculate time intervals from clocks and timetables."

Year 5 Objective

"Read timetables and time using 24-hour clock notation; use a calendar to calculate time intervals."

Objective Coverage

Units and Measures

Page Number

Sheet 3 .... **108**

Year 3 Objective

"Know the relationships between kilometres and metres, metres and centimetres, kilograms and grams, litres and millilitres; choose and use appropriate units to estimate, measure and record measurements."

Sheet 4 .... **109**

Year 4 Objective

Key Objective

"Choose and use standard metric units and their abbreviations when estimating, measuring and recording length, weight and capacity; know the meaning of 'kilo', 'centi' and 'milli' and, where appropriate, use decimal notation to record measurements (e.g. 1.3 m or 0.6 kg)."

Sheet 5 .... **110**

Year 4 Objective

Key Objective

"Choose and use standard metric units and their abbreviations when estimating, measuring and recording length, weight and capacity; know the meaning of 'kilo', 'centi' and 'milli' and, where appropriate, use decimal notation to record measurements (e.g. 1.3 m or 0.6 kg)."

Sheet 6 .... **111**

Year 5 Objective

"Read, choose, use and record standard metric units to estimate and measure length, weight and capacity to a suitable degree of accuracy (e.g. the nearest centimetre); convert larger to smaller units using decimals to one place (e.g. change 2.6 kg to 2600 g)."

Section 7 — Handling Data

Data

Sheet 2 .... **112**

Year 3 Objective

"Answer a question by collecting, organising and interpreting data; use tally charts, frequency tables, pictograms and bar charts to represent results and illustrate observations; use ICT to create a simple bar chart."

Sheet 3 .... **113**

Year 4 Objective

Key Objective

"Answer a question by identifying what data to collect; organise, present, analyse and interpret the data in tables, diagrams, tally charts, pictograms and bar charts, using ICT where appropriate."

Sheet 4 .... **114**

Year 5 Objective

"Answer a set of related questions by collecting, selecting and organising relevant data; draw conclusions, using ICT to present features, and identify further questions to ask."

Objective Coverage

Tables and Charts

Page Number

Year 3 Objective

"Answer a question by collecting, organising and interpreting data; use tally charts, frequency tables, pictograms and bar charts to represent results and illustrate observations; use ICT to create a simple bar chart."

Year 4 Objective

Key Objective

"Answer a question by identifying what data to collect; organise, present, analyse and interpret the data in tables, diagrams, tally charts, pictograms and bar charts, using ICT where appropriate."

Year 4 Objective

"Compare the impact of representations where scales have intervals of differing step size."

Year 5 Objective

Key Objective

"Construct frequency tables, pictograms and bar and line graphs to represent the frequencies of events and changes over time."

Explaining Problem Solving

1 **Louise has invited 26 children to her birthday party.**

17 of the children are girls. Cross off 17 people in the picture to find out how many boys there are.

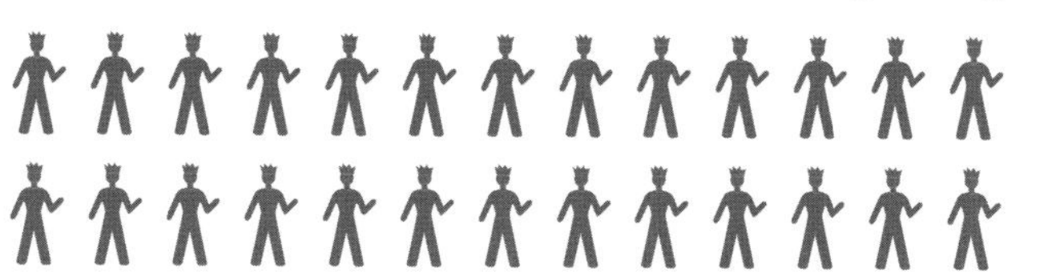

Number of boys = 

2 **Louise has 6 cakes. Each cake is cut into 5 slices.**

a) What is the total number of slices that she has? Draw a picture to help you work it out.

b) 13 slices are eaten. How many whole cakes are left? Use your picture to help you.

Whole cakes left: ☐

3 **Find a quick way to add and subtract these numbers. The first one has been done for you.**

Subtract 20. Then add 1.

a) $48 - 19 = 48 - 20 + 1 = 28 + 1 = 29$

b) $54 + 27 =$

c) $148 - 95 =$

Activity Joshua has 44 stickers. He keeps 23. He gives the rest to Ruth and David. He gives <u>at least</u> 5 stickers to Ruth and <u>at least</u> 8 to David. Write down all the ways he can give out the stickers.

Learning Objective:

"I can explain how I solve problems."

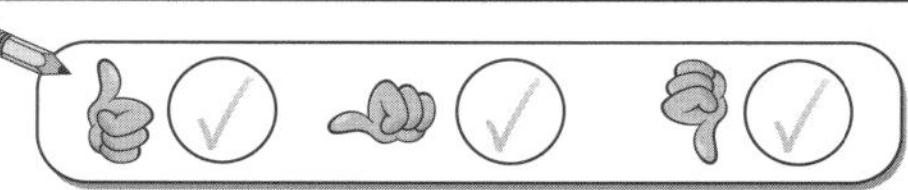

 Name: .... Date: ....

Explaining Problem Solving

1 **Here are some signs:** 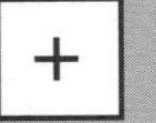 − ÷ 

Use the signs to make these calculations correct:

a) 18 ☐ 3 = 6

b) 24 ☐ 9 = 15

c) 42 ☐ 12 ☐ 54

2 **Grace has saved up £4.30 to buy a new basketball. Her mum gives her £2.45 more.**

How much money does she have altogether? Show your working.

3 **A sports shop has the following offers:**

Naseen wants to buy 6 tennis balls.
Which is the cheapest offer?
Explain your answer.

Activity Write a word problem that could be solved using the calculation 7 × 4.

Learning Objective:

"I can explain to someone else how I solved a problem or puzzle."

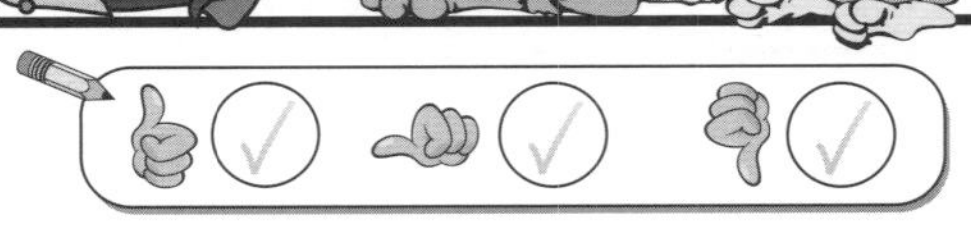

Explaining Problem Solving

1 There are 3 different types of chocolate in a jar. Rosie takes out a chocolate without looking.

a) Which chocolate is Rosie most likely to pull out? Explain how you know.

b) Rosie puts the chocolate back and adds three more orange chocolates to the jar. Which type is she most likely to pull out now? Explain why.

2 25 is a square number.

Draw a diagram to explain how you know this.

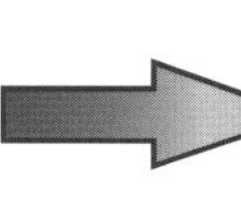

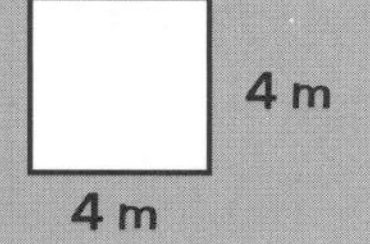

3 A garden centre sells square concrete slabs like this: Romina buys 6 square concrete slabs for her patio.

4 m

4 m

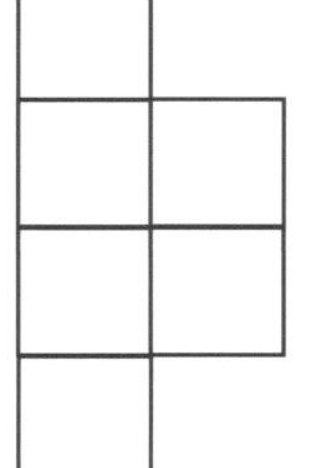

She lays the slabs in the pattern shown. What is the perimeter of Romina's patio? Show your working.

Activity Zach rolls two dice (numbered 1 to 6). Write down all the number combinations that he could have rolled for the following scores:

3 5 6 8 10 11 12

Learning Objective:

"I can write down how I solved a problem, showing every step."

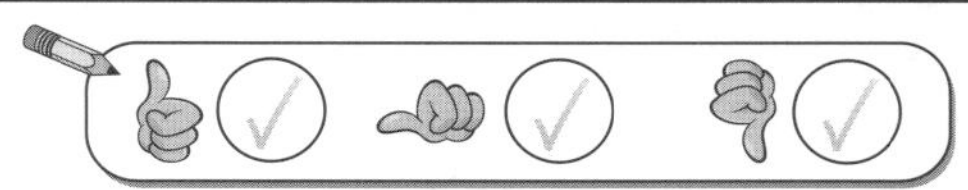

 Name: .... Date: ....

Number Patterns

1 Complete the sequence and work out the rule:

a) 70 60 ☐ ☐ 30 ☐ ☐ The rule is subtract 10.

b) 4 6 ☐ 10 ☐ ☐ ☐ The rule is ☐

c) 8 11 ☐ ☐ 20 ☐ ☐ The rule is ☐

d) 35 30 25 ☐ ☐ ☐ ☐ The rule is ☐

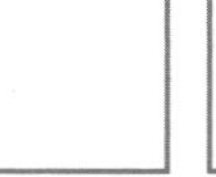
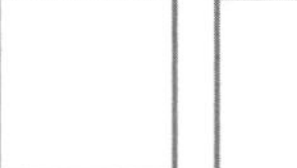

2 Helen makes a sequence. She doubles the number each time.

2 4 8 ☐ ☐ ☐

a) Fill in the empty boxes.

b) Will there ever be an odd number in this pattern? Give a reason.

☐

3 Look at this pattern made with matches:

3 matches 5 matches 7 matches 9 matches

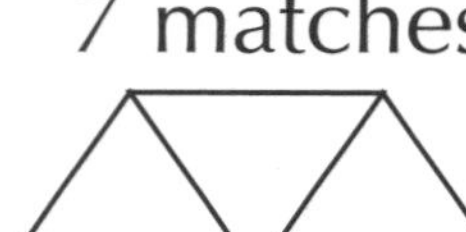
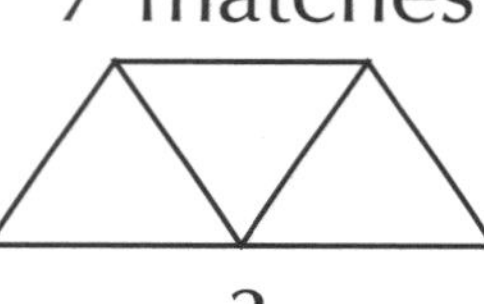
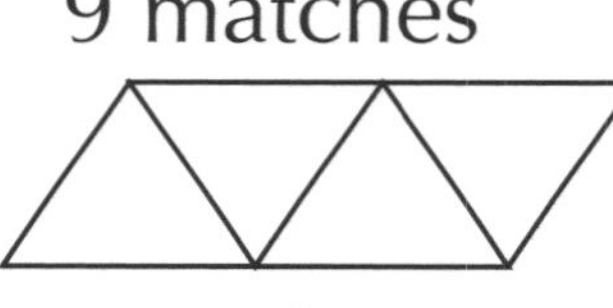

1 2 3 4

a) How many matches will Shape 5 use? ☐

b) What is the pattern for the number of matches?

☐

Activity Draw as many shapes as you can with exactly <u>2 right angles</u>. You should use <u>straight lines</u>.

Learning Objective:

"I can predict what the next value will be in a sequence."

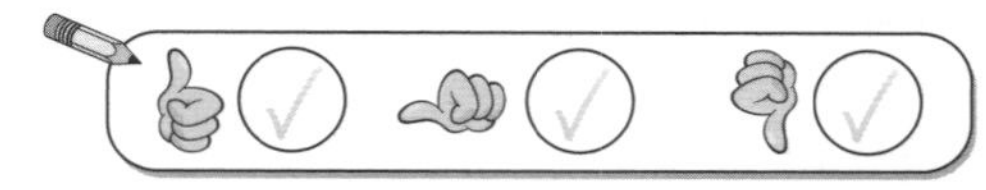

Number Patterns

1 Fill in the missing numbers and work out the rule:

a) 32 36 40 ☐ ☐ ☐ The rule is ☐

b) 450 400 350 ☐ ☐ ☐ The rule is ☐

c) ☐ ☐ ☐ ☐ 80 100 120 The rule is ☐

2 Alex has some numbered cards:

2 3 4 7

Use the cards to make 2 sums where the answers are <u>odd</u> numbers.

a) ☐☐ + ☐☐ b) ☐☐ + ☐☐

c) Complete the rule by circling the correct word in each box:

Odd / Even + Odd / Even = Odd Number

3 Grid A is a pattern on your classroom window.

In Grid B draw how the pattern would look from the other side of the glass.

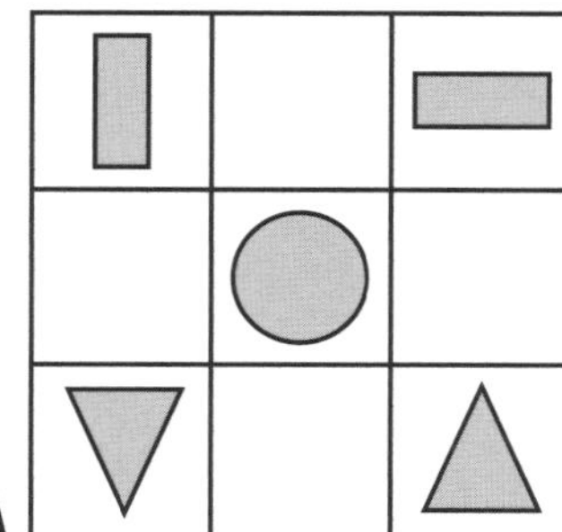

Grid A

Grid B

Use the line of reflection to help.

Activity You need to make <u>less than 20p</u> using <u>only 2 coins</u>. Record the different <u>amounts</u> and which <u>coins</u> you have used.

Learning Objective:

"I can identify patterns between numbers and test them with my own examples."

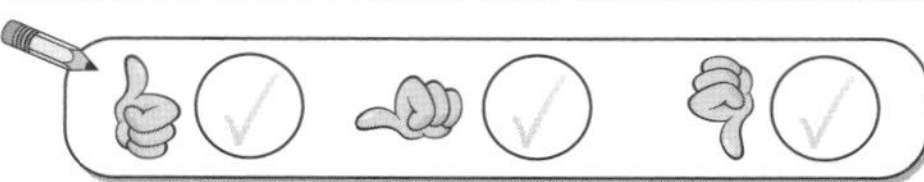

Number Patterns

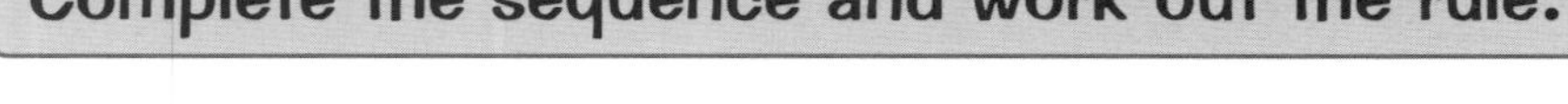
1 Complete the sequence and work out the rule:

a) 63 51 ☐ ☐ ☐ ☐ The rule is ☐

b) 80 105 ☐ ☐ ☐ ☐ The rule is ☐

c) 3 6 12 ☐ ☐ ☐ The rule is ☐

2 Jane says "Any number ending in 28 will always be divisible by 4."

Do you agree with Jane? Explain your answer.

☐

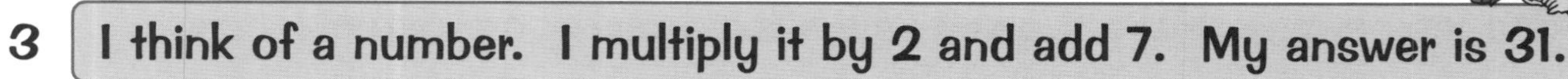
3 I think of a number. I multiply it by 2 and add 7. My answer is 31.

What was my original number? Remember to show your working.

☐

4 Katie draws two shapes.

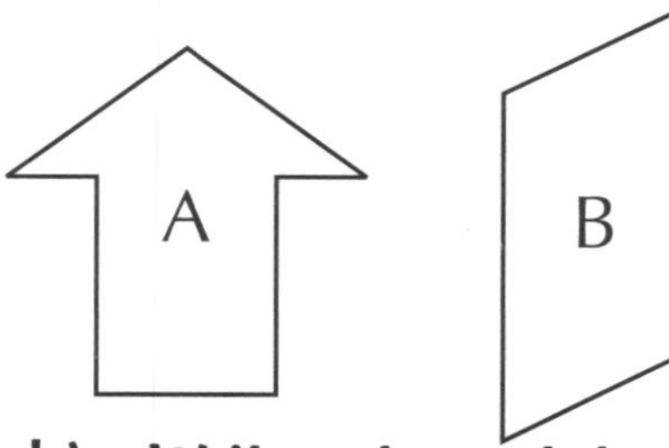

a) True or False?

Shape A is a hexagon. ☐

Shape B has 2 pairs of parallel lines. ☐

b) Write a true statement about the angles in Shape A.

☐

c) Write a false statement about the lines of symmetry in Shape B.

☐

Activity Lewis thinks of a number. It's odd, less than 50 and a multiple of 3. List all the numbers Lewis could be thinking of.

Learning Objective:

"I can make up my own statements about patterns of numbers and shapes using examples."

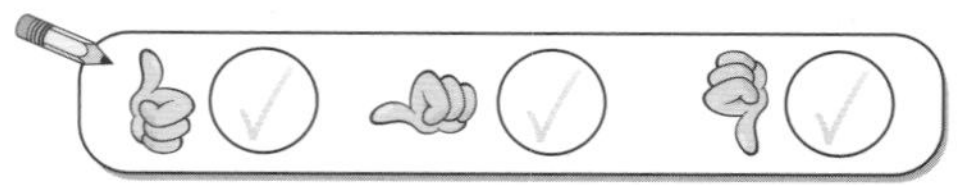

Planning Problem Solving

1 **Draw each shape in the correct place on the diagram. The first two have been done for you.**

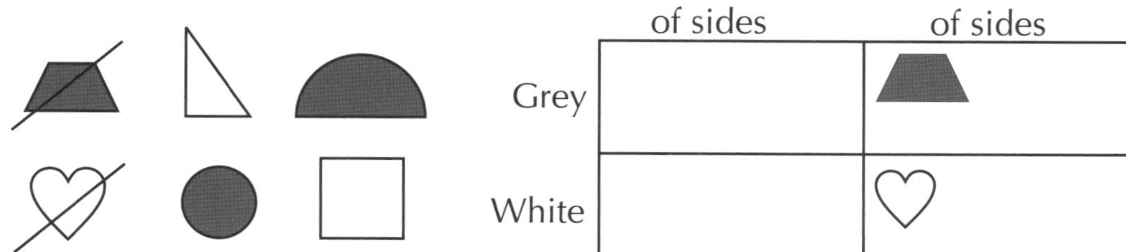

2 **Use this diagram to complete the table.**

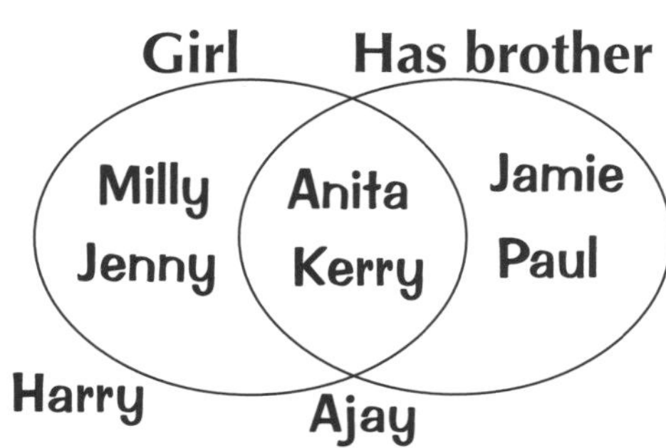

Boys		Girls	
Name	**Has brother**	**Name**	**Has brother**
Ajay	✗	Anita	✓
Harry		Jenny	
Jamie		Kerry	
Paul		Milly	

3 **The table shows how much money an ice-cream kiosk made.**

Day	Number of ice-creams sold	Money collected
Monday	19	£32
Tuesday	27	£40
Wednesday	31	£39
Thursday	42	£48
Friday	34	£53

a) On which day did they collect the most money?

b) How many ice-creams were sold that day ?

c) How many more ice-creams were sold on Thursday than on Tuesday?

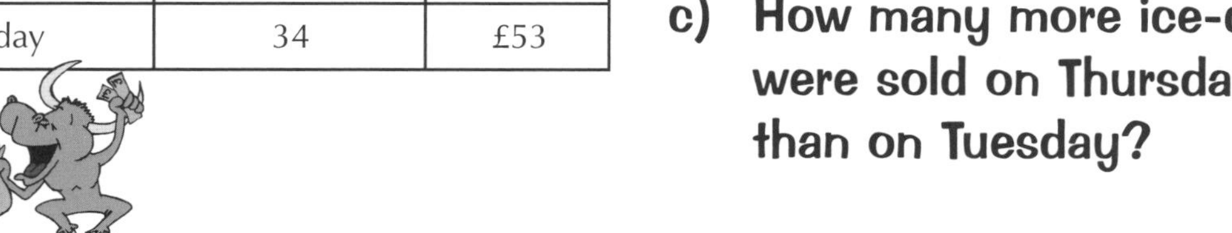

What different shapes can you make by shading four squares that are side-by-side? Here's one to get you started.

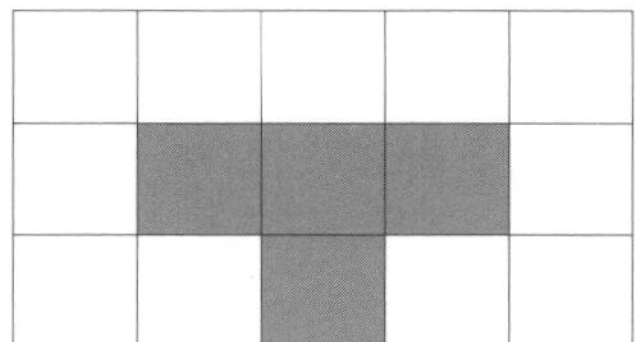

Learning Objective:

"I can decide what information to use to answer questions involving tables and diagrams."

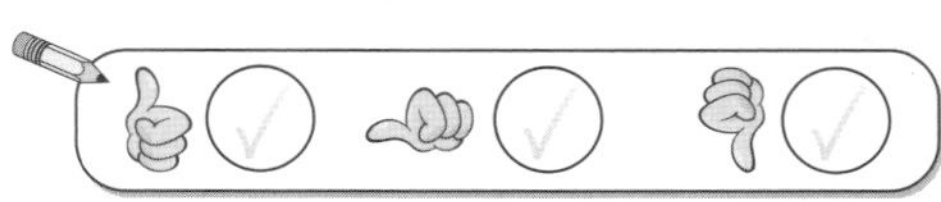

 Name: .... Date: ....

Planning Problem Solving

1 **Put each letter in the correct place on the diagram. The first two have been done for you.**

~~N~~ ~~D~~ A

S C G

	Only straight lines	Only curved lines	Straight and curved lines
No lines of symmetry	N		
One or more lines of symmetry			D

2 **The children in Class 4 did a survey about their favourite types of newt. They started to put their results in a frequency table.**

Type of newt	Tally	Total
Smooth	~~IIII~~ II	7
Palmate	~~IIII~~ ~~IIII~~ I	
Crested		
Banded		

a) Complete the total for palmate newts.

b) One more child liked crested newts than liked palmate newts. Complete the tally and total for crested newts.

c) There are 32 children in the class. Complete the banded newt information.

3 **Charlotte needs to buy 10 buns. She has £2.**

Cherry — 15p
Iced — 25p
Cream — 20p

a) If she buys 5 cherry buns, can she also buy 5 iced buns?

b) Charlotte buys 4 cream buns, 4 cherry buns and 2 iced buns. How much change will she get from £2?

Activity In question 1 you sorted some letters. Find some other ways of sorting letters of the alphabet. E.g. letters in your name and letters not in your name. Make a table or diagram to show your sorting.

Learning Objective:

"I can organise information and use it to answer questions."

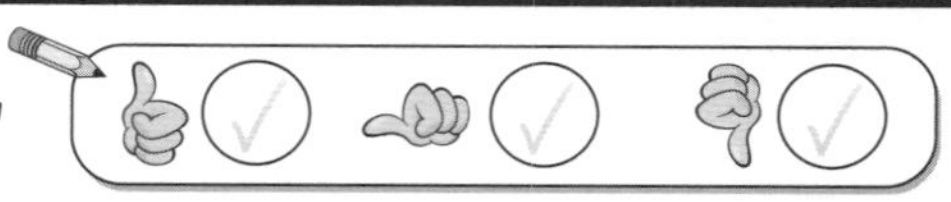

Planning Problem Solving

1 Some children have recorded their ages and heights.

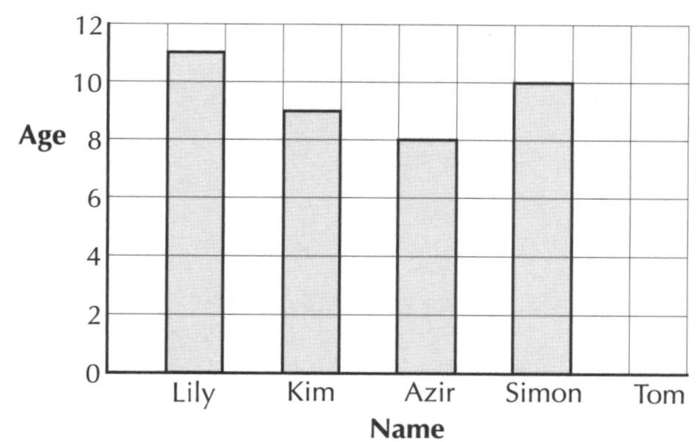

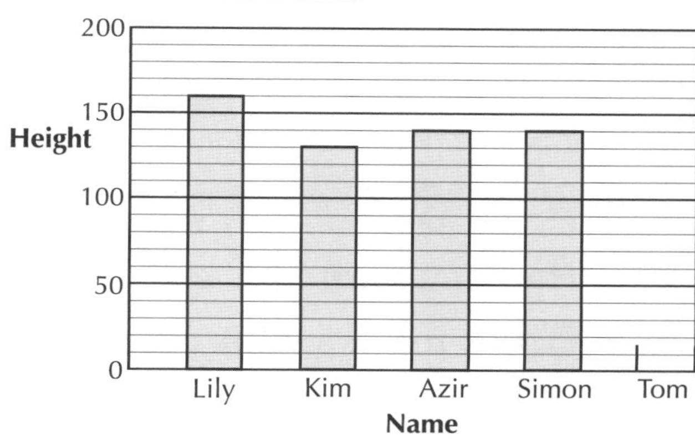

a) Tom is 9 years old and is 150 cm tall. Record this information on the two graphs above.

b) Use the graphs to complete the table on the right.

	Shorter than 150 cm	150 cm or taller
10 or older		Lily
Younger than 10		

2 This table shows which pets belong to a group of children.

Name	Cat	Dog	Rabbit	Fish	Snake
Charlie		✓			✓
Ella	✓	✓			
Holly			✓		
Archie				✓	
Amy	✓	✓		✓	

a) Which child owns the most pets?

b) Who owns a dog but not a cat?

c) Write down another question that could be answered using this chart, then answer it.

Activity

Here is the menu at the Pudding Parlour:

Vanilla or Strawberry Ice Cream
Chocolate or Toffee Sauce
Marshmallow or Jelly bean toppings

Using an ice cream, a sauce and a topping each time, how many different puddings can you make from these choices?

Learning Objective:

"I can organise and understand information."

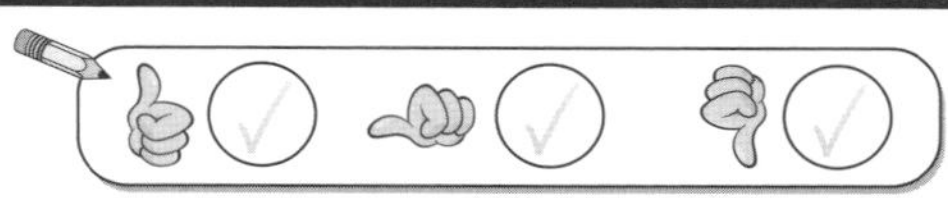

Problem Solving

1 **Sam bought a book and a pen.**

£1.60

95p

a) How much did he spend altogether?

£

b) He pays with £5.
Circle the coins he would get in his change.

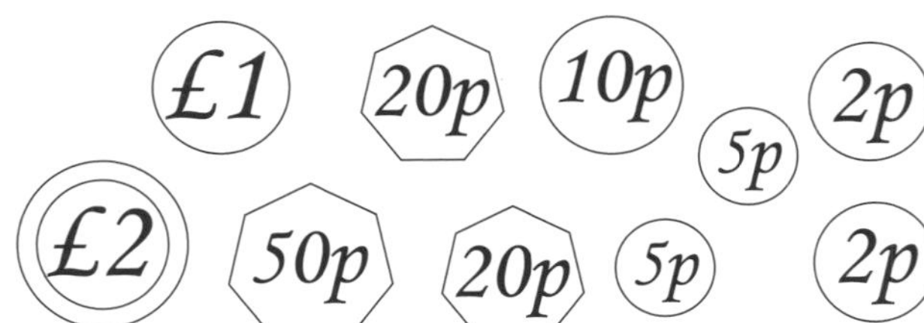

2 **My watch reads 11:03.**

a) What time was it 5 minutes ago? :

b) What time will it be in 1 hour and 5 minutes? :

3 **Chairs are 30 cm wide. How many will fit across a 330 cm room?**

4 **Anna sleeps for 8 hours each night and 2 hours each afternoon.**

How many hours does she sleep each week? Show how you work it out.

Activity

How long do you spend at school each day?
How many hours is this a week?
Work out how long you spend on other activities.

Learning Objective:

"I can work out what calculations to do to solve a word problem."

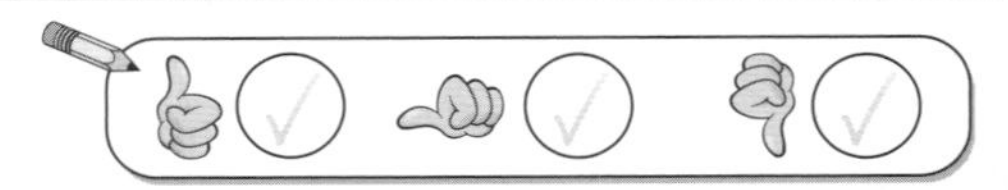

Problem Solving

You can use a calculator for this sheet

1 Chloe needs £34.99 to buy a game.
Gran gives her £15.75 and dad gives her £17.23.

a) How much money does she have?

b) How much more does she need?

2 Andy runs 100 m each day of the week. Here are his times in seconds:

16.6 s 17.0 s 16.8 s 17.2 s 17.4 s 16.7 s 17.1 s

a) What is the difference between his best and worst times?

b) How long in seconds does he spend running that week?

3 3rd prize in a competition is £167.
2nd prize is double this amount.
1st prize is the 2nd and 3rd prizes added together.

How much are the 2nd and 1st prizes.

2nd prize = £ 1st prize = £

Activity Ask 5 friends how long it takes them to get to school.
Find the difference between the longest and shortest times.

Learning Objective:

"I can solve problems with one or two steps."

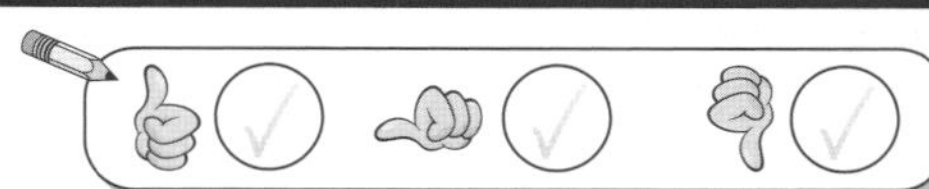

 Name: .... Date: ....

Problem Solving

1 This list shows how far some skiers jumped.

Liz Leap	215.3 m
Sam Snow	87.4 m
Fred Fly	161.5 m
Jane Jump	231.6 m

How much further did Liz Leap jump than Sam Snow?

[ ] m

2 This chart shows how Year 4 children came to school in May and December.

	May	December
Walk	39	11
Cycle	31	14
Bus	23	51
Car	16	33

a) How many children are there in Year 4?

b) How many more children cycled in May than December?

c) How many children come by either bus or car in May?

3 Here is the price of a games console and the game "Hamster Attack" in two shops:

Shop A	
Games console	£179.99
Hamster Attack	£39.99

Shop B	
Games console	£189.95
Hamster Attack	£36.50

How much more would you pay in Shop B for the console and the game together?

Activity Find out how much a litre of petrol costs.
Ask a car driver how much it costs them to fill up their tank.
Use a calculator to work out how many litres their tank holds.

Learning Objective:

"I can solve problems with one or two steps."

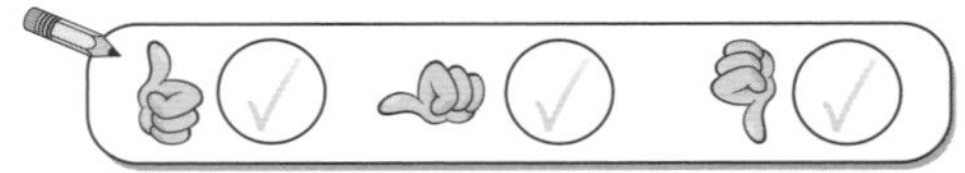

Problem Solving

You can use a calculator for this sheet

1 **A 1.5 litre bottle of lemonade is poured into 12 glasses.**

How much lemonade goes into each glass?

2 **Bread costs 86p per loaf.**

a) Anne has £6. How many loaves can she buy?

b) How much change will she get?

3 **Mary goes to the supermarket.**

Bananas	42p per kg
Apples	39p per kg
Grapes	87p per kg

a) Mary buys 1.5 kg of each kind of fruit.
What is the total cost?

b) Mary buys 2 kg of bananas, 3 kg of grapes and 2 kg of apples.
This is enough to make 10 glasses of a fruit drink.
Calculate the cost of one glass of the fruit drink.

Activity Find and weigh some apples. If they cost 29p per kilogram, how much would these apples cost?

Learning Objective:

"I can identify the steps I need to take to solve problems."

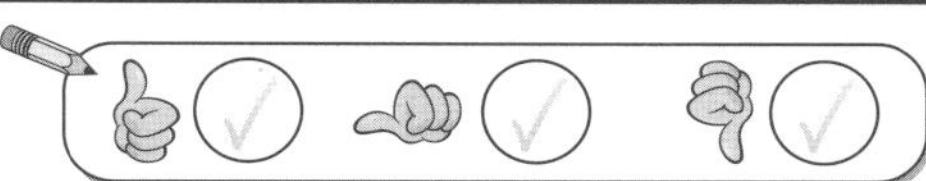

Write and Draw to Solve Problems

1 Complete the number patterns:

a) 1 3 ☐ 7 9 ☐ ☐ 15

b) 1 5 ☐ 13 17 ☐ 25

2 Look at this shape:

a) Colour half of the shape.

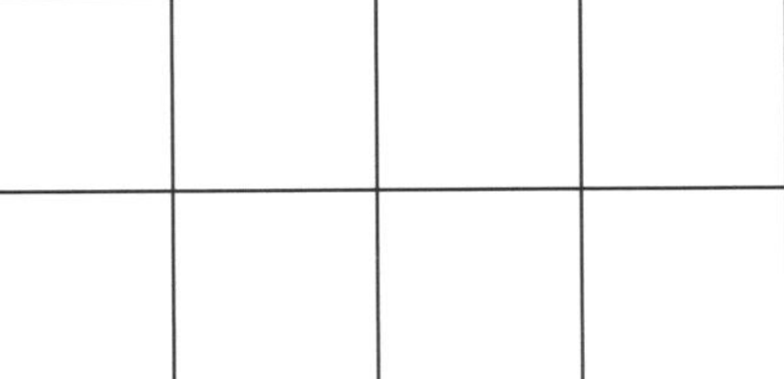

I put 20p on each small square.

b) How much money is there altogether? £ .

c) I spend half of the money.
How much do I spend? p

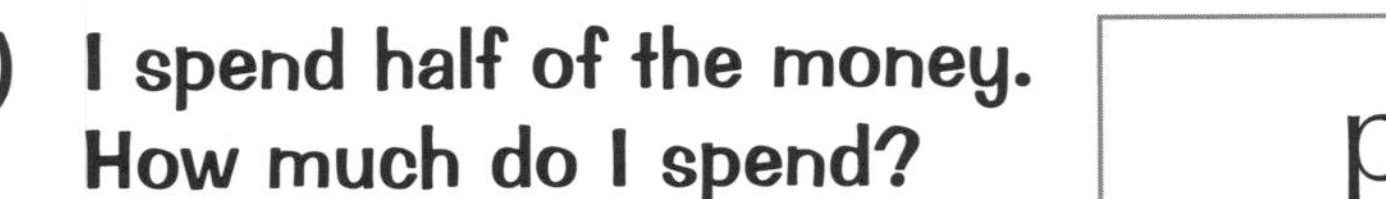

3 Here are some number cards: **8** **3** **6**

a) Make the biggest number you can with them.

b) Make the smallest number you can with them.

c) Make an odd number with them.

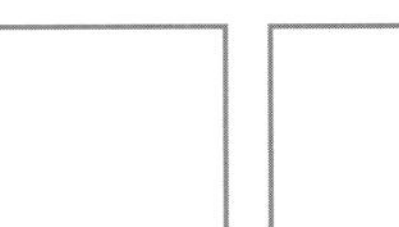

Activity Draw a chart to show how much pocket money you get each week for four weeks. Can you make a chart for a 20 weeks?

Learning Objective:

"I can solve problems using numbers and diagrams."

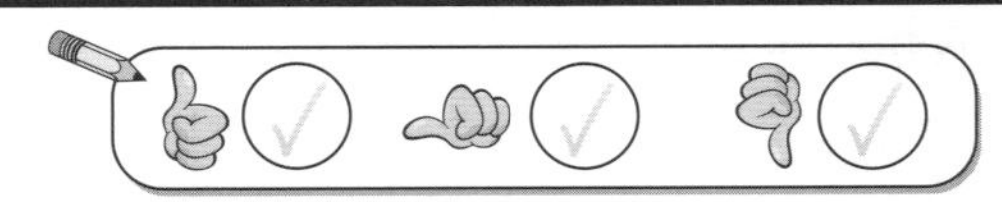

Write and Draw to Solve Problems

1 **This pattern is made using matchsticks.**

a) Draw the next triangle.

b) How many matchsticks would you use for the fourth triangle?

2 **The sum of Pete's and Dan's ages is 12. Dan is 5.**

a) How old is Pete? Circle how to work out the answer.

12 + 5   17 – 5   17 – 12   12 – 5

b) In how many years will Dan be 22? Circle how to work out the answer.

12 + 5   22 – 5   17 + 5   22 + 5

3 **A chocolate bar costs 25p.**

a) How much do 2 chocolate bars cost?

b) How much do 3 chocolate bars cost?

c) Write a number sentence to work out how much 7 chocolate bars cost.

Activity Use matchsticks or pens and pencils to make this pattern. How many more of them do you need each time?

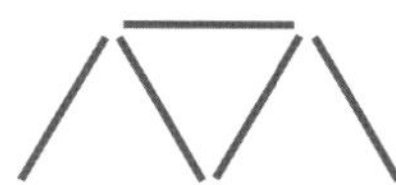

Learning Objective:

"I can solve problems using numbers and diagrams."

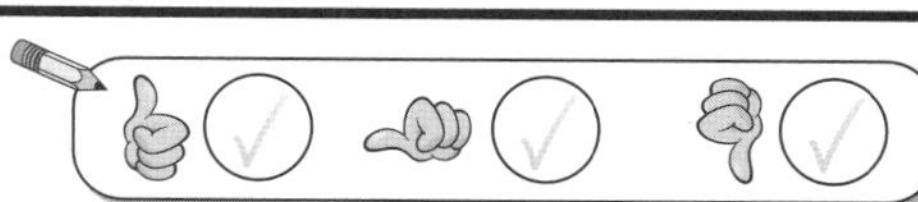

 Name: .... Date: ....

Write and Draw to Solve Problems

1 **220 children go on a school trip. 12 teachers go with them. They go on 53-seater coaches.**

Draw a diagram to work out how many coaches they will need.

They will need ☐ coaches.

2 **Sam is going to stay at a hotel for 6 nights.**

a) Fill in the table to show the cost of just a bed at the hotel.

Number of nights	1	2	3	4	5	6
Total cost	£35	£70				

b) How much will 6 breakfasts at Sid's Cafe cost?

c) How much money will Sam save by eating breakfast at Sid's Cafe instead of at the Hotel every day?

Activity

Some children are playing a game.
They jump up 2 steps and down 1 step.
Draw the rest of the jumps to get up these 5 steps.
How many jumps are needed?
Try it with different numbers of steps.

Learning Objective:

"I can solve problems using numbers and diagrams."

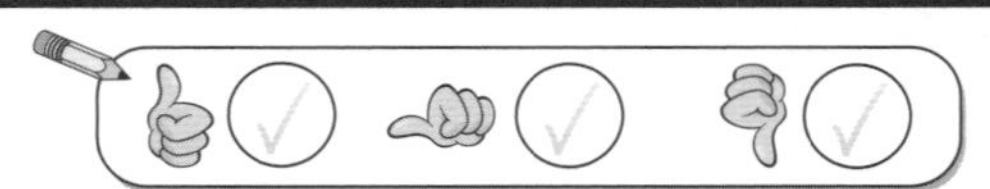

Counting and Sequences

1 **Write these numbers in order of size.**

31 8 24 111

smallest largest

12 112 21 102

2 **Write the correct numbers in the boxes. Some are done for you.**

a)

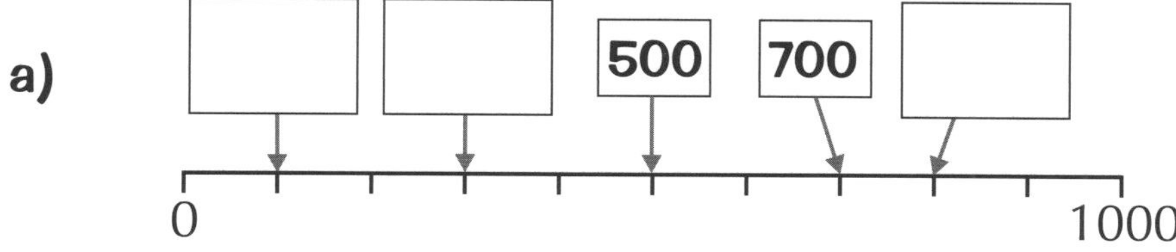

b)

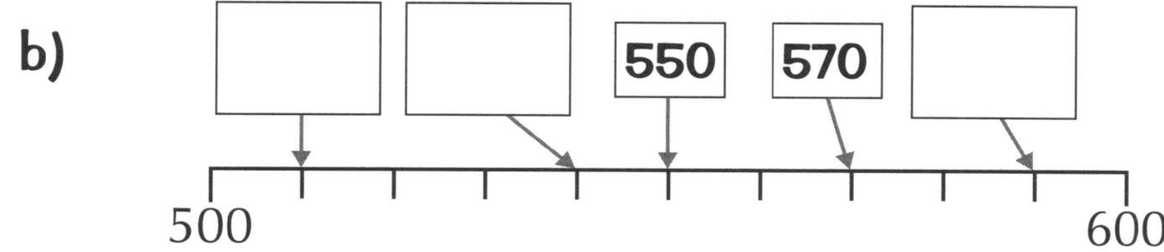

3 **Here are some digit cards:**

4 6 2 7

Use them to make:

a) The largest 3-digit number you can.

b) The smallest 3-digit number you can.

c) A 3-digit number larger than 750.

Activity

How many different 3-digit numbers can you make with these cards? Write them down. Now write them in order.

3 8 1

Learning Objective:

"I can read and write numbers to 1000 and put them in order."

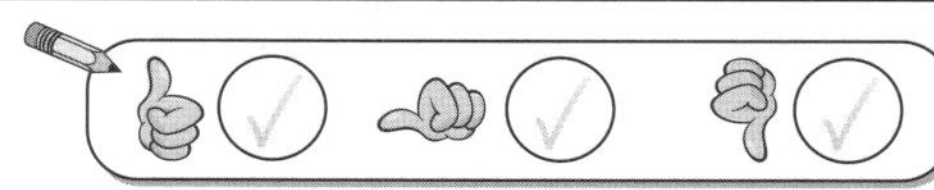

Name: .... Date: ....

Counting and Sequences

1 Write the next three numbers in these sequences:

a) 48 52 56 60 ☐ ☐ ☐

b) 700 725 750 775 ☐ ☐ ☐

2 What number is each insect hiding?

a)

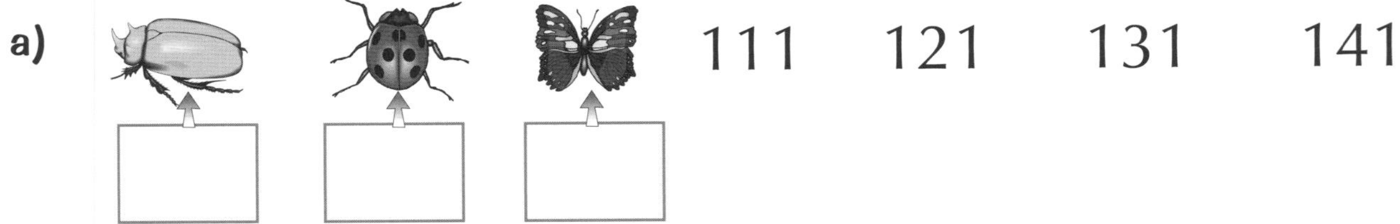

b)

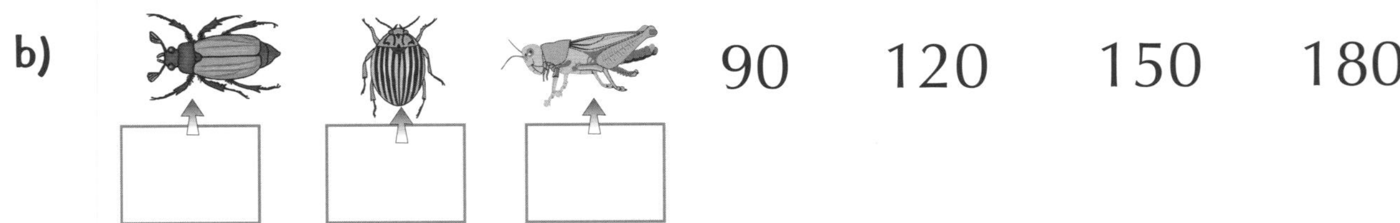

3 Jump along the number line in the steps given.

a) 20

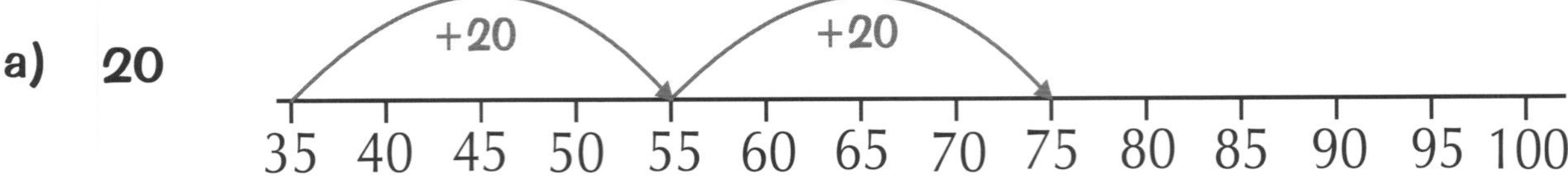

b) 10

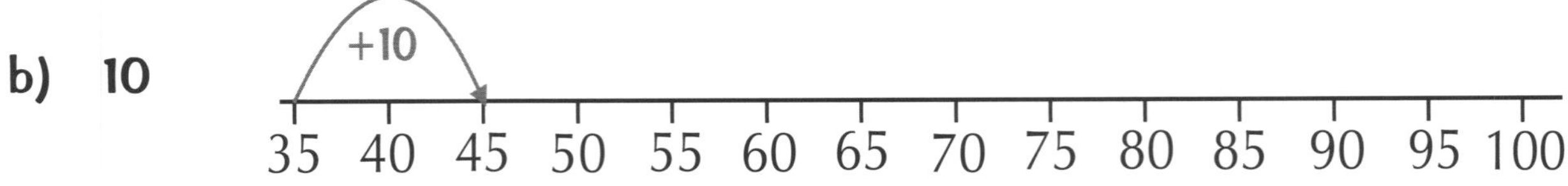

c) 15

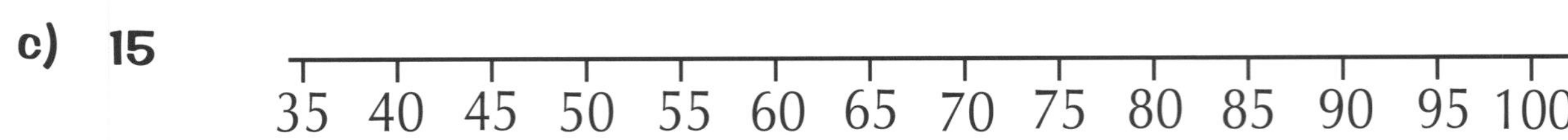

Activity Start from 0 on a number line and hop along in steps of 2. Do you always land on even numbers or on odd numbers? What about if you jump along in steps of 3?

Learning Objective:

"I can count up or down in steps of different sizes."

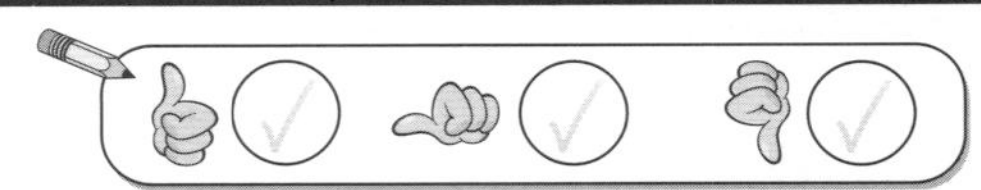

Counting and Sequences

1 Fill in the missing numbers in these sequences:

a) ☐ ☐ ☐ –1 1 3 5

b) ☐ ☐ –1 2 5 8 ☐

c) 9.6 10.2 10.8 11.4  ☐ 

d) 3.6 3.3 3.0 2.7   

2 On Monday the temperature is 15 °C.

Every day it gets colder by 3 °C. Fill in the temperatures below.

Day	Monday	Tuesday	Wednesday	Thursday	Friday	Saturday	Sunday
Temperature	15 °C						

3 Write the first two numbers in this sequence in figures.

☐ ☐ minus two, plus seven, plus sixteen, plus twenty-five

4 Stu lifts giant doughnuts.

Each doughnut weighs 0.6 kg. Complete this table.

Number of doughnuts	1	2	3	4	5
Mass	0.6 kg				

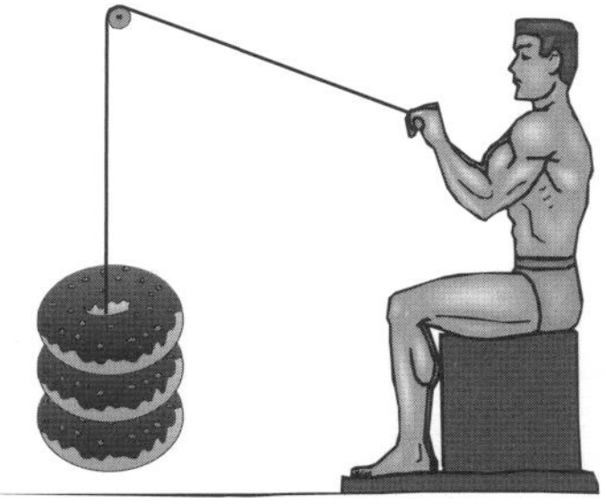

Activity An average 10 year old is about 1.4 m tall. Giraffes are about 5.6 m tall. Make a sequence to find out how many times taller a giraffe is than a 10 year old. It will start like this: 5.6, 4.2, ...
Find out the heights of some buildings and do the same thing.

Learning Objective:

"I can find missing numbers in sequences that include negative and decimal numbers."

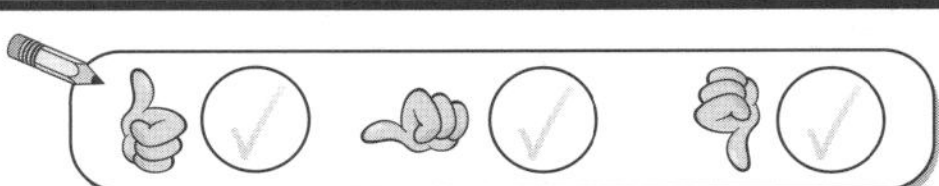

 Name: .... Date: ....

Decimals

1 **In the number 5.64 there are 5 units, 6 tenths and 4 hundredths.**

What is the value of the 3 in each of these numbers?

a) 3.45 ☐ b) 2.37 ☐

c) 6.93 ☐ d) 32.42 ☐

2 **Look at the number line below.**

Draw an arrow to show where 2.45 is.

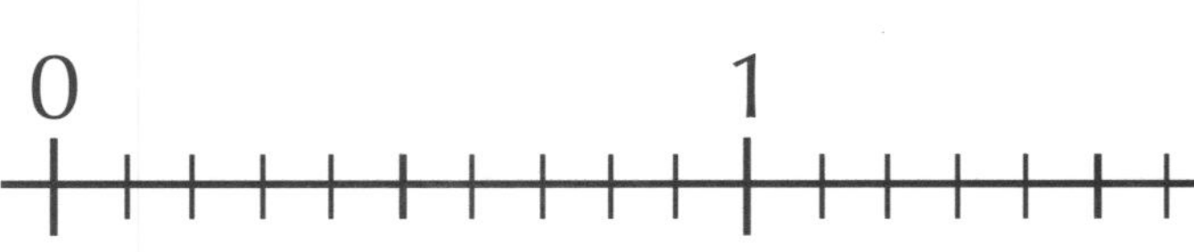

3 **Put these amounts of money in order. Start with the smallest.**

£6.40 £6.14 £6.04 £6.44 £6.11

☐ ☐ ☐ ☐ ☐

Smallest → Largest

4 **Put these measurements in the correct order. Start with the smallest.**

146 cm 1.04 m 1.42 m 1.40 m 143 cm

☐ ☐ ☐ ☐ ☐

Smallest → Largest

Activity Find 5 food items that show their weight. Put them into order, starting with the lightest.

Learning Objective:

"I can use decimals when I work with money and measurement."

Decimals

1 **Jess has a ribbon measuring 2.4 m. She cuts it into 10 cm strips.**

How many strips will Jess be able to cut from the ribbon?

2 **Put these amounts of money in order. Start with the smallest.**

£1.21 21p £1.02 120p £1.22

Smallest → Largest

3 **Draw a line from each decimal to its place on the number line.**

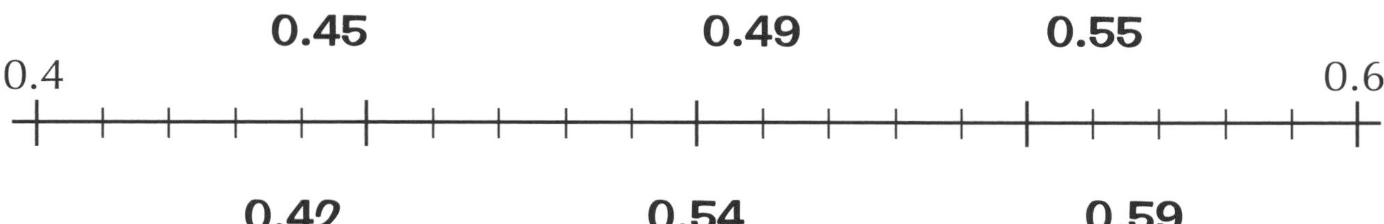

4 **Fill in the boxes to show the decimals on the number line.**

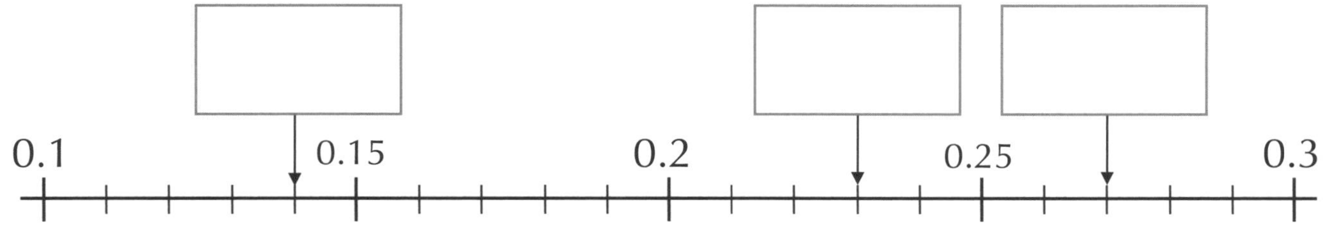

Activity Find a receipt from the supermarket.
Choose any 10 items and put them in order of cost.

Learning Objective:

"I can use decimals when I work with money and measurement."

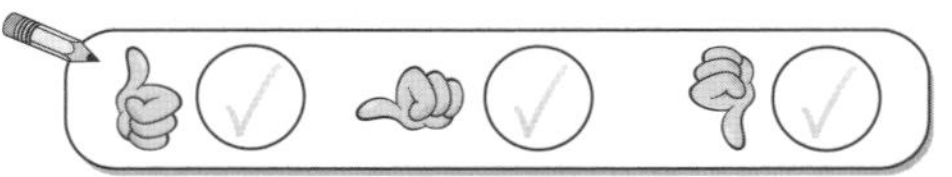

 Name: .... Date: ....

Key Objective

Decimals

1 Six frogs measured how far they could jump.

Debbie	1.85 m
Rob	1.96 m
Gill	2.23 m
Pete	2.05 m
Julia	2.19 m
David	2.16 m

a) Put them in order. Start with the furthest jump.

b) Who jumped closest to 2 metres?

2 2.63 partitions into 2 + 0.6 + 0.03.

Partition the following decimals.

a) 6.82

b) 9.16

3 In the number 35.2 the value of the 3 is 3 tens.

What is the value of the underlined digit in each of the numbers?

a) 320

b) 2561 

c) 14.9

d) 73.8 

e) 59.25 

f) 38.16 

Activity Find a shopping receipt. Choose 3 items from the list and partition their prices. £2.99 would partition to 2 + 0.9 + 0.09.

Learning Objective:

"I can say the value of each digit in a number, including decimals."

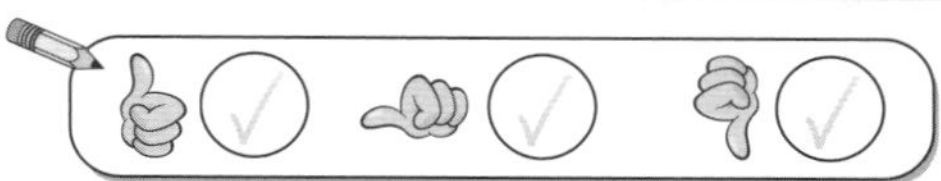

Fractions

1 **What fraction of each shape is shaded?**

a) 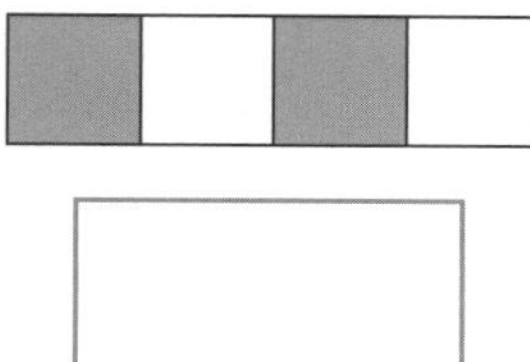

b) 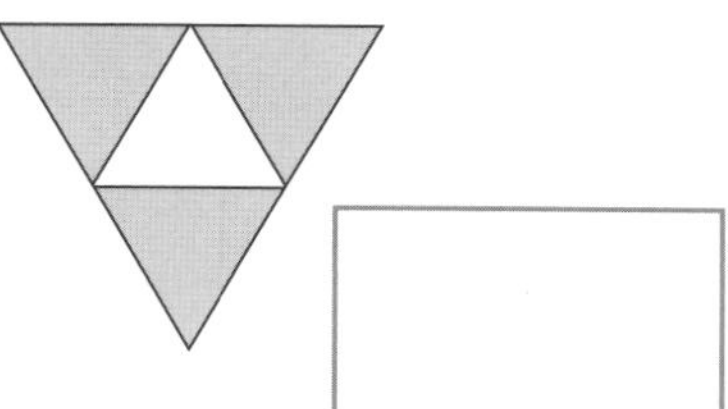

c) 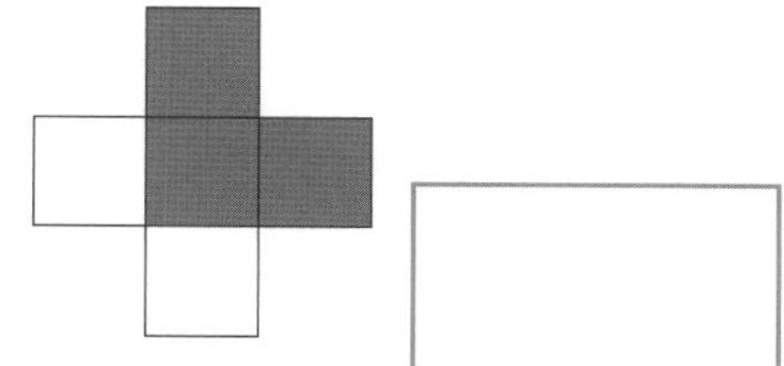

2 **Estimate how much of the pie has been eaten.**

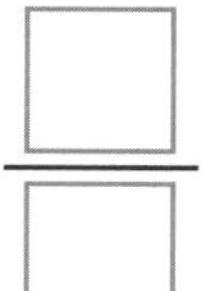 of the pie has been eaten.

3 **Tick the shapes that have one third shaded.**

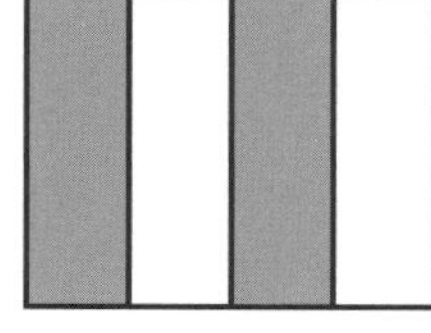
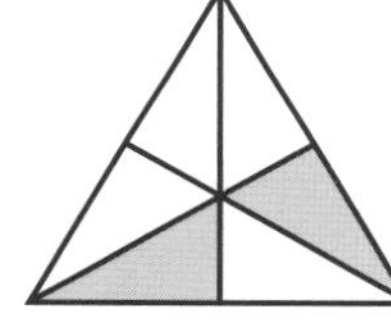
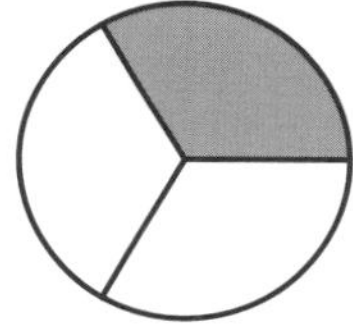
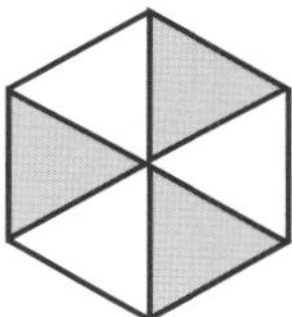
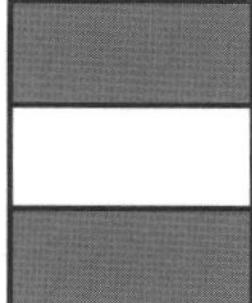

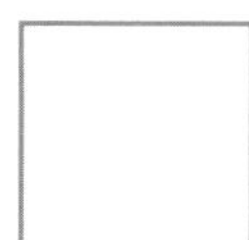

4 **Circle the shape that has the same fraction shaded as the shape in the box.**

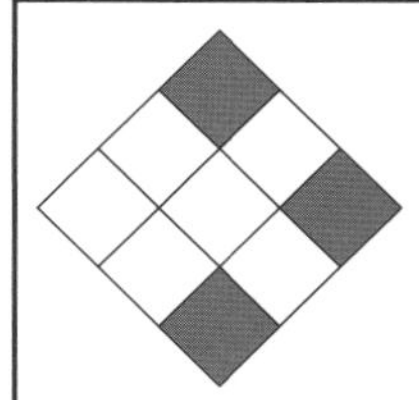
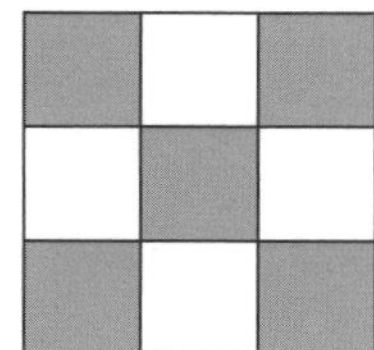
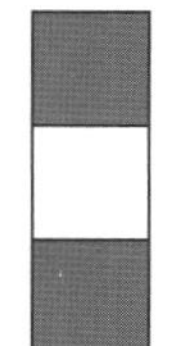
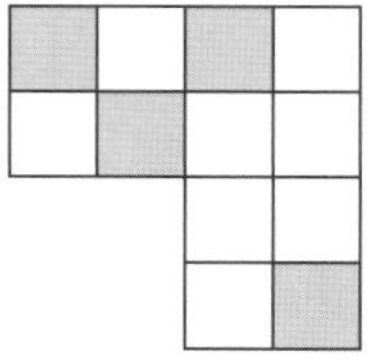

Activity Draw 3 rectangles on squared paper.
Find three ways to shade 3 tenths of each rectangle.

Learning Objective:

"I can say what fraction of a shape is shaded."

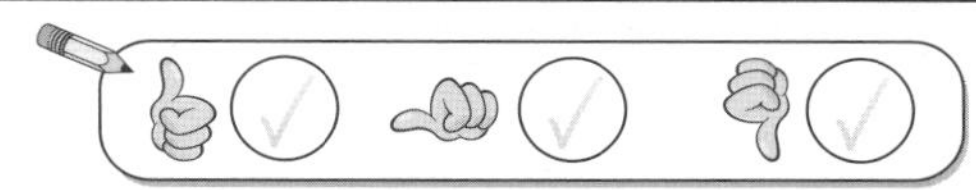

 Name: .... Date: ....

Key Objective

Fractions

1 Circle all the shapes that are three quarters shaded.

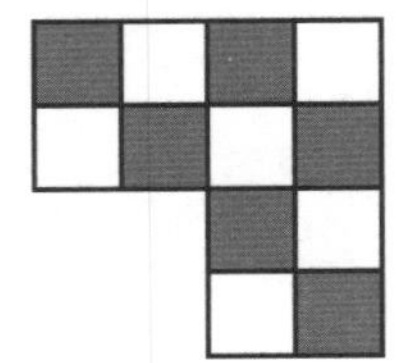

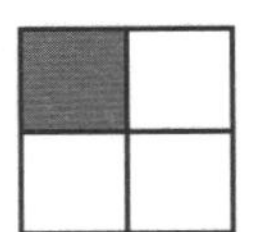
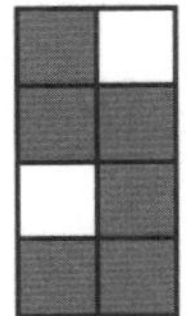
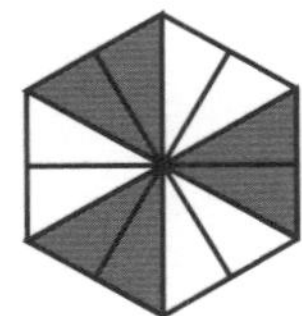

2 Draw an arrow from each mixed number to its place on the number line.

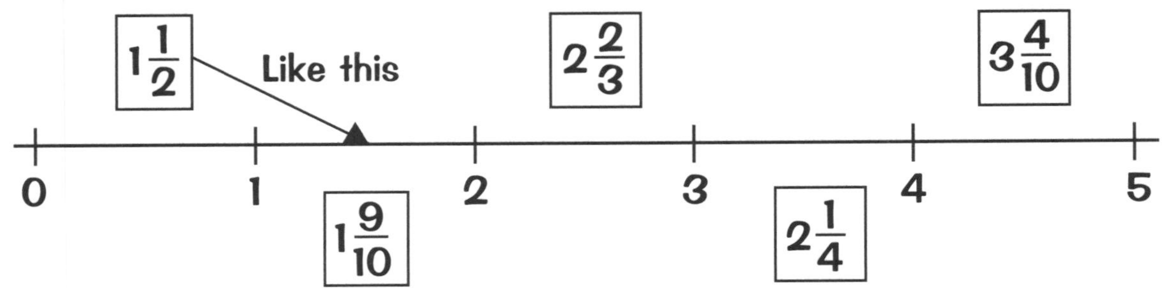

3 Put the mixed numbers in order. Start with the smallest.

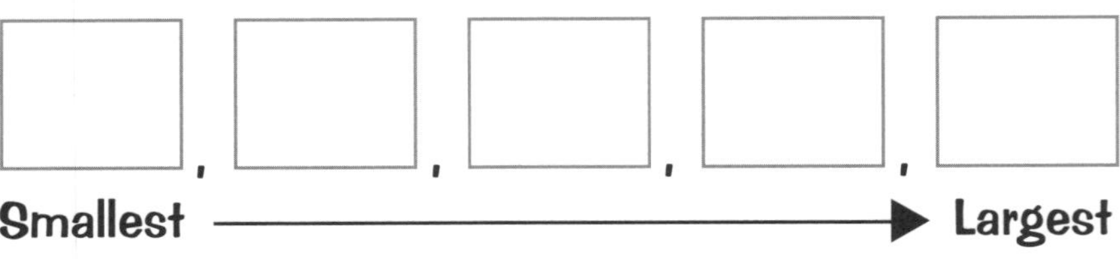

4 Draw lines to join the fractions to the right shapes.

$\frac{4}{12}$ shaded $\frac{3}{8}$ shaded $\frac{7}{10}$ shaded

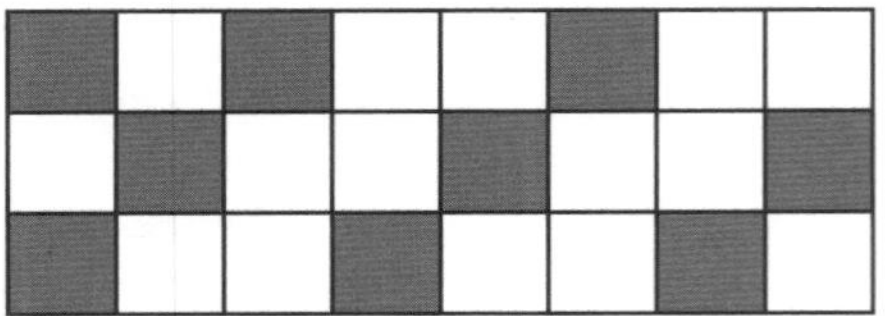
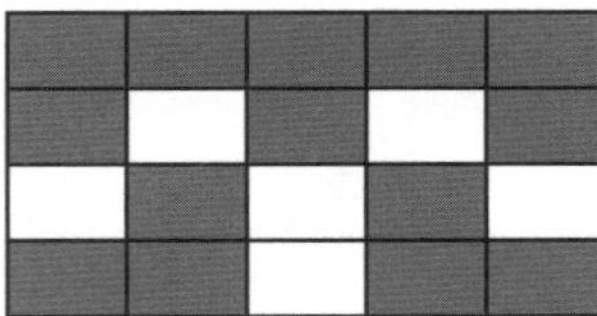

Activity Draw a circle and colour three quarters.
Repeat this with a quarter, a third and a half.

Learning Objective:

"I can put mixed numbers like $1\frac{3}{4}$ on a number line."

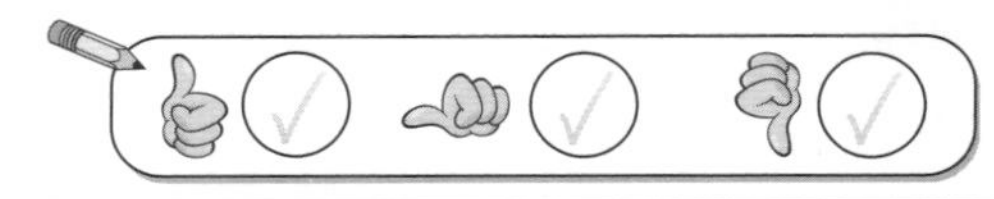

Fractions

1 **A birthday cake is cut into 8 pieces. Five pieces are eaten.**

a) What fraction of the cake has been eaten? 

b) What fraction of the cake is left? 

2 **Draw lines to match the fractions with the equivalent mixed number.**

$\frac{3}{4}$ $\frac{2}{3}$ $\frac{4}{5}$ $\frac{5}{8}$

$\frac{10}{16}$ $\frac{9}{12}$ $\frac{4}{6}$ $\frac{8}{10}$

3 **Draw rings around the two equivalent fractions.**

$\frac{5}{6}$ $\frac{2}{3}$ $\frac{1}{4}$ $\frac{10}{15}$ $\frac{3}{4}$

4 **Fill in the gaps to complete the equivalent fractions.**

a) $\frac{3}{4} = \frac{\square}{8}$

b) $\frac{3}{5} = \frac{15}{\square}$

c) $\frac{\square}{25} = \frac{80}{100}$

d) $\frac{9}{\square} = \frac{27}{30}$

Activity Here are some equivalent fractions: $\frac{1}{5}$, $\frac{2}{10}$, $\frac{3}{15}$.
How many more can you find in 5 minutes?

Learning Objective:

"I can find fractions that are equivalent to each other."

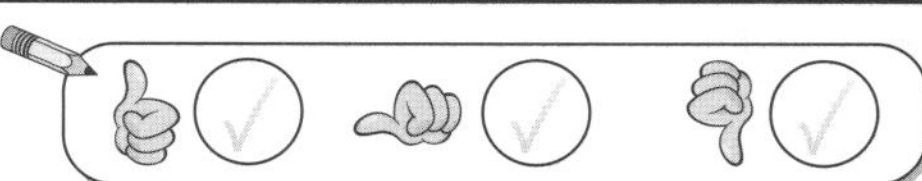

 Name: .... Date: ....

Fractions and Decimals

1 **Draw a line to join each fraction to its decimal equivalent.**

a) $\frac{1}{2}$ — 0.3, 0.25, 0.1, 0.5

b) $\frac{1}{10}$ — 0.3, 0.25, 0.1, 0.5

c) $\frac{4}{100}$ — 0.3, 0.04, 0.12, 0.5

2 **Complete the pairs so that each fraction is matched to its decimal equivalent.**

a) $\frac{7}{10}$ = ☐

b) $\frac{3}{4}$ = ☐

c) ☐ = 0.05

d) $\frac{1}{4}$ = ☐

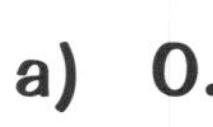

3 **Write one fraction that is equivalent to each decimal.**

a) 0.6 ☐ b) 0.35 ☐ c) 0.08 ☐

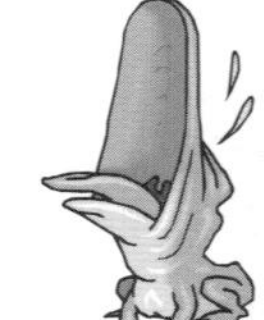

4 **Write three fractions that are equivalent to 0.4.**

0.4 = ☐ 0.4 = ☐ 0.4 = ☐

Activity

Pairs Game for 2 or more players

Make cards with these fractions and decimals on:

$\frac{3}{10}$, $\frac{1}{2}$, $\frac{1}{4}$, $\frac{3}{4}$, $\frac{6}{10}$, $\frac{1}{100}$, $\frac{8}{100}$, $\frac{1}{10}$ 0.3, 0.5, 0.25, 0.75, 0.6, 0.01, 0.08, 0.1

Lay the cards face down. Take turns to pick 2 cards. If they are equivalent you keep them. If not, put them back. The winner has the most cards at the end.

Learning Objective:

"I can recognise decimals and fractions that are equivalent."

Fractions and Decimals

1 For each decimal write an equivalent fraction.

a) 0.04 ☐ b) 0.75 ☐ c) 0.6 ☐ d) 0.25 ☐

2 Use a line to join each fraction to its equivalent decimal.

$\frac{2}{10}$ $\frac{3}{4}$ $\frac{10}{100}$ $\frac{5}{100}$

0.75 0.1 0.2 0.05

3 Look at the calculator displays below.

Write the equivalent fraction to the decimal shown on each screen.

a) 0.25 ☐

b) 

4 Write each fraction as a decimal.

a) six tenths 

b) four hundredths 

c) three quarters 

d) twelve hundredths 

Activity 0.001 is equivalent to $\frac{1}{1000}$. 0.002 is equivalent to $\frac{2}{1000}$.
Can you spot the rule for this?
Give the fractions that 0.009 and 0.023 are equivalent to.
Check your answers on a calculator.

Learning Objective:

"I can recognise decimals and fractions that are equivalent."

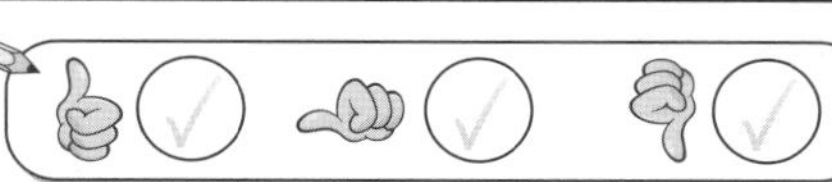

Fractions and Decimals

1 Complete the two grids so that the fractions on the left are equivalent to the decimals on the right.

$\frac{1}{2}$		$\frac{6}{10}$
	$\frac{2}{10}$	
$\frac{5}{20}$		$\frac{15}{100}$
	$\frac{3}{4}$	

	0.95	
0.7		0.25
	0.35	
0.8		0.4

2 Shade the correct amount of each shape.

a) 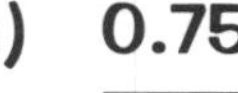 0.75

b) 0.6

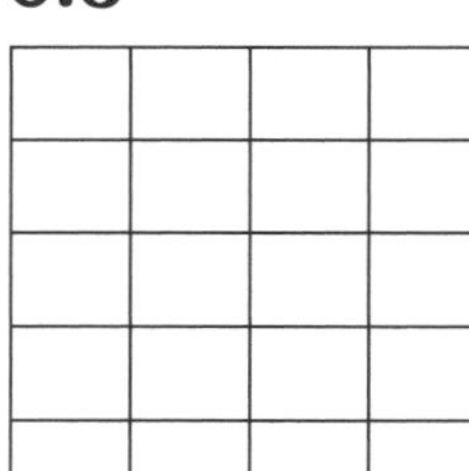

c) 0.25

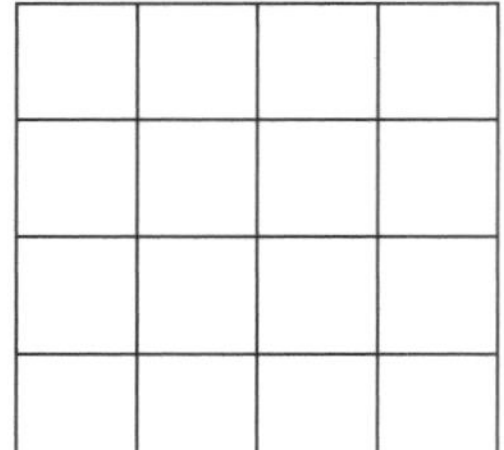

3 Write a decimal to describe how much of each shape has been shaded.

 a)

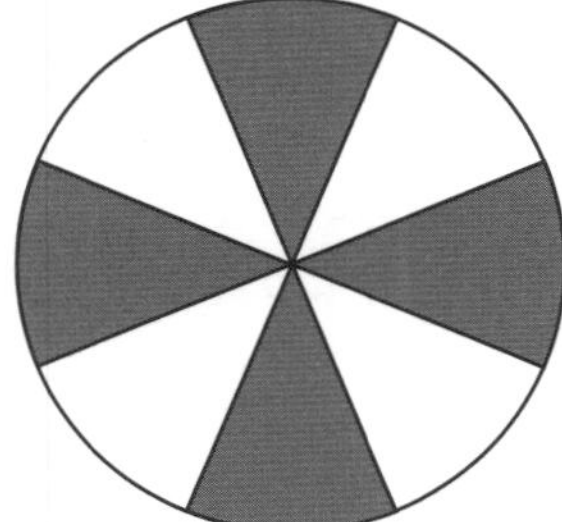

b)

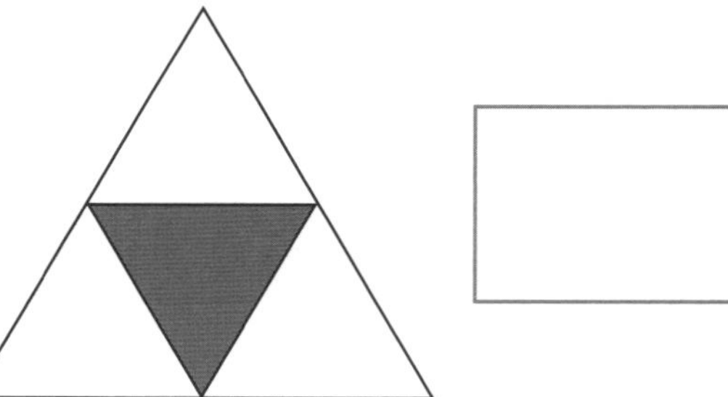

Activity Practise using your calculator to convert fractions to decimals. Try these ones, and then make up some fractions of your own.

a) $\frac{23}{100}$ b) $\frac{4}{13}$ c) $\frac{71}{90}$ d) $\frac{339}{1100}$

Learning Objective:

"I can give the decimal equivalent of a simple fraction."

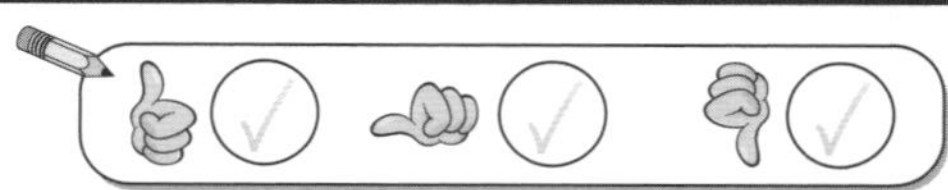

Name: .... Date: ....

Numbers and Number Lines

1 Write these numbers in words:

a) 960

b) 737

2 Write these numbers in figures:

a) Eight hundred and forty five

b) Two hundred and ninety seven

3 Use these digits to make the biggest number you can:

6 3 9 2

4 Order these numbers:

251 316 198 1011 901 18

a) biggest → → → → → smallest

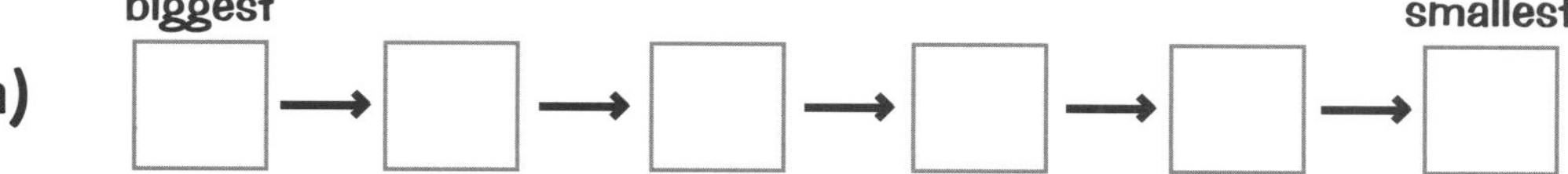

611 220 1040 217 601 125

b) smallest → → → → → biggest

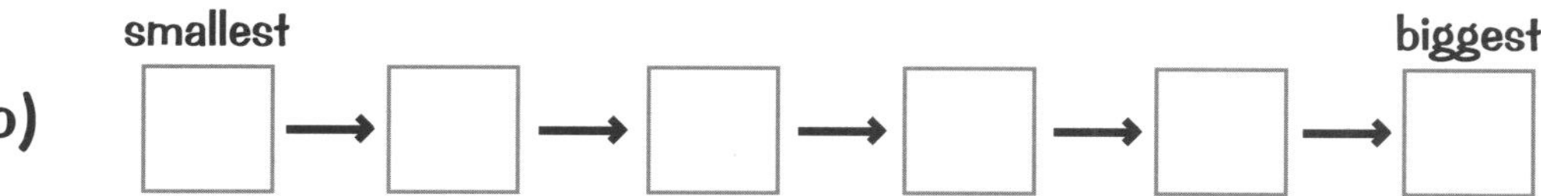

5 Draw an arrow from each number to its place on the number line:

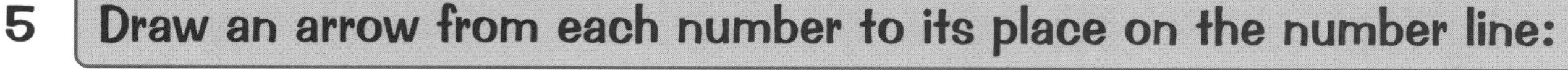

740 830 890 990

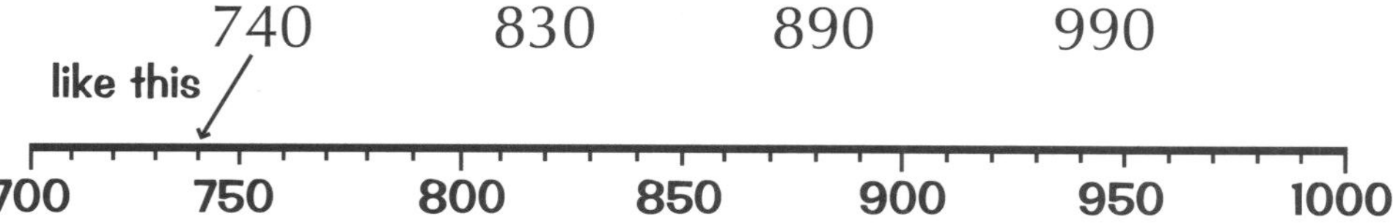

Activity <u>Guess</u> how many books are on each bookcase in your school library. Put the numbers in <u>size order</u>.

Learning Objective:

"I can read and write numbers to 1000 and put them in order."

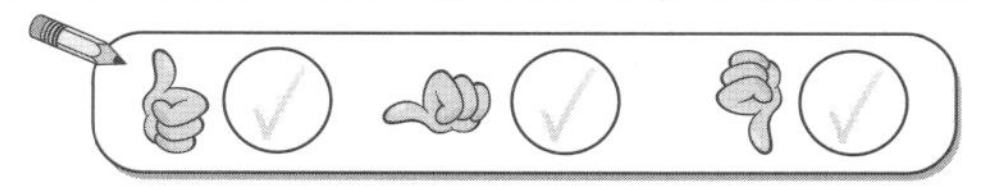

 Name: .... Date: ....

Numbers and Number Lines

1 **Write these numbers in order, smallest first:**

–4 6 –2 2 10 0

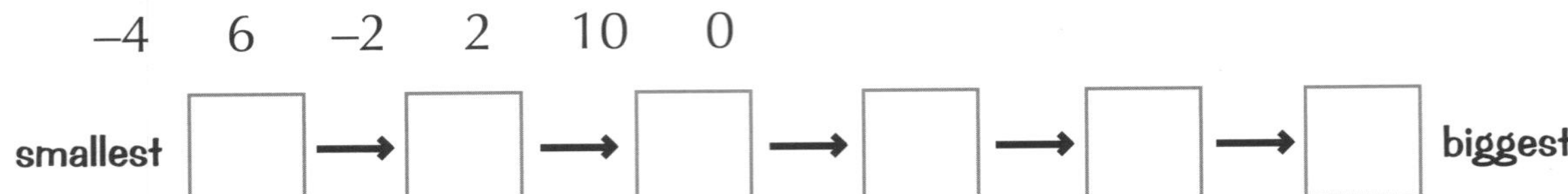

2 **Fill in the labels on this number line:**

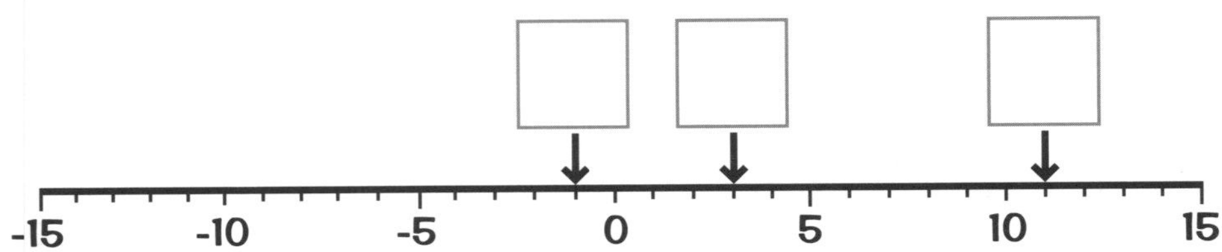

3 **Put the correct sign (> or <) in the boxes. Use the number line to help.**

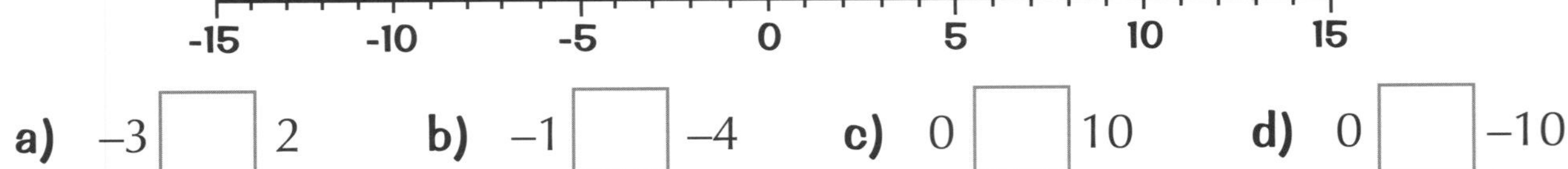

a) –3 ☐ 2 b) –1 ☐ –4 c) 0 ☐ 10 d) 0 ☐ –10

4 **Write the correct numbers in the boxes below this thermometer.**

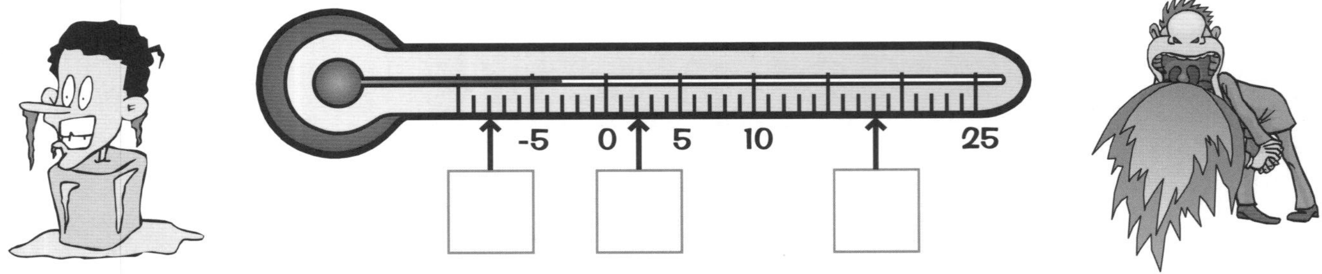

The numbers below go in the empty boxes. Use the thermometer to help fill them in.

–1 –10

a) ☐ < –5 b) 0 > ☐

Activity The temperature of a freezer is shown on the number line (–18). Mark on a fridge (4) and an oven (200). Mark two other temperatures on this line.

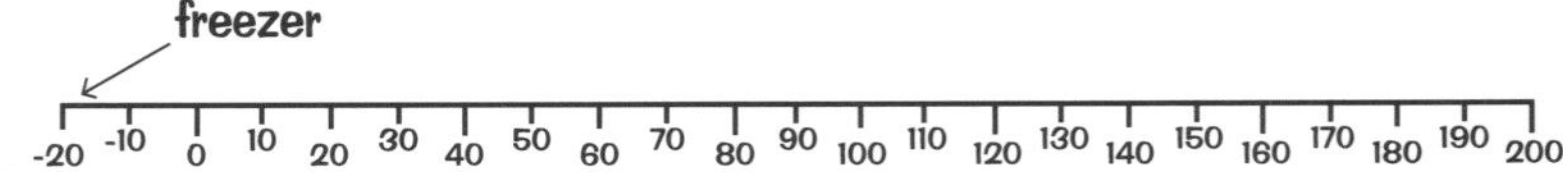

Learning Objective:

"I can put positive and negative numbers into order.
I can use the < and > signs."

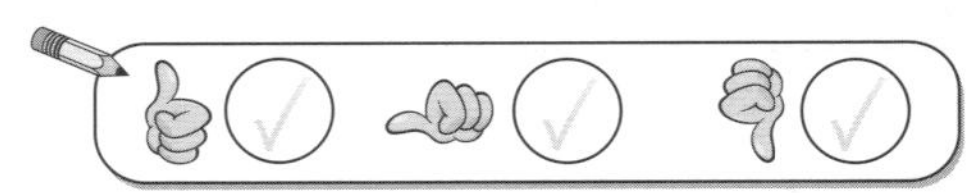

Numbers and Number Lines

1 **Put these numbers in order, smallest first.**

5.6 6.1 6.3 5.4 5.2

smallest ☐ → ☐ → ☐ → ☐ → ☐ biggest

2 **Fill in the missing numbers in these sequences:**

a) 7.2 7.5 7.8 ☐ 8.4 ☐ ☐

b) ☐ 27.4 27.0 ☐ 26.2 25.8 25.4

c) 4 –1 –6 ☐ ☐ –21 –26

d) 1.2 0.7 0.2 ☐ ☐ –1.3 –1.8

3 **Write the missing numbers in these boxes:**

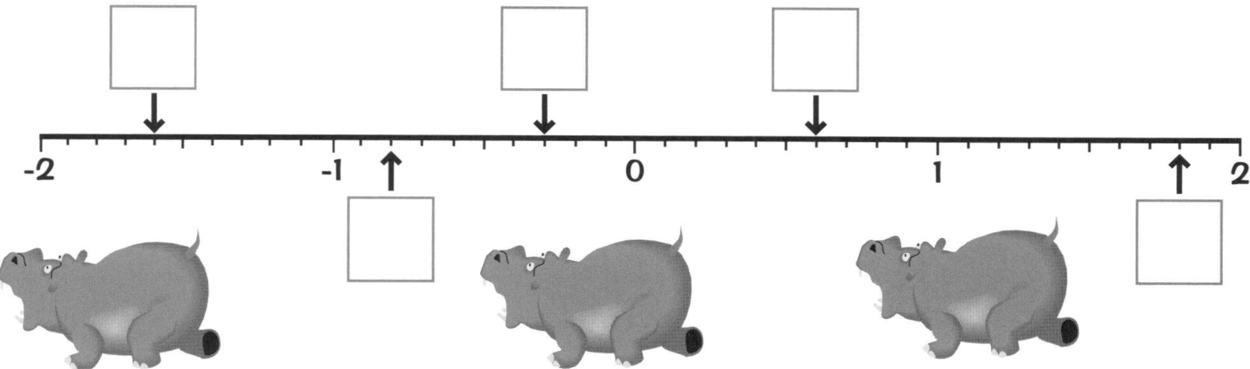

Activity Make up some <u>number sequences</u> and show them on <u>number lines</u>. Like this:

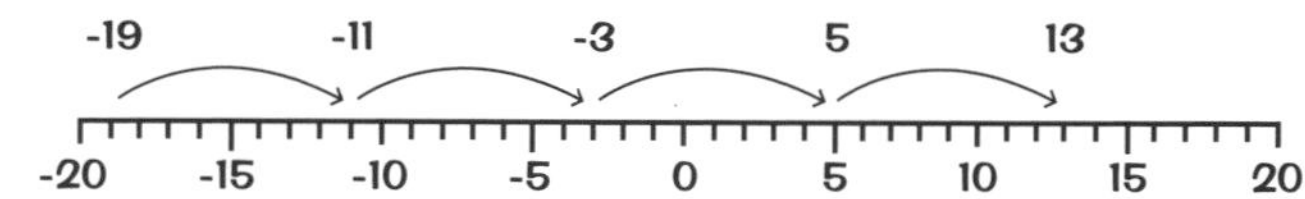

Learning Objective:

"I can count up or down in decimal steps with positive and negative numbers."

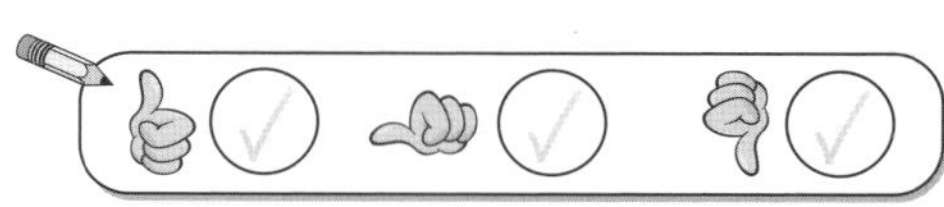

Key Objective

Partitioning

1 **235 has been partitioned in three ways. Fill in the missing numbers.**

a) 235 = ☐ + 30 + 5

b) 235 = 200 + ☐

c) 235 = 100 + 100 + 32 + ☐

d) **Write another way of partitioning 235.**

☐

2 **Fill in the empty boxes on this number line.**

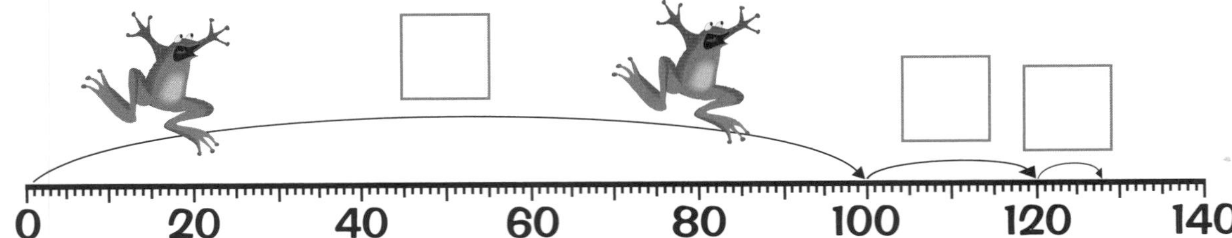

What number is shown on the number line?

3 **Fill in the missing numbers.**

a) 264 = 150 + ☐ + 60 + 4

b) 772 = 300 + ☐ + 30 + 40 +2

c) 859 = 250 + 550 + 40 + 10 + ☐

d) 168 = 68 + 32 + 60 + ☐ + ☐

Activity Think of a number bigger than 100.
<u>Partition</u> this number in different ways using 100s, 10s and 1s.

Learning Objective:

"I can partition a number into hundreds, tens and ones."

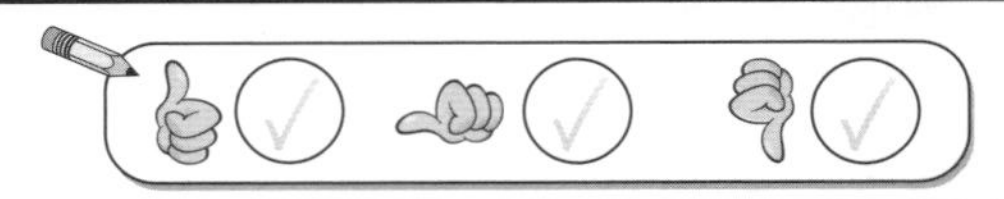

Partitioning

1 **Write these numbers in figures.**

a) Five thousand four hundred and twenty six.

b) Six thousand three hundred and thirty nine.

c) Nine thousand eight hundred and seventy one.

2 **What is the value of the underlined digits?**

a) 3654 b) 9625

c) 2007 d) 8217

3 **Use these digits to make the biggest four digit number you can.**

2 5 1 6

What's the smallest number you can make using these digits?

4 **This is an example of how the number 7482 could be partitioned:**

7482 = 6000 + 1100 + 379 + 3

Write down three other ways that 7482 could be partitioned.

a)

b)

c)

Activity Think of a year. Can you use the digits to make a bigger and a smaller number? What are they?

Learning Objective:

"I can partition a number into thousands, hundreds, tens and ones."

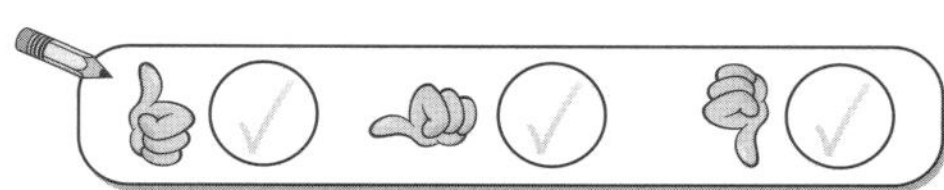

 Name: .... Date: ....

Partitioning

1 **Partition these numbers by filling in the boxes:**

a) 2615 = 2000 + 300 + ☐ + 10 + 5

b) 9725 = 4000 + 5000 + 700 + ☐ + 5

c) 7645 = 7000 + 400 + ☐ + 40 + 5

d) 3207 = 3000 + 200 + 4 + ☐

2 **Marjorie has collected forty 10p pieces, fifteen £1 coins and three 5p pieces.**

How much money has she got in pence?

3 **Holly has 19 m 26 cm of ribbon.**

a) How many centimetres of ribbon does Holly have?

b) How many 100 cm lengths of ribbon could be made?

c) How many 10 cm lengths of ribbon could be made?

Activity Think of a four digit number. Try and partition it using 3, 4, 5 or more numbers. Can you find five different ways?

Learning Objective:

"I can partition 4 digit numbers."

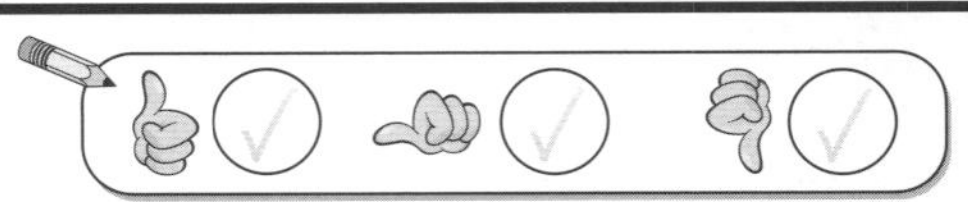

Proportion and Ratio

1 **Look at this pattern of shapes:**

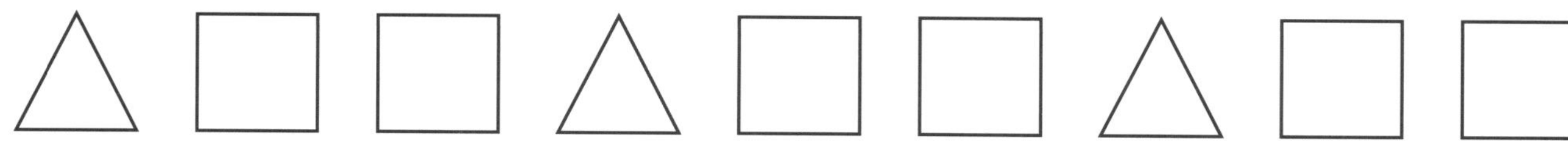

a) Complete these sentences by filling in the boxes:

1 in every 3 shapes is a [ ]

There is 1 triangle for every [ ] squares.

b) Draw a pattern of 8 shapes where there is 1 square for every 3 triangles.

2 **Work out the answers to the following problems. Show your working.**

a) Sally cycles 34 km a day. How far does she cycle in 2 days?

b) Sasha has 1 pencil for every 4 pens in her pencil case.
If she has 12 pencils, how many pens does she have?

c) Noel uses 3 free range eggs for every cake he bakes.
If he uses 18 eggs, how many cakes has he baked?

d) Lewis has collected 63 apples. His basket is about half full.
Estimate how many apples will fit into a full basket. Circle the answer.

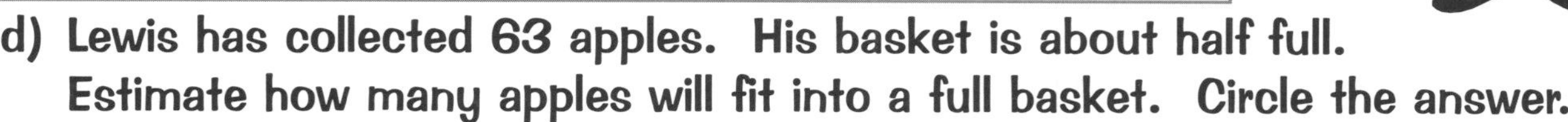

Activity Draw a shape pattern which uses 1 circle for every 4 squares.
Then write 2 sentences about the ratio in the pattern.

Learning Objective:

"I can work out ratios in patterns of shapes and numbers."

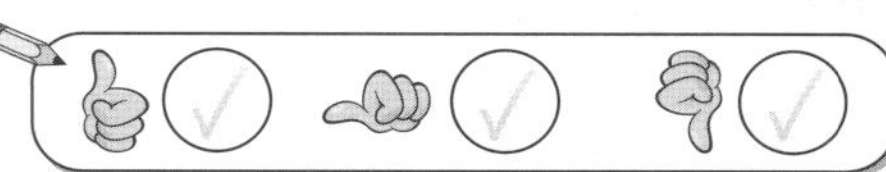

 Name: .... Date: ....

Proportion and Ratio

1 **Here are two hotels:**

a) What fraction of lights are off at the Seafront Hotel? ☐

b) Shade the windows of Jo's Motel so that 3 in every 4 lights are off.

2 **Solve the following problems. Show your working for each.**

a) An ice lolly costs 56p. How much would 3 ice lollies cost?

b) A bucket holds 100 shells when it's full. Martha has 27 shells. Estimate what fraction of the bucket Martha can fill.

3 **In a harbour there are 2 yachts for every 3 fishing boats.**

How many fishing boats are in the harbour if there are:

a) 6 yachts?

b) 10 yachts?

Activity Ask 5 people if they like banana milkshakes. Write down how many said yes to how many said no. Use this to estimate how many of 20 people would like banana milkshakes. Try it for different numbers of people.

Learning Objective:

"I can estimate proportions and fractions."

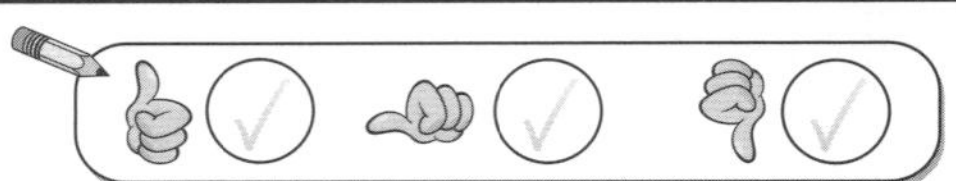

Proportion and Ratio

1 **Ruby's scarf has 15 stripes.**

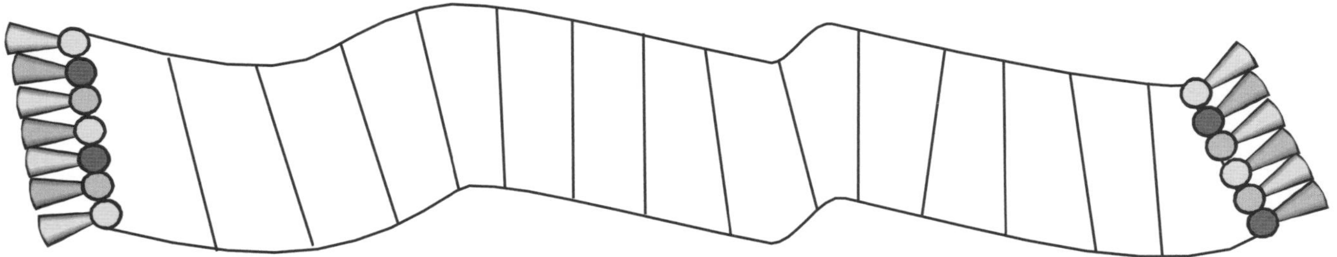

a) Colour in the scarf so there are 2 blue stripes for every 3 yellow stripes.

b) Fill in the boxes to complete these rules:

2 in every 5 stripes are coloured [ ]

[ ] in every 5 stripes are coloured yellow.

2 **At a football match there are 3 away fans for every 5 home fans.**

a) Complete the table.

b) If there are 80 fans in total, how many away fans are there ?

Away	Home	Total
3	5	
	10	
12		
		40

3 **Here is a list of ingredients for curry sauce:**

Recipe for curry sauce
Serves 6 people

150g tomatoes
600ml water
3 small onions
12g curry powder

Ethan wants to make curry sauce for 12 people.

a) How many grams of tomatoes will he need?

b) How many millilitres of water will he need?

Activity A chef needs 1 onion for every 4 hotdogs. Make a table showing how many onions he needs for 4, 8, 12, 16 or 20 hotdogs.

Learning Objective:

"I can express ratios in numbers and words."

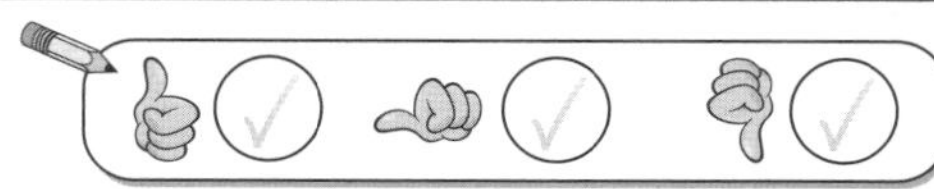

Rounding

1 Round these numbers to the nearest 10.

a) 26 ☐

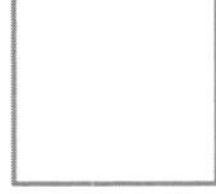

b) 83 ☐

c) 25 ☐

d) 121 ☐

e) 758 ☐

f) 909 ☐

2 Round the numbers on the left to the nearest 100.

Match them to the numbers on the right.

579	400
780	600
445	800
950	1000

3 About how many presents are there altogether?

Circle the right answer:

90 40 30 70

4 Circle the number which is about the same as:

a) the <u>sum</u> of 22 and 59. 90 40 30 80 140

b) the <u>difference</u> between 69 and 28. 20 40 30 10 140

Activity Look in the food cupboard and make a list of the weights of different foods. Then round them to the nearest 10 g and to the nearest 100 g.

Learning Objective:

"I can round numbers to the nearest 10 or 100."

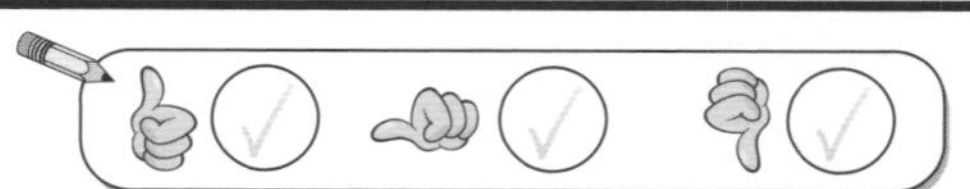

Rounding

1 **Round these numbers to the nearest 1000.**

a) 2370 ☐ b) 3614 ☐

c) 5732 ☐ d) 6197 ☐

2 **Round these numbers to the nearest 100.**

a) 5714 ☐ b) 2657 ☐

c) 5794 ☐ d) 6779 ☐

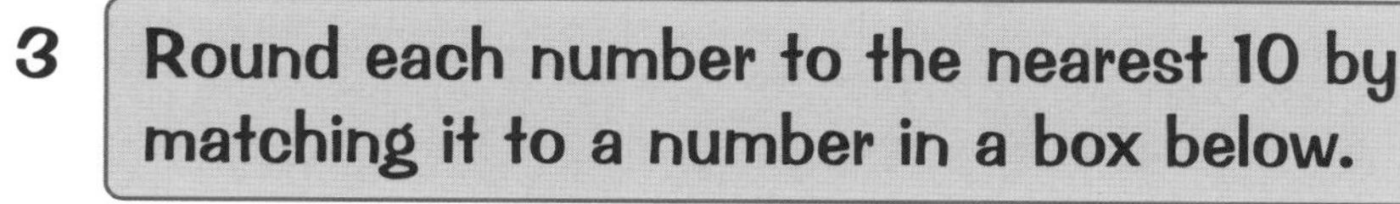

3 **Round each number to the nearest 10 by matching it to a number in a box below.**

5327   5372   5355   5318

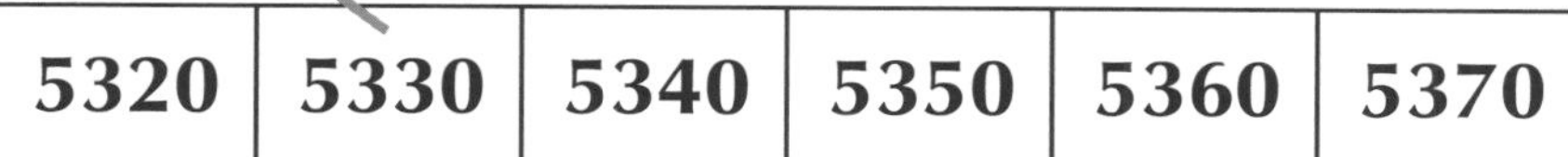

5320	5330	5340	5350	5360	5370

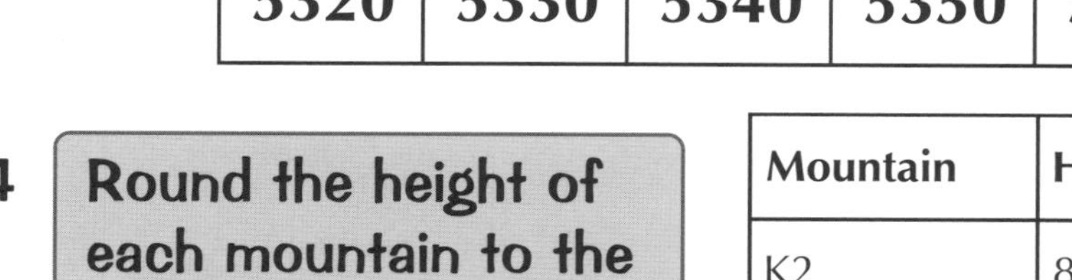

4 **Round the height of each mountain to the nearest 1000 m and to the nearest 100 m.**

Mountain	Height	Nearest 1000 m	Nearest 100 m
K2	8611 m		
Annapurna I	8091 m		
Snowdon	1085 m		
Mont Blanc	4810 m		

Activity 2950 rounds to 3000 to the nearest 1000.
Find 5 other numbers which round to 3000 to the nearest 1000.
Find 5 numbers which round to 3000 to the nearest 10.

Learning Objective:

"I can round a 4-digit number to the nearest 10, 100 or 1000."

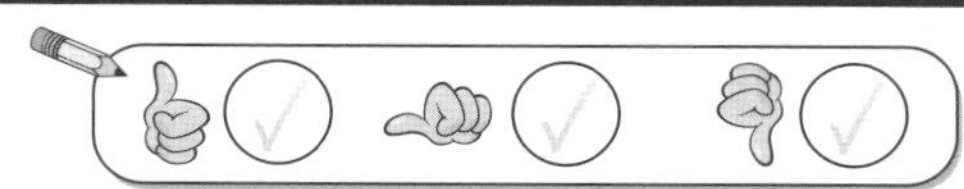

 Name: .... Date: ....

Key Objective

Rounding

1 **Round these numbers to the nearest 100.**

a) 267 ☐ b) 8542 ☐ c) 3881 ☐

2 **Round each number to 1 decimal place and then to the nearest whole number.**

Number	to 1 decimal place	to the nearest whole number
14.71		
7.29		
21.98		

3 **Round the cost of each surfboard to the nearest pound and then to the nearest 10p.**

surfboard	to the nearest pound	to the nearest 10p
£23.99		
£31.50		
£50.25		

Activity Look in the food cupboard and find a tin or packet which shows nutritional information. Round each weight to the nearest gram.

For example:
Protein 4.3 g ➩ 4 g
Fat 0.5 g ➩ 1 g

Learning Objective:

"I can round numbers with up to 2 decimal places."

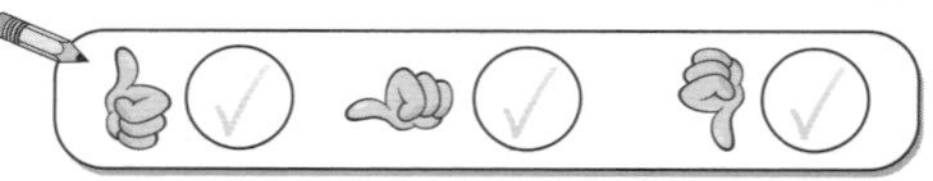

Key Objective

Adding and Subtracting

1 **Fill in the boxes:**

a) ☐ + 47 = 100 b) 81 + ☐ = 100

c) 17 + ☐ = 100 d) ☐ + 33 = 100

e) ☐ + 11 = 100 f) 73 + ☐ = 100

2 **Three children are knitting scarves.**

How many more cm must each knit to make their scarf 100 cm long?

a)  80 cm b)  68 cm c)  52 cm

☐ cm ☐ cm ☐ cm

3 **Find a pair of numbers in this shape with:**

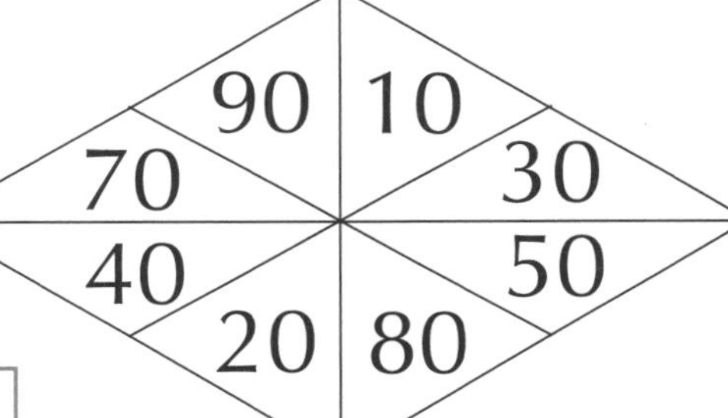

a) a sum of 150. ☐ and ☐

b) a difference of 40. ☐ and ☐

c) a sum of 110. ☐ and ☐

Activity Throw two dice and make a 2-digit number. Write down the number which you need to add to make 100. Repeat this 3 times.

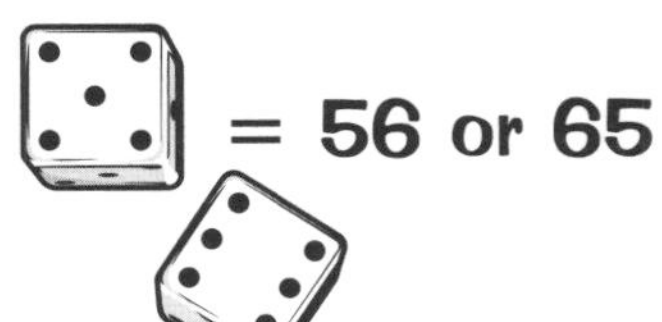

Learning Objective:

"I can add and subtract multiples of 10 in my head. I can find what to add to a number to make 100."

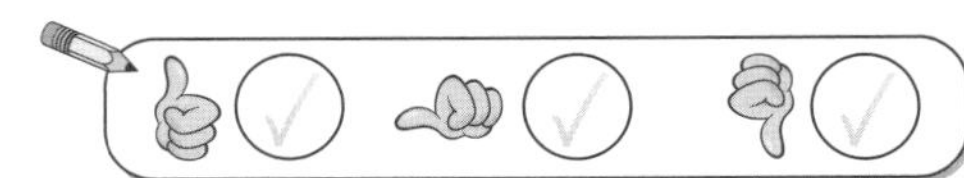

Name: .... Date: ....

Adding and Subtracting

1 **Write in the missing numbers:**

a) 5000 is 1000 more than 

b) 3000 is 200 more than 

c) 700 is 90 less than 

2 **Find the change from £10.00 if I buy:**

a) A book for £4.50

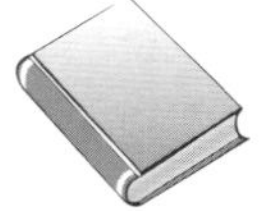

£

b) A bus ticket for 90p.

£

c) A DVD for £8.40.

£

3 **Fill in the boxes:**

a) $240 + 90 =$ ☐

b) $2070 + 3020 =$ ☐

c) $1010 - 80 =$ ☐

d) $540 - 330 =$ ☐

4 **Join pairs of numbers with a difference of 80.**

110	940
250	560
640	1030
950	170
1020	30

Activity

Look at the map.
Find the lengths of different routes.
E.g. House to shop, via church
= 200 m + 410 m = 610 m
Then make up your own map and do the same.

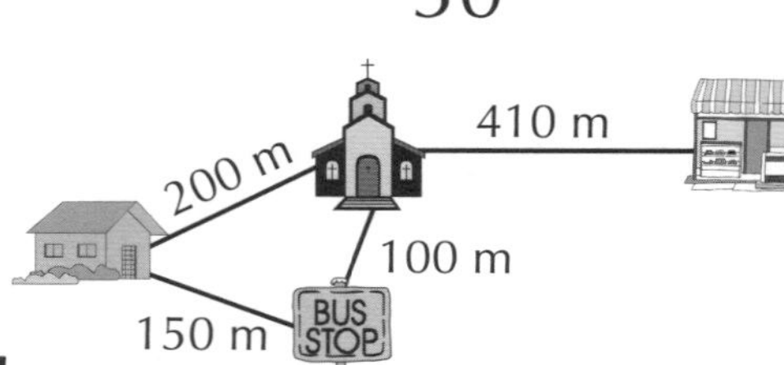

Learning Objective:

"I can add and subtract multiples of 10, 100 and 1000."

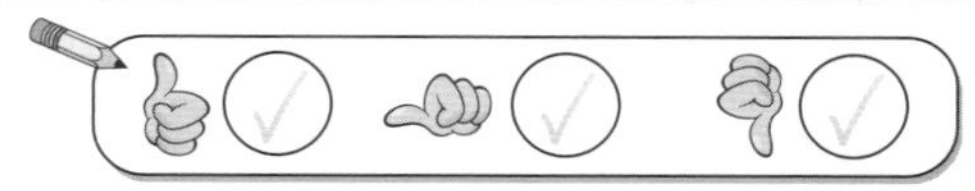

Key Objective

Adding and Subtracting

1 **Fill in the boxes:**

a) $2.2 + 1.7 =$ ☐

b) $7.4 + 1.3 =$ ☐

c) $5.1 - 4.9 =$ ☐

d) $8.4 - 7.7 =$ ☐

2 **The slug race track is 10 cm long.**

How much further must each slug go?

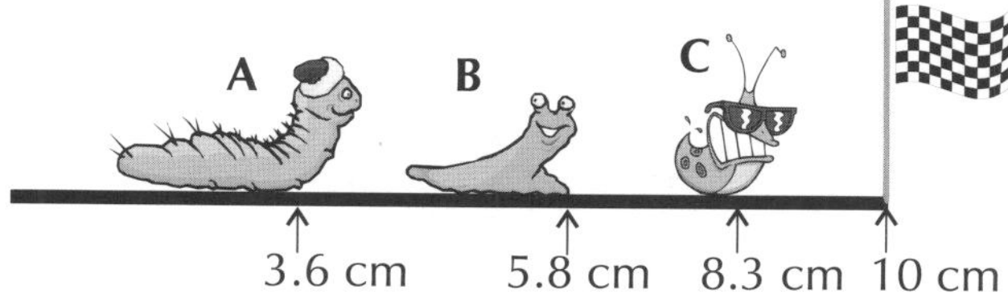

A = ☐ cm B = ☐ cm C = ☐ cm

3 **Make all these additions and subtractions equal 7.**

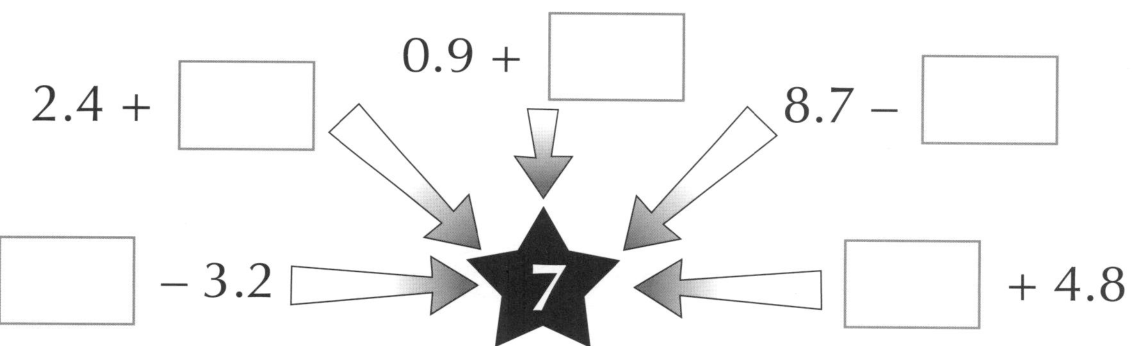

4 **Circle the two numbers which add together to make 27.**

11.9 12.7 13.5 14.3 14.1

5 **Circle the two numbers with a difference of 3.6.**

5.2 6.3 7.5 8.7 9.9

Activity Pick a number between 1 and 10.
Write down 5 decimal sums that equal this number.
Can you write down your sums in a pattern to do this more quickly?

Learning Objective:

"I can add and subtract decimals in my head by using a related two-digit addition or subtraction."

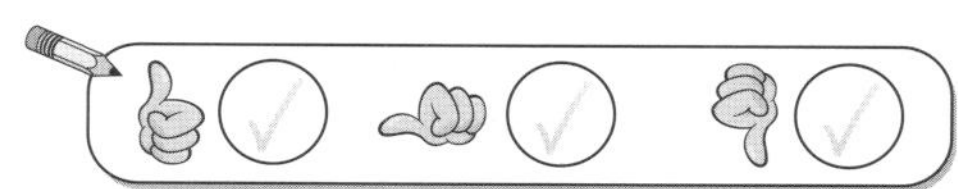

 Name: .... Date: ....

Checking Calculations

Don't use a calculator unless the question tells you to

1 **Write the correct number in each box:**

13 + 7 = 20 Check: 20 – 7 = 13

a) 12 + 11 = 23 Check: 23 – 11 = ☐

b) 4 + 6 = 10 Check: 10 – ☐ = ☐

c) 22 + 31 = 53 Check: ☐ – ☐ = ☐

2 **Multiply each number. Check your answer by dividing.**

One is done for you.

	1 →	×2	2	÷2	1
a)	4 →	×2	☐	÷2	☐
b)	6 →	×5	☐	÷5	☐
c)	8 →	×10	☐	÷10	☐

3 **Circle a number which is about the same as 61 – 29.**

10 20 30 40 50 60

4 **Circle a number which is about the same as 42 ÷ 5.**

1 3 5 7 8 11

Activity Start with number 15. Use a calculator to multiply 15 by another number. Then do a division calculation so that you get back to 15. Write down which buttons you press.

Learning Objective:

"I can estimate and check my calculations using inverses."

Checking Calculations

Don't use a calculator for this sheet

1 Show how you could check this division sum:

$81 \div 9 = 9$ Check: $9 \times \square = \square$

2 Estimate the total cost to the nearest pound.

a) 

99p £1.99

 £ ☐

b) 

£1.99 £4.98

 £ ☐

c) 

£1.99 £2.99

£ ☐

3 Circle a number which is about the same as 38 + 39.

30 60 70 80 100 130

4 Circle a number which is about the same as 51 × 4.

50 100 150 200 250 300

5 Fill in boxes to make each statement correct.

One is done for you.

$4 + \boxed{3}$  (–)  $\boxed{3} = 4$

a) $9 + \square$  ◯ $\square = 9$

b) $7 \times \square$  ◯ $\square = 7$

Activity

You can get from 5 to 30 by doing ×10, then ÷2, then +5.
How can you get back from 30 to 5 using reverse calculations?
Find a way of getting from 2 to 15 using 3 steps.
Then go from 15 to 2 using reverse calculations.

Learning Objective:

"I can use reverse calculations and rounding to help me check calculations."

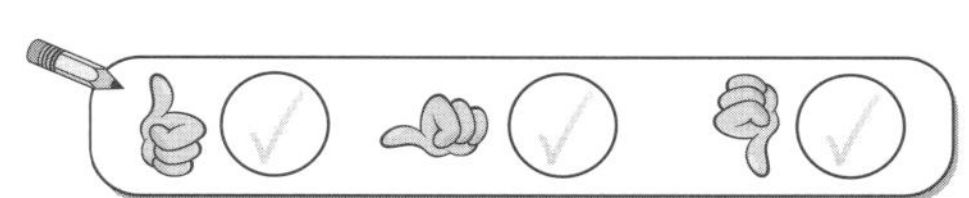

 Name: .... Date: ....

Checking Calculations

Don't use a calculator for this sheet

1 Do the two step calculation and then check your answer.

E.g. 3 $\xrightarrow{\times 2}$ [6] $\xrightarrow{+3}$ [9]   [9] $\xrightarrow{-3}$ [6] $\xrightarrow{\div 2}$ 3

10 $\xrightarrow{-5}$ [ ] $\xrightarrow{\times 2}$ [ ]   [ ] $\xrightarrow{\div 2}$ [ ] $\xrightarrow{+5}$ 10

2 Paul and Amy went to a car boot sale.

Estimate how much they each spent and circle the correct amount.

Paul

£3.94
£5.94
£7.94
£8.94

Amy

£2.95
£9.98
95p

£10.88
£11.88
£13.88
£16.88

3 Jim says that four 52-seater coaches are needed to take 210 children to the zoo.

a) Round the numbers and do a calculation to check this is about right.

b) Work out the actual number of seats on 4 coaches to see if Jim is right.

Activity Find a receipt from a shopping trip.
Use estimation to check that the total looks about right.

Learning Objective:

"I can use reverse calculations and rounding to help me check calculations."

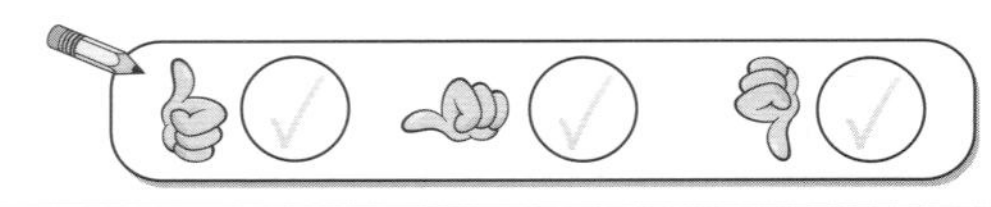

Checking Calculations

Don't use a calculator for this sheet

1 **Jenny has worked out that 13 + 14 = 27.**

Using only those numbers, and the symbols for adding (+) and subtracting (–), write two other calculations that can be made from this number sentence.

a) [ ]

b) [ ]

2 **Using rounding, estimate an answer to these divisions and circle the sensible estimate:**

a)	119 ÷ 61 =	20	2	15	4
b)	265 ÷ 28 =	9	11	6	14
c)	842 ÷ 19 =	34	38	42	50
d)	92 ÷ 6 =	12	15	18	20

3 **Emma has worked out that 265 + 318 = 583.**
Circle the equation you might use to check her answer.

318 × 265 583 – 318 583 ÷ 265

4 **Fill in the empty boxes below.**

If I know that **32 ÷ 4 = 8**, then I also know that:

a) 8 [ ] 4 = 32 b) 32 = 4 [ ] 8 c) 32 [ ] 8 = 4

5 **Round these numbers to the nearest hundred to work out roughly what the answer is. Show your working in the box:**

1687 – 926 = [ ]

Activity How far do you and your friends have to travel to get to school? Can you estimate the total distance?

Learning Objective:

"I can use inverse operations and rounding to help me check calculations."

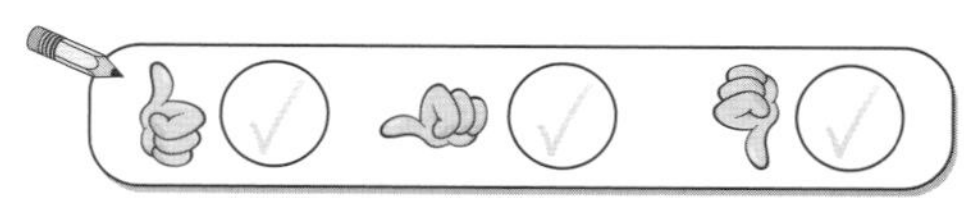

 Name: .... Date: ....

Doubling and Halving

Don't use a calculator for this sheet

1 Choose numbers to put in the boxes to make the calculations right. The first one has been done for you.

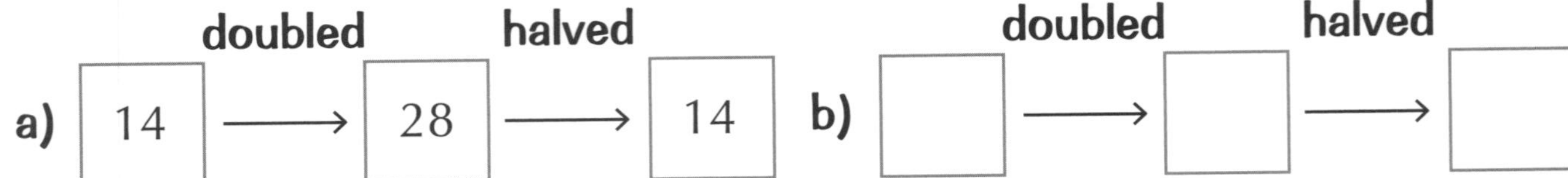

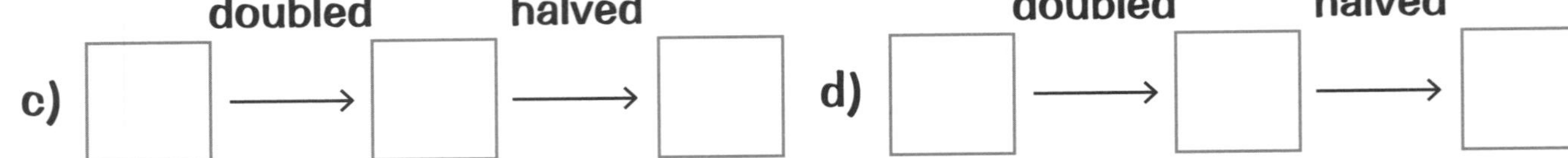

2 Double 17 is 34. Check that this is true by filling in the boxes:

a) $17 + \square = 34$ b) $34 \div \square = 17$

3 Each day, a bug splits in two to make 2 new bugs. Fill in the boxes to find out how many there are after 6 days.

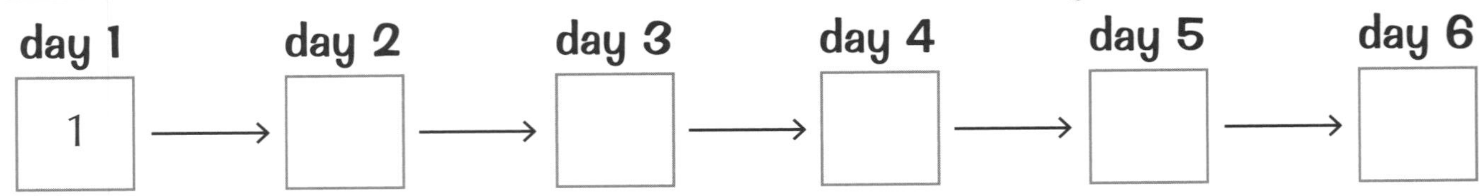

Check your calculations by starting with the total on day 6 and halving each day instead of doubling.

day 6	day 5	day 4	day 3	day 2	day 1
					1

Activity Take the shoe sizes of your friends and double them. Can you halve them to check you're right each time?

Learning Objective:

"I can check the calculations I do with doubling and halving."

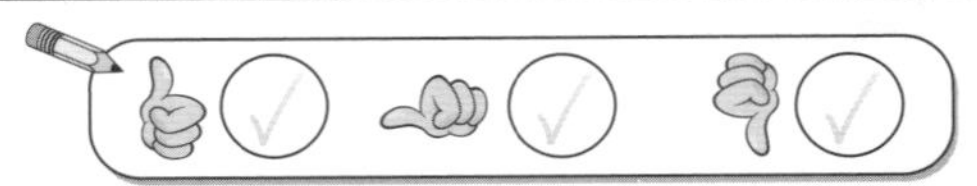

Doubling and Halving

1 Fill in the empty boxes below.

a) double
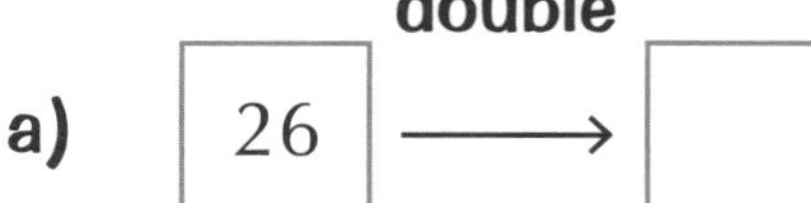

b) 110 —double→ ☐

c) double
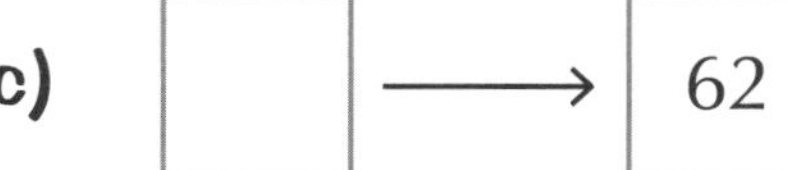

d) double

2 Here are the full prices of some shopping items.
Some are on special offer.

Tuna 190p

Bread 150p

Half price

Pears usually 18p

Bananas usually 26p

Write how much it costs for Anne to buy these items, and show your working:

a) 2 tins of tuna. ☐

b) 2 loaves of bread. ☐

c) 10 pears. ☐

d) 10 bananas. ☐

3 Ben has a jar with 240 sweets in.
He buys another jar that's exactly the same.

a) How many sweets does he have? ☐

b) Ben gives half a jar of sweets to his sister.
How many sweets does she have? ☐

Activity How many children are in your class? Try doubling and halving this number. Then try the same with some bigger numbers.

Learning Objective:

"I can double and halve two and some three digit numbers."

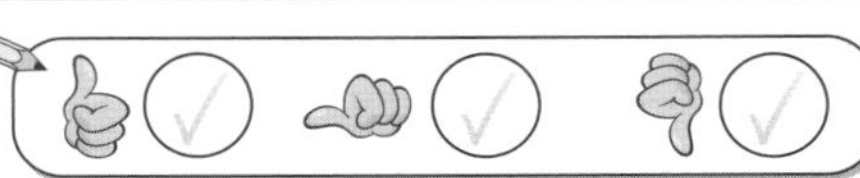

Name: .... Date: ....

Doubling and Halving

Don't use a calculator for this sheet

1 Use the digits below to make the calculations correct.

7.2 8.4 8.2 7.8 0.6 7.6

a) 3.8 + 3.8 = ☐

b) 3.6 + 3.6 = ☐

c) ☐ – 4.2 = 4.2

d) ☐ – 4.1 = 4.1

e) 0.6 + ☐ = 1.2

f) 15.6 – ☐ = 7.8

2 What is half of 74?

a) ☐

b) What is half of 7.4? 

3 What is double 24?

a) 

b) What is double 2.4? ☐

4 What is half of these numbers?

a) 6.8 ☐ b) 8.2 ☐ c) 0.2 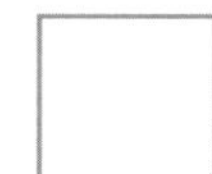 d) 14.4 

5 What is double these numbers?

a) 3.8 ☐ b) 4.8 ☐ c) 9.7  d) 0.5 

Activity Add up all the spare change you can find at home in pounds and pence. How much would there be if you <u>double</u> or <u>halve</u> it?

Learning Objective:

"I can double and halve using decimals."

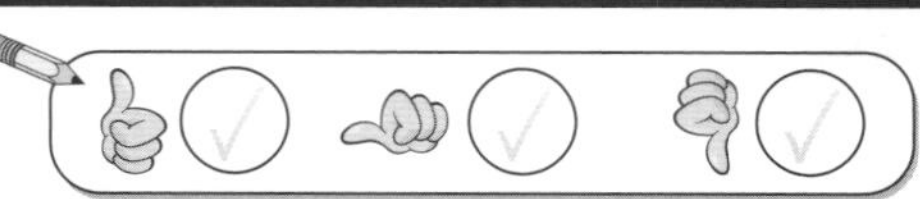

Fraction Pairs

1 **Three cakes have had a piece cut out. Draw a line to match each cake with its missing piece:**

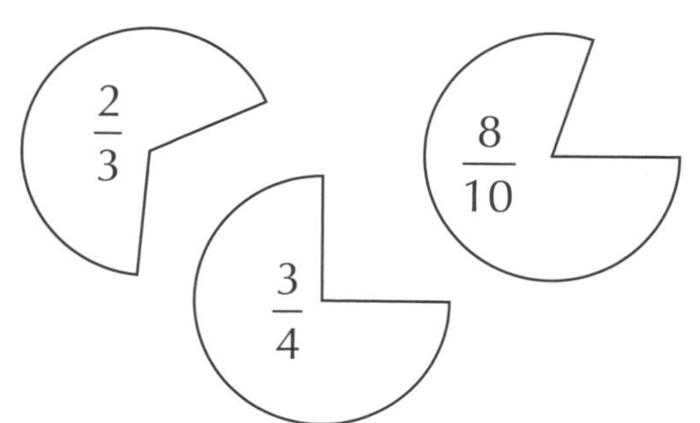

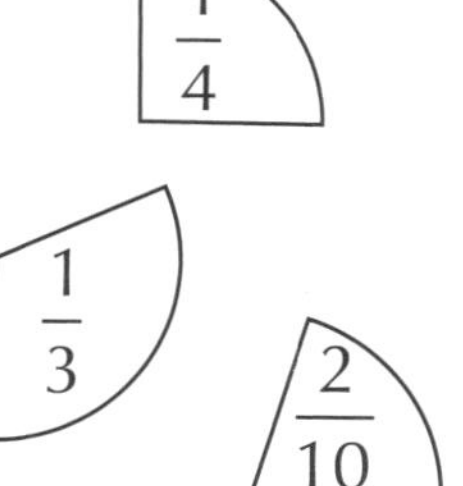

2 **In each group, circle two fractions that make up a whole:**

a) $\frac{1}{3}$ $\frac{1}{2}$ $\frac{1}{4}$ $\frac{1}{2}$

b) $\frac{1}{2}$ $\frac{2}{3}$ $\frac{3}{4}$ $\frac{1}{3}$

c) $\frac{1}{5}$ $\frac{3}{4}$ $\frac{2}{5}$ $\frac{3}{5}$

3 **Say what fraction of each shape is white and what fraction is shaded. Then add the fractions together.**

Fraction that is white | Fraction that is shaded

a)

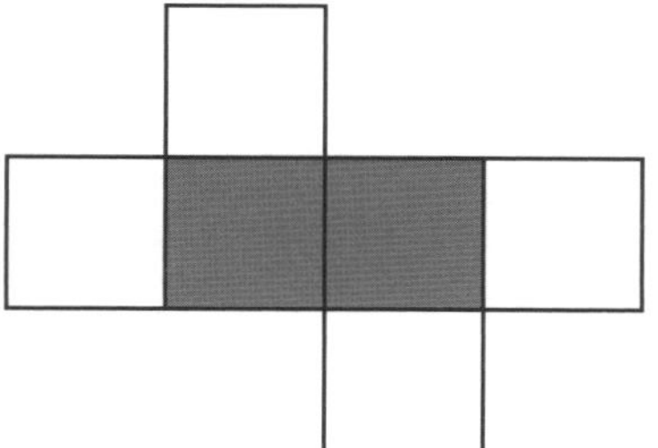

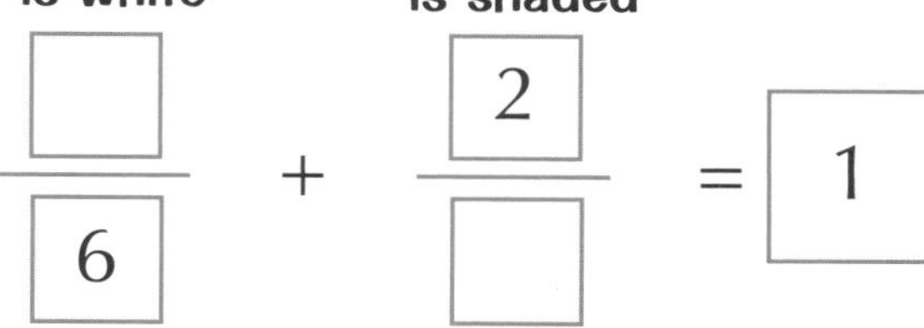

b)

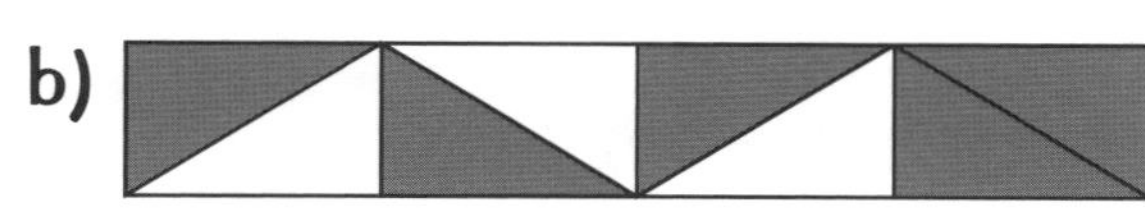

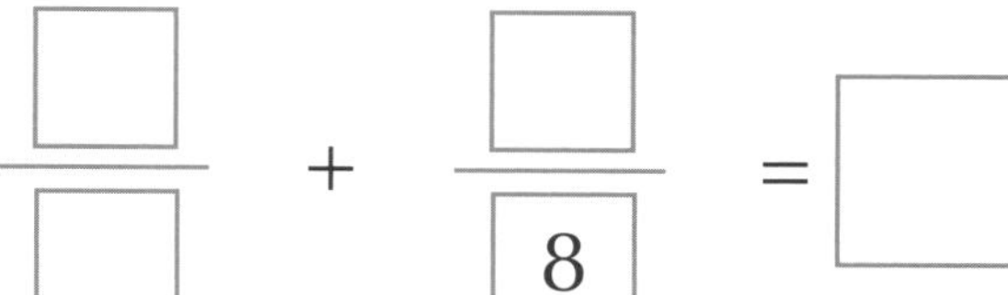

c)

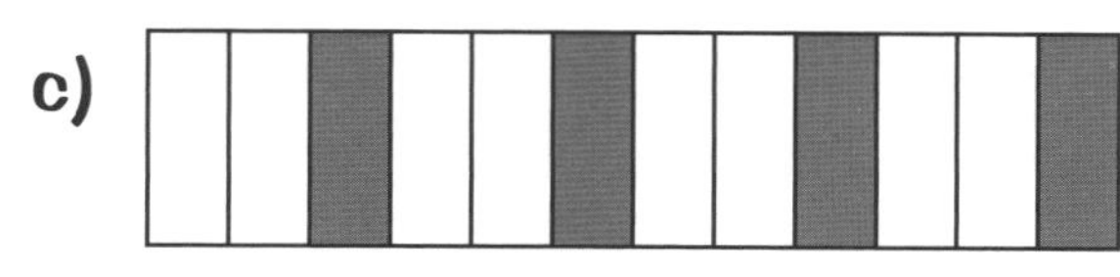

$\frac{\square}{\square} + \frac{\square}{\square} = \square$

Activity Collect pens from around your home. What fraction are blue? What fraction are <u>not</u> blue? What do these fractions <u>add to</u>? Try the same with other objects and colours.

Learning Objective:

"I can identify fractions that add up to 1."

Fraction Pairs

1 **Eight pizzas were cut up. They were put onto three plates. Complete these sums to find out how many pizzas are on each plate:**

$\frac{3}{4} + \frac{1}{4} =$

$1\frac{1}{2} + 2\frac{1}{2} =$

$2\frac{2}{3} + \frac{1}{3} =$

a) ☐ b) ☐ c) ☐

2 **Complete these fractions:**

a) $\frac{2}{8} + \frac{\square}{8} = 1$

b) $\frac{1}{3} + \frac{2}{\square} = 1$

c) $1\frac{3}{4} + 1\frac{1}{\square} = 3$

d) $3\frac{7}{10} + \frac{\square}{10} = 4$

3 **Sam dropped a bag of 20 marbles. Five marbles fell out. Fill in the boxes below.**

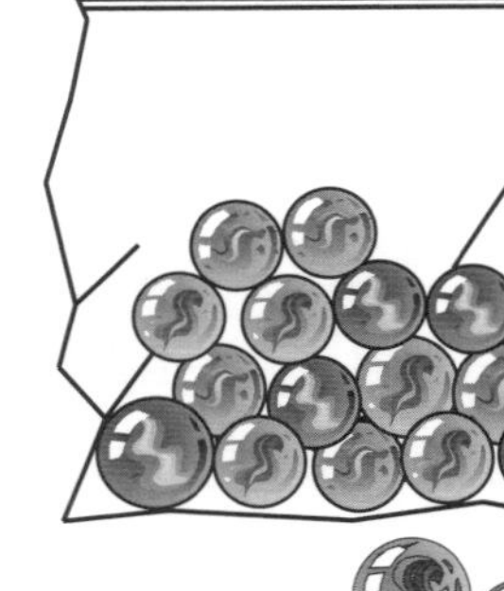

$\frac{\square}{\square}$ of the marbles fell out. $\frac{\square}{\square}$ were left in the bag.

Adding the fractions gives: $\frac{\square}{\square} + \frac{\square}{\square} = \square$

Activity Count the books on a shelf. Put them into two groups — big books and small books. Write down the fraction of big books and the fraction of small books. Add the fractions. Try the same for different groups, like light and dark colours.

Learning Objective:

"I can identify fractions that add up to 1."

Fraction Pairs

1 Two thirds of the class went to the school disco. What fraction didn't go?

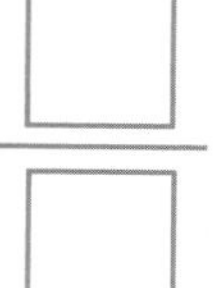

2 Half of the children at a school have school dinners. A quarter have packed lunches. What fraction go home?

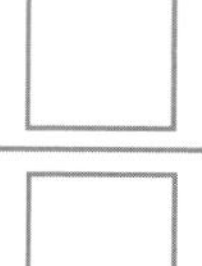

3 I want to share a cake fairly between myself and three friends. Should I cut it into quarters or thirds? Show how you know.

4 Bill breaks a chocolate bar into 12 equal pieces. He gives five pieces to his brother. What fraction does he keep for himself?

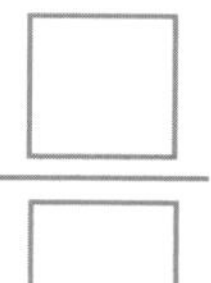

5 Look at this square. Label parts A-D as fractions of the square.

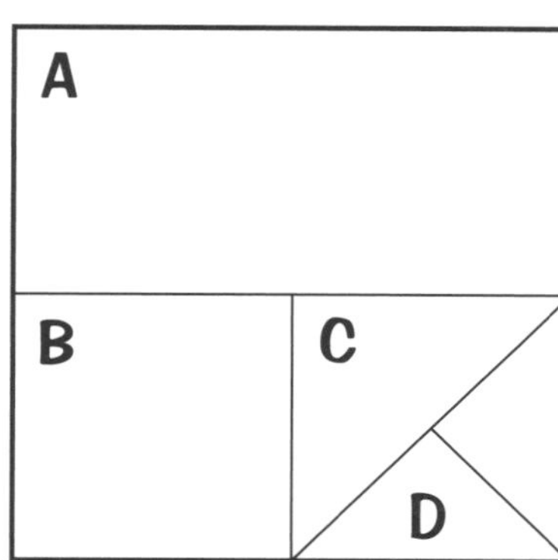

A= ☐/☐ C= ☐/☐

B= ☐/☐ D= ☐/☐

Activity Write your name on a piece of paper.
What fraction of the letters are vowels?
What fraction are consonants?
Add the fractions together.
Now try it with other names.

The 5 vowels are a, e, i, o and u. Consonants are all the other letters in the alphabet.

Learning Objective:

"I can identify fractions that add up to 1."

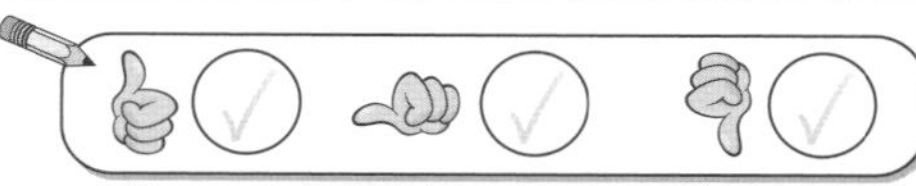

Multiplication and Division

1 Circle the numbers which are multiples of two.
Underline the numbers which are multiples of five.

487 236 900 865 404 788 634

2 Complete these sentences by putting a number in the box.

a) If you multiply  by 6 you get 36.

b) If you divide ☐ by 5 you get 4.

c) If you times ☐ by 3 and then double it you get 36.

3 Complete these calculations.

a) Thirty children sit at tables in groups of five. How many groups are there?

30 ÷ 5 = ☐

b) Zoe has twenty flowers. She divides them equally between four vases. How many flowers go in each vase?

20 ○ ☐ = ☐

c) Joe has a bag of marbles. He divides the marbles into nine groups of three. How many marbles were in the bag?

☐ × 3 = ☐

d) Rachel gives three cakes each to eight friends. She has two left. How many did she start with?

☐ ○ ☐ = 24

24 + ☐ = ☐

Activity Write out the 6 times table from $6 \times 1 = 6$ to $6 \times 10 = 60$.
Use each multiplication to write down two divisions.
Like this: $6 \times 2 = 12$ gives $12 \div 2 = 6$ and $12 \div 6 = 2$.

Learning Objective:

"I know my 2, 3, 4, 5, 6 and 10 times tables and can work out the division facts that go with them."

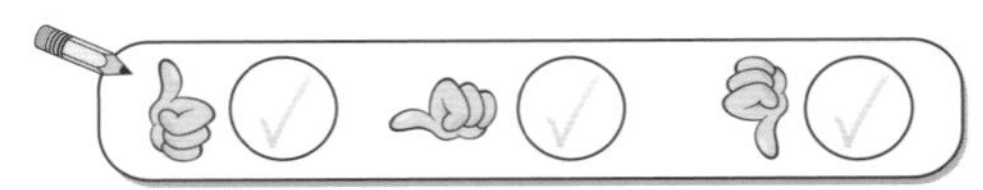

Key Objective

Multiplication and Division

1 Circle the diagram which would help you to work out 3 × 8.

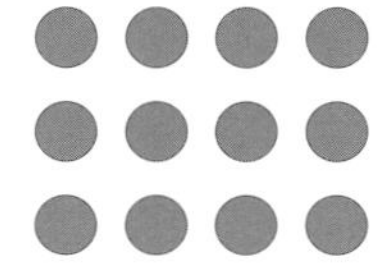

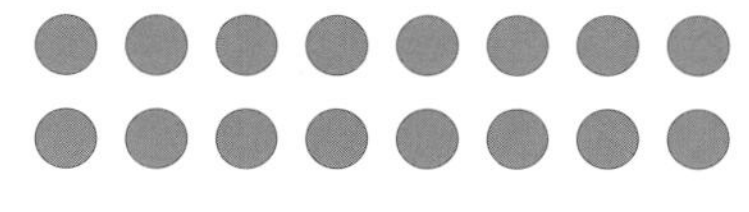

2 Draw diagrams that would help you work out:

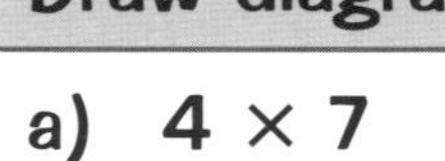

a) 4 × 7

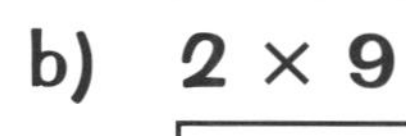

b) 2 × 9

3 I know that 10 × 8 = 80.

Use this fact to help you work out:

a) 5 × 8 = ☐ 10 × 4 = ☐ 5 × 4 = ☐

Now use your answers to help you work out these:

b) 40 ÷ 8 = ☐ 40 ÷ 10 = ☐ ☐ ÷ ☐ = 5

4 Use these digit cards once each to make:

2 3 4 5 6 9

a) a multiple of 7 and 8. b) a multiple of 7. c) a multiple of 8.

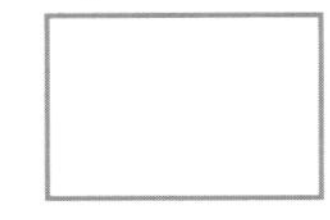

Activity All numbers that end in 8 are multiples of 4. True or false? Explain how you know.

Learning Objective:

"I know all my multiplication and division facts up to 10×10. I can spot multiples of numbers up to 10."

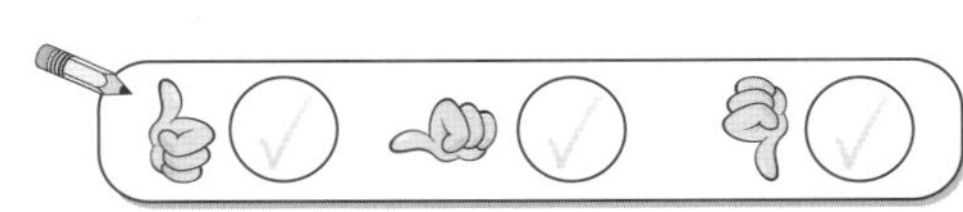

 Name: .... Date: ....

Key Objective

Multiplication and Division

1 **Circle the multiples of 8 in this list of numbers.**

14 32 40 55 64 72 79 80

2 **Look at this sum: 6 × 8 = 48.**

Use it to help you work out:

a) 3 × 8 = ☐ b) 6 × 4 = ☐ c) 48 ÷ 8 = ☐

3 **Write different multiples of each number on the petals of each flower.**

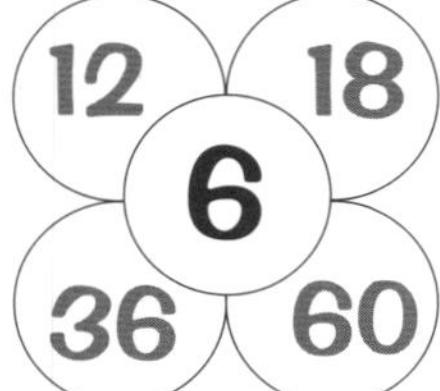

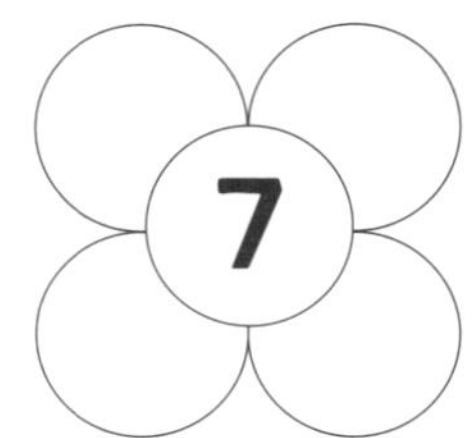

4 **Find a pair of numbers with a product of 27 and a sum of 12.**

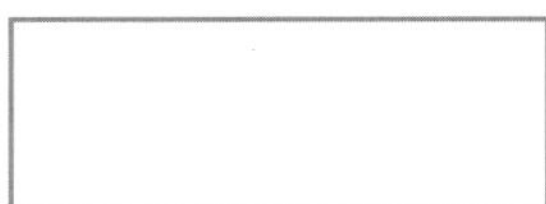

5 **All the children in a school went to a pantomime. At the theatre they were seated in rows of 9. 8 rows were filled and 4 children in wheelchairs sat in the front.**

How many children went on the trip?

Three bears have 40 small steps that lead to their front door. Boris climbs 8 steps in each stride. Doris climbs 4 steps in each stride, and Noris climbs 2 steps in each stride.
How many steps must each bear take to reach the door?
Now go and find some real steps and count them. How many steps of different sizes would it take to exactly reach the top step?

Learning Objective:

"I know all my multiplication and division facts up to 10×10. I can spot multiples of numbers up to 10."

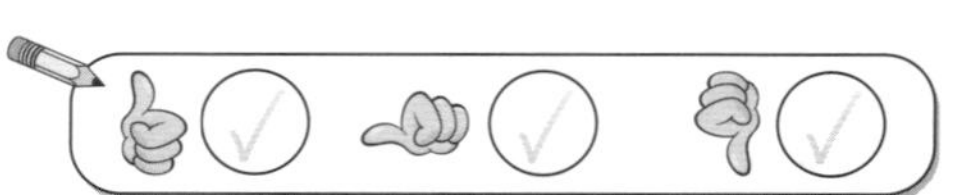

Key Objective

Multiplication and Division

1 Complete these calculations.

a) 9 × ☐ = 63

b) 6 × 9 = ☐

c) ☐ × 4 = 32

d) 45 ÷ ☐ = 5

e) 48 ÷ 6 = ☐

f) 56 ÷ 7 = ☐

2 Solve these problems. Show your working.

a) Twenty-one sprouts are shared between some children.
Each gets five and there is one left over. How many children are there?

b) Bill gives four rollerskates to each of his six zebras. He has three rollerskates left over. How many rollerskates did he have?

c) Sam has six books. They each have six pages. He reads four pages a night. How many nights will it take him to finish all the books?

3 Find the mystery numbers.

a) I am a multiple of both 8 and 6. I am less than 30.

b) If you multiply me by 10 then divide me by 4 you get 5.

Activity Find 5 numbers less than 20 that can only be divided exactly by themselves and 1.
E.g. 7 can only be divided by 1 and 7.
It can't be divided by 2, 3, 4, 5 or 6.

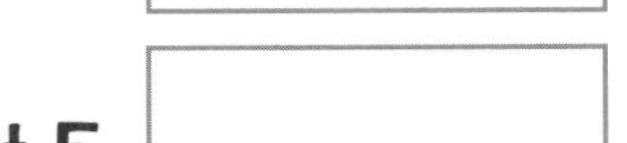

Learning Objective:

"I know all my multiplication and division facts up to 10×10. I can spot multiples of numbers up to 10."

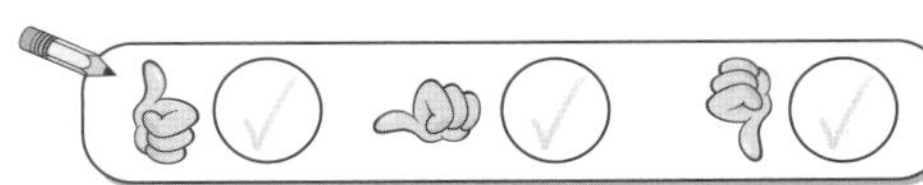

 Name: .... Date: ....

Multiplication and Division

Don't use a calculator for this sheet

1 Do these divisions. Check your answer by multiplying.

a) $24 \div 6 = \square$ b) $63 \div 7 = \square$ c) $32 \div 8 = \square$

$\square \times 6 = 24$ $\square \times 7 = 63$ $\square \times \square = 32$

2 Work out these multiplications.

a) $20 \times 4 = \square$ b) $200 \times 4 = \square$

c) $3 \times 60 = \square$ d) $3 \times 600 = \square$

3 Work out these divisions.

Check your answers by multiplying.

a) $120 \div 4 = \square$ b) $2100 \div 30 = \square$

c) $250 \div 50 = \square$ d) $280 \div 70 = \square$

4 Write the numbers below in the correct box.

Some numbers go in more than one box.

60 120 150 160 200 240

Multiples of 20	Multiples of 30	Multiples of 40	Multiples of 50

Activity Find as many multiplications and divisions as you can that give an answer between 30 and 40.

Learning Objective:

"I can use tables facts to multiply multiples of 10 and 100 and to find linked division facts."

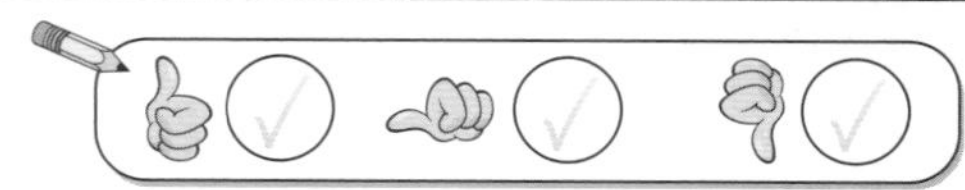

Calculators

1 Use a calculator to work out the following problems:

a) $132 \times 27 =$ ☐ c) $517 + 231 =$ ☐

b) $432 \div 18 =$ ☐ d) $457 - 272 =$ ☐

2 Jo buys 5 boxes of strawberry-flavoured worms for £3.32 each.

a) How much does she pay altogether? ☐

b) The shopkeeper takes 9p off each box. How much will Jo pay now? ☐

3 Len buys Ruby a gift for every day of the week.

They cost 75p, £1.12, 9p, £1, 3p, 76p and £3.45.

If he had £20 on Monday, how much does he have after Sunday? ☐

4 Work out the answers using your calculator:

a) $-13 \times 12 =$ ☐ c) $-474 \div 6 =$ ☐

b) $187 - 292 =$ ☐ d) $48 \times -13 =$ ☐

5 Dragon eggs cost £3.72 for 12 at the local market.

a) How much does it cost for 1 egg? 

b) How much does it cost for 25 eggs? 

Activity Using 10 calculator keys can you make an answer of 50?

For example: 1 1 × 3 + 1 4 + 3 = 50

Learning Objective:

"I can use a calculator to work out problems."

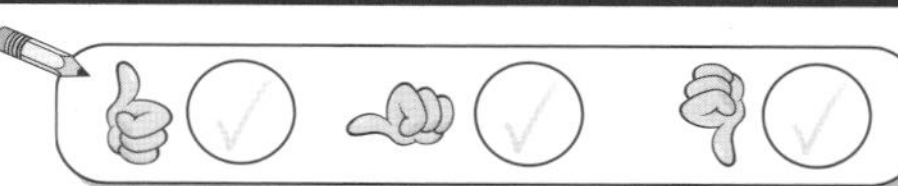

 Name: .... Date: ....

Calculators

1 **Use a calculator to work out these equations:**

a) $652 \times 71 =$ ☐

b) $3861 \div 27 =$ ☐

c) $437 \times 58 =$ ☐

d) $7 + 131 + 782 =$ ☐

e) $737 + 17 - 57 =$ ☐

f) $3617 - 7762 =$ ☐

2 **Lindsey has £14. She shares it equally between herself and 4 friends.**

Using your calculator, work out how much money they will each get.

☐

3 **Calculate the answers to these money problems:**

a) £1.70 – 48p = ☐

b) £7.32 ÷ 6 = ☐

c) £4.74 ÷ 6 = ☐

d) £87 – £2.92 = ☐

e) 96p + £1.03 = ☐

f) £13.10 × 12 = ☐

4 **Try these questions involving negative numbers:**

a) $-2 \times 71 =$ ☐

b) $-27 \div 3 =$ ☐

c) $-52 + 131 =$ ☐

d) $-5 \times -3 =$ ☐

5 **My piggy bank has £10.92 in it. If I take 13p out every day for sweets, how many weeks will it take for me to empty it?**

☐

Activity Find some adverts in a newspaper that are selling things. Try to find 5 objects which have prices that add up to £30.

Learning Objective:

"I can use my calculator to work out problems involving money and negative numbers."

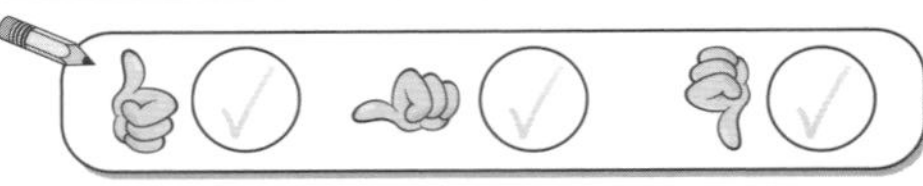

Calculators

1 Use a calculator to work out the following problems:

a) $1.3 \times 1.3 =$ ☐

c) $75 \div 12 =$ ☐

b) $125 \div 4 =$ ☐

d) $13.5 - 8.05 =$ ☐

2 Find the answers to these fractions using your calculator:

a) $\frac{1}{4}$ of 272 = ☐

e) $\frac{1}{8}$ of 176 = ☐

b) $\frac{3}{4}$ of 272 = ☐

f) $\frac{5}{8}$ of 176 = ☐

c) $\frac{1}{5}$ of 395 = ☐

g) $\frac{1}{12}$ of 252 = ☐

d) $\frac{3}{5}$ of 395 = ☐

h) $\frac{7}{12}$ of 252 = ☐

3 Lisa owns a pencil factory. One pencil is 13.2 cm long.

a) How long would a line of 75 pencils be? ☐

b) How many centimetres less than 10 metres is this? ☐

4 Calculate the answer to these problems. Give your answer in the most appropriate units (millimetres, centimetres, metres or kilometres).

a) $15.6 \text{ cm} \times 12 =$ ☐

d) $1.03 \text{ km} \div 36 =$ ☐

b) $15.6 \text{ m} \div 12 =$ ☐

e) $76 \text{ mm} \times 143 =$ ☐

c) $12.7 \text{ m} \times 923 =$ ☐

f) $12 \text{ mm} + 1.2 \text{ m} =$ ☐

Activity

Measure the length of your stride to the nearest centimetre.
How far would you walk in 2000 steps? Or 3000 steps?

Learning Objective:

"I can calculate problems involving decimals or fractions."

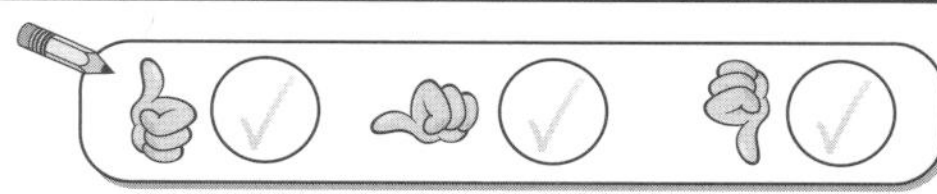

 Name: .... Date: ....

Key Objective

Mental Maths

Don't use a calculator for this sheet

1 Do these sums in your head.

a) $12 - 6 + 4 =$ ☐

b) $73 - 9 + 2 =$ ☐

c) $53 + 20 + 10 =$ ☐

d) $18 + 2 - 15 =$ ☐

2 Sam partitioned these sums into tens and units.

Draw a line to match each sum with the method, then fill in the answers.

a) $53 + 27$ $\qquad$ $30 + 20 + 8 + 5 =$ ☐

b) $38 + 25$ $\qquad$ $27 - 10 - 2 =$ ☐

c) $27 - 12$ $\qquad$ $50 + 20 + 3 + 7 =$ ☐

3 A class of children compared the temperature over the same week in 2 different years. The table shows what they found.

	Year 1	Year 2
Monday	8 °C	14 °C
Tuesday	9 °C	28 °C
Wednesday	11 °C	22 °C
Thursday	7 °C	11 °C
Friday	15 °C	18 °C

a) What was the difference in temperature between the Thursdays? ☐ °C

b) Which day showed the greatest rise in temperature? ☐

c) On which day was the rise in temperature less than 4 degrees? ☐

Activity Use each of these numbers once: 1, 10, 30, 40. Make a calculation which equals 59 by adding and taking them away. Use the same numbers to make a calculation which equals 21.

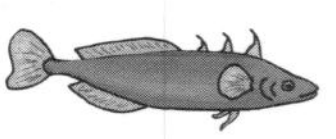

Learning Objective:

"I can add and subtract numbers in my head."

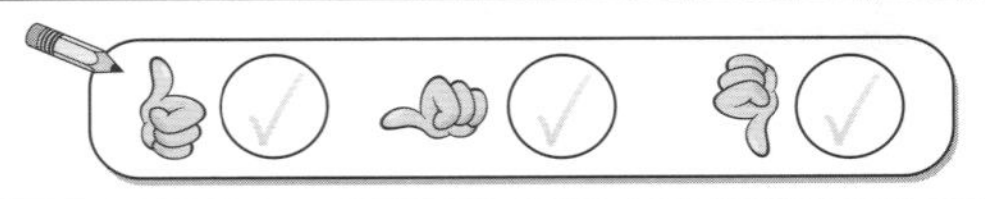

Key Objective

Mental Maths

Don't use a calculator for this sheet

1 Fill in the missing numbers.

a) 42 – ☐ = 30 b) 28 + 36 = ☐

c) ☐ + 72 = 100 d) 15 + ☐ = 50

e) 94 – 82 = ☐ f) ☐ – 31 = 8

2 Circle the pairs that have a difference of 12.

37 and 50 41 and 29 74 and 82

15 and 17 58 and 36 25 and 37

3 Use rounding and adjusting to complete these sums.

Round one or both numbers to the nearest 10, then adjust at the end.
Then show what you did to work them out.

a) 19 + 35 = ☐ What I did: ☐

b) 31 + 17 = ☐ What I did: ☐

c) 78 + 20 = ☐ What I did: ☐

4 Now try these questions:

a) I have 43p and Bob has 36p.
How much more money do I have than Bob?

b) I have completed 43 skips.
How many more do I need to do before I reach 100?

Activity Choose a list of numbers out of the phone book. See if you can add the last two digits of some of them to get as close as you can to 100 without going over.

Learning Objective:

"I can add and subtract two two-digit numbers in my head."

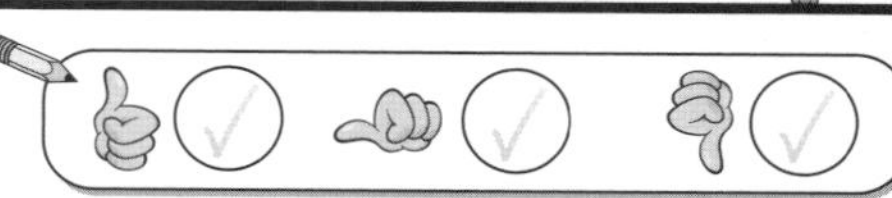

 Name: .... Date: ....

Mental Maths

Don't use a calculator for this sheet

1 **Use the times tables you know to complete these sums.**

Explain how you did them.

a) $12 \times 9 =$ 108 — I added 9 × 10 to 9 × 2 = 90 + 18 = 108

b) $20 \times 3 =$

c) $50 \times 5 =$

2 **Use your rounding skills to help solve these sums.**

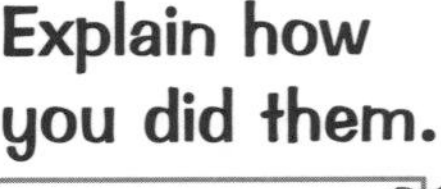

Explain how you did them.

a) $5030 - 2997 =$

b) $2003 - 900 =$

3 **Solve these problems. Use jottings to help you.**

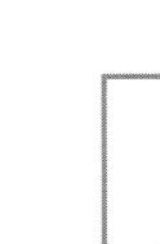

a) One lolly costs 15p. How much would five cost?

b) Four apples cost 68p. How much would one cost?

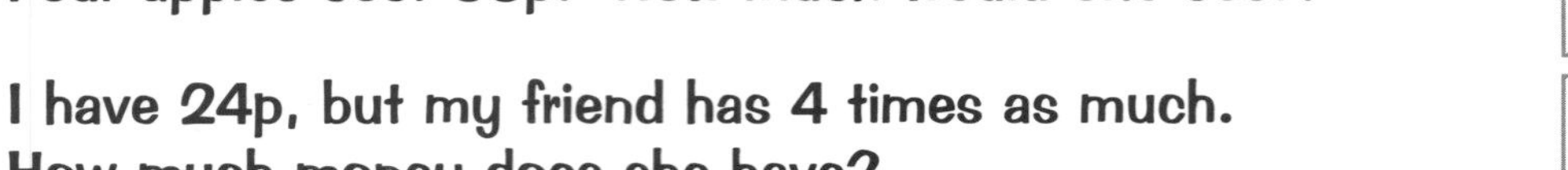

c) I have 24p, but my friend has 4 times as much.
How much money does she have?

4 **Solve each sum in your head.** Explain how you did them.

a) $11 \times 25 =$

b) $2834 + 2999 =$

c) $14 \times 4 =$

Activity Find 3 consecutive numbers that add up to 162 (consecutive means 1 after another).

Learning Objective:

"I can multiply one and two digit numbers, and add and subtract numbers near to whole thousands in my head."

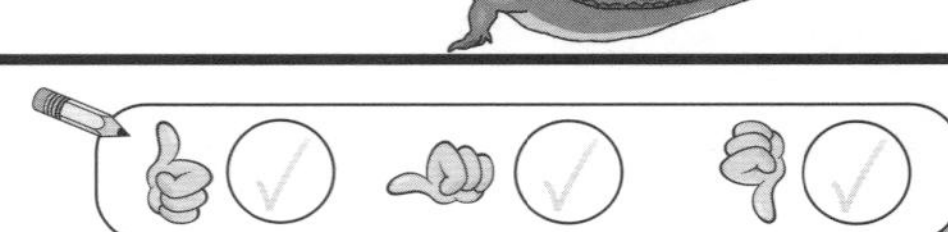

Multiply by 10, 100 and 1000

Don't use a calculator for this sheet

1 **Fill in the missing numbers:**

2 **Sally fills 21 boxes with biscuits.**

A box holds 10 biscuits. How many biscuits does Sally have altogether?

3 **Tom has sixteen 10p coins and ten 20p coins.**

How much money does he have altogether?

4 **72 × 100 = 7200.**

Explain what happens to the value of 7 when 72 is multiplied by 100.

Activity Choose 3 numbers between 1 and 10. Multiply each number by 100 and add your answers together. Can you find 3 answers that will give a total of 800? Or 1000?

Learning Objective:

"I can explain how the place value of a number changes when I multiply by 10 or 100."

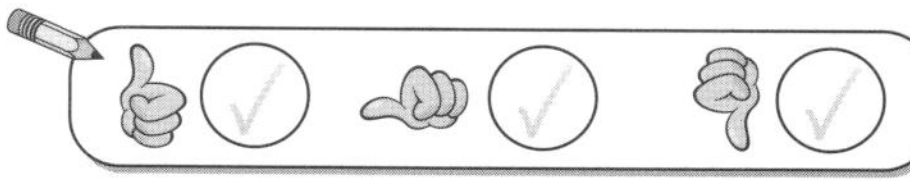

Multiply by 10, 100 and 1000

Don't use a calculator for this sheet

1 **What is eight hundred and forty divided by ten?**

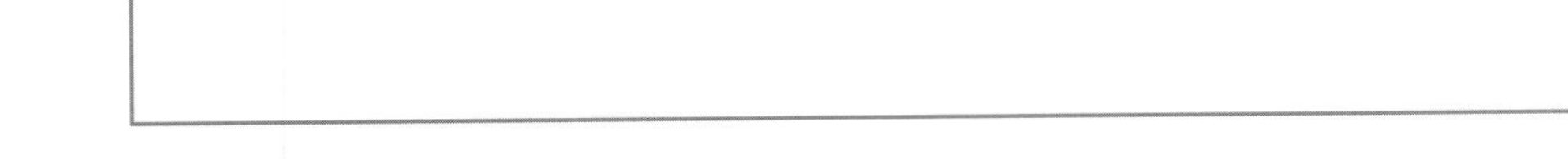

2 **Fill in the missing numbers.**

a) $17 \times \square = 1700$

b) $\square \div 10 = 157$

c) $100 \times \square = 2300$

d) $3600 \div \square = 36$

3 **Work out the answers to these problems:**

a) What number is 100 times bigger than 45?

b) What number is 10 times smaller than 5620?

c) What number is 10 times bigger than 27?

d) What number is 100 times smaller than 8600?

4 **Stickers are sold in sheets of 10.**

I need six hundred and eighty stickers. How many sheets must I buy?

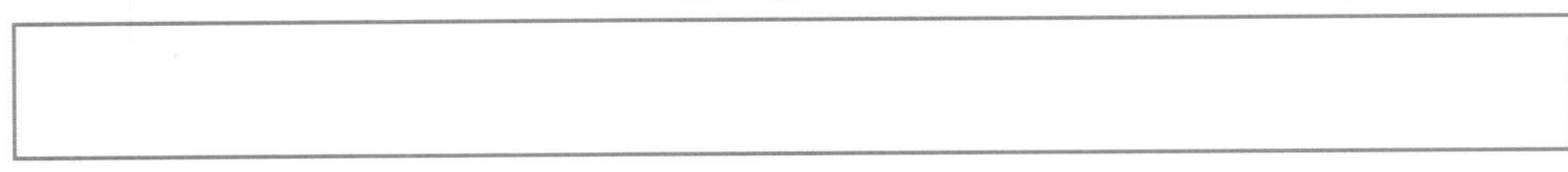

Activity

$60 \times 7 = 420$ is based on $6 \times 7 = 42$. List three other <u>multiplications</u> based on $6 \times 7 = 42$ and work out the answer to each. Now do the same with $3 \times 8 = 24$.

Learning Objective:

"I can multiply and divide numbers by 10 and 100."

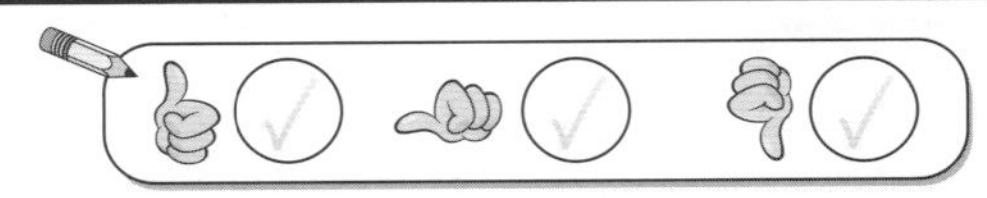

Multiply by 10, 100 and 1000

Don't use a calculator for this sheet

1 **Answer these questions:**

a) How many tens are there in one hundred?

b) How many hundreds are there in one thousand?

c) How many tens are there in one thousand?

2 **Fill in the missing numbers.**

a) $25 \times 10 = \square$

b) $5400 \div \square = 5.4$

c) $420 \div \square = 100$

d) $56.4 \times 10 = \square$

e) $73.6 \times 100 = \square$

f) $17.8 \div \square = 1.78$

g) $\square \times 1000 = 16\,000$

3 **Katie puts 100 2p coins edge to edge across a playground.**

Each coin is 2.5 cm wide. How long is the line of coins?

4 **Greg is thinking of a number.**

He divides the number by 100 and then by 10. His answer is 61.
What number was he thinking of? Show your working.

Activity Find a simple cake recipe. Calculate how much of each ingredient you would need to make a hundred cakes. How much would you need to make one tenth of one cake?

Learning Objective:

"I can multiply and divide decimals by 10, 100 and 1000."

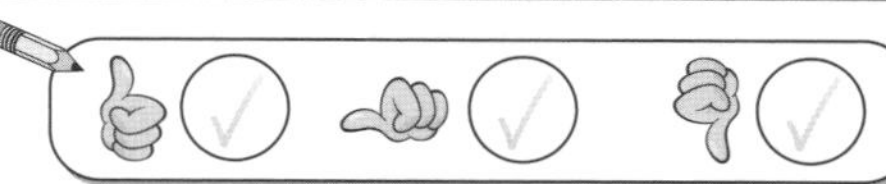

 Name: .... Date: ....

Using Fractions

Don't use a calculator for this sheet

1 **4 people try to run a 20 km race, but they all get tired before they finish.**

The table shows the fraction of the race that each person runs. Fill in the missing distances.

Runner	Fraction of 20 km race completed	Distance run
Ahmed	$\frac{1}{2}$	10 km
Alison	$\frac{1}{4}$	
Jenny	$\frac{1}{5}$	
Roland	$\frac{1}{10}$	

2 **Complete the number sentences below. One has been done for you.**

a) $\frac{1}{2}$ of [16] = 8 b) $\frac{1}{3}$ of [ ] = 3 c) $\frac{1}{4}$ of [ ] = 3

3 **Lucy has 4 types of fruit juice. She gives an equal amount of each type of juice to 5 classes at her school. Fill in the missing numbers.**

a) Orange juice: $\frac{1}{5}$ of 15 litres = [ ] litres

b) Apple juice: $\frac{1}{5}$ of 25 litres = [ ] litres

c) Pineapple juice: $\frac{1}{5}$ of [ ] litres = 7 litres

d) Mango juice: $\frac{1}{5}$ of 20 litres = [ ] litres

Activity Using the numbers below, how many ways can you make this number sentence correct? Write them down.

$\frac{1}{2}$ of [ ] = [ ]

Use these numbers: 1 2 3 4 5 6 7 8 9 10 11 12 13 14

Learning Objective:

"I can find fractions of numbers using division."

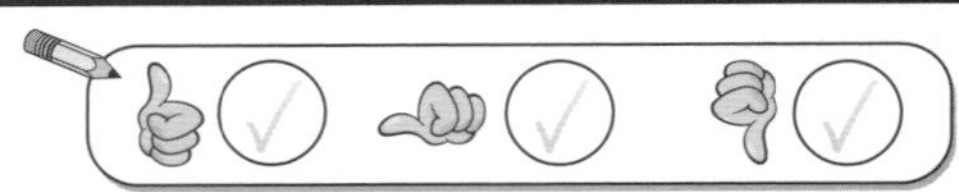

Using Fractions

Don't use a calculator for this sheet

1 30 guests are at a party. $\frac{1}{5}$ of the guests are boys. $\frac{4}{5}$ are girls.

How many boys and girls are there? ☐ boys ☐ girls

2 Calculate these fractions.

a) $\frac{3}{8}$ of 24 g = ☐

b) $\frac{2}{7}$ of 21 cm = ☐

3 A basketball team scores 32 points in a game.

Jason scores $\frac{1}{4}$ of the points.
Joanne scores $\frac{5}{8}$ of the points
and Lee scores $\frac{1}{8}$ of the points.

Complete the points chart.

Player	Jason	Joanne	Lee
Points scored	8		

4 Elton has 50p. He spends $\frac{1}{10}$ of his money on sweets, $\frac{1}{5}$ on a pencil, $\frac{3}{10}$ on stickers and $\frac{2}{5}$ on a comic. How much does each item cost?

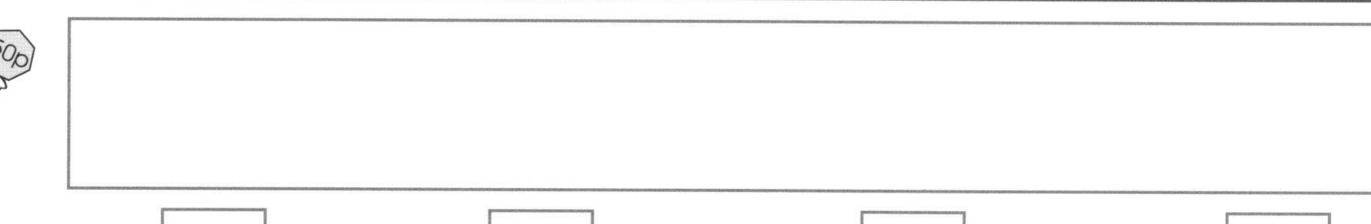

Sweets: ☐ p Pencil: ☐ p Stickers: ☐ p Comic: ☐ p

Activity Write some fraction sentences about things you find in your house. For example:
$\frac{3}{8}$ of the rooms contain beds. $\frac{2}{5}$ of the toothbrushes are blue.

Learning Objective:

"I can find a fraction of a number or an amount."

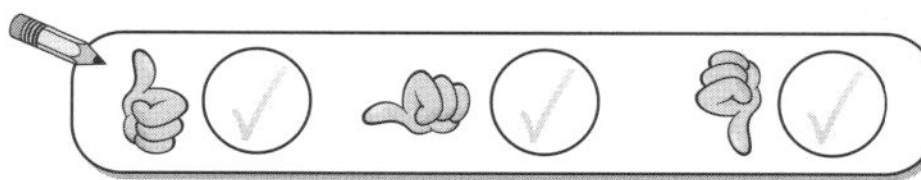

 Name: .... Date: ....

Using Fractions

Don't use a calculator for this sheet

1 **Work out these fractions.**

a) $\frac{2}{3}$ of 120 =

b) $\frac{7}{10}$ of 120 =

2 **Professor Digit's Number Machine can find 5% of any number.**

It has already worked out 5% of 20.
What answer will it give for the other numbers? Write your answers in the correct shapes.

Remember that 5% is half of 10%

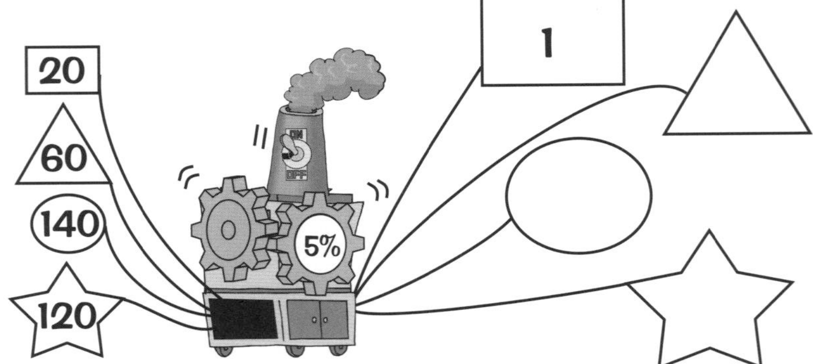

3 **Fill in the gaps in the table. Show your working in the box below.**

Whole amount	20 m	40 kg	80 mins	£1.20
$\frac{3}{5}$				72 p
25%	5 m			

Activity Find one fifth of each of these numbers: 35 100 75 150 60.
Which ones give answers of 15 or less?
Find 3 other numbers where the value of $\frac{1}{5}$ is a whole number that is less than 15.

Learning Objective:

"I can find a fraction or percentage of an amount."

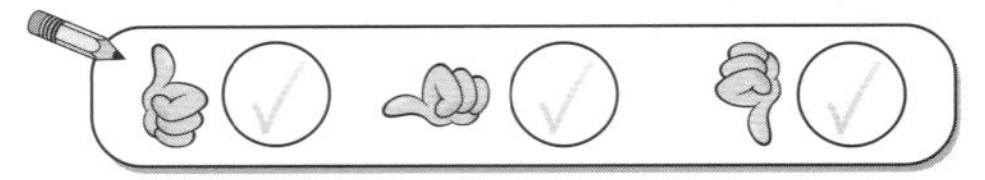

Written Adding and Subtracting

1 **Write the totals:**

a) 25 + 11 =

b) 46 + 32 =

c) 142 + 85 =

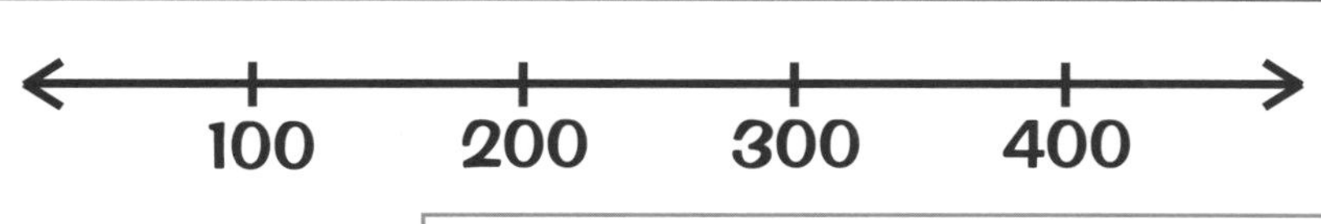

2 **Work out the difference between 153 and 409.**

100 200 300 400

Use the number line to help.

difference =

3 **Write the answers:**

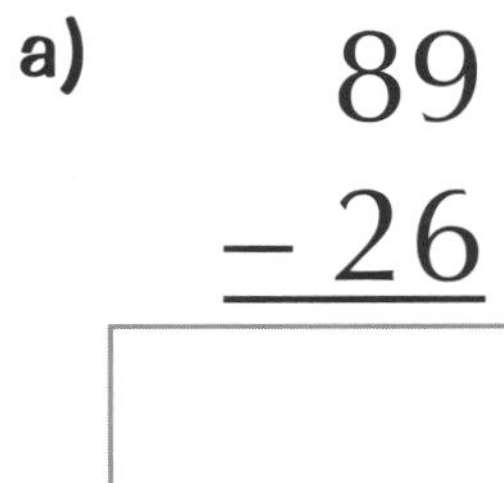

a) 89 − 26 =

b) 385 − 184 =

c) 72 − 26 =

4 **Mary's book is 58 pages long. Her Dad's book is 110 pages long.**

What is the difference between the lengths of their books?

Activity What is the difference between 62 and 15?
Find five more pairs of numbers with the same difference.

Learning Objective:

"I can add or subtract two-digit or three-digit numbers."

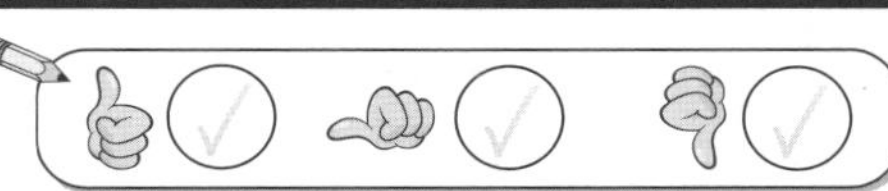

Written Adding and Subtracting

1 **Write the totals:**

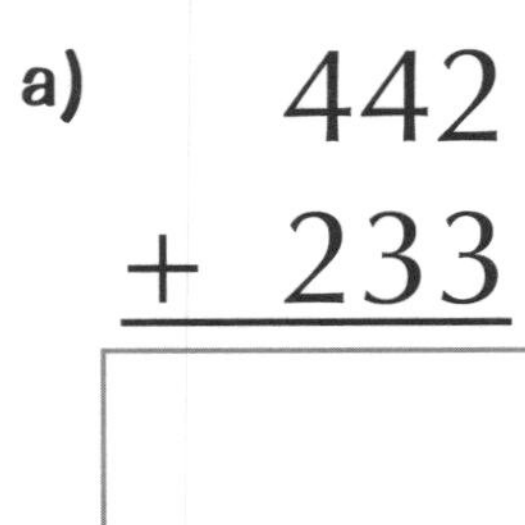

a) $\begin{array}{r} 442 \\ +\ 233 \\ \hline \end{array}$ ☐

b) $\begin{array}{r} 714 \\ +\ 125 \\ \hline \end{array}$ ☐

c) $\begin{array}{r} 173 \\ +\ 418 \\ \hline \end{array}$ ☐

2 **James got 845 points in a quiz. Oliver got 386 points. How many more points did James get than Oliver? Show your working.**

3 **Find the total cost of a bat costing £2.25, a ball costing 12p and a net costing £1.95. Show your working.**

4 **Fill in the missing digits.**

a) 24☐ + 1☐4 = 400

b) ☐42 – 23☐ = 705

c) 1☐4 + 39☐ = 528

d) ☐87 – 1☐6 = 661

Activity Using only 2 of the numbers <u>342</u>, <u>634</u> and <u>478</u>, what is the <u>largest difference</u> and the <u>smallest total</u> you can make? Choose <u>another</u> set of 3-digit numbers. Using only 2 of them, what is the largest difference and the smallest total this time?

Learning Objective:

"I can add and subtract two-digit and three-digit numbers using a written method."

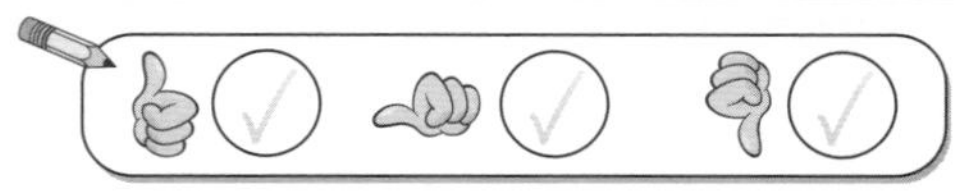

Key Objective

Written Adding and Subtracting

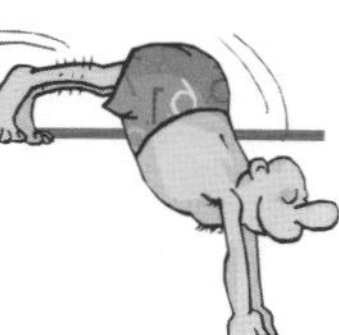

1 **Calculate:**

a) $\begin{array}{r} 225 \\ +\ 169 \\ \hline \end{array}$

b) $\begin{array}{r} 2.46 \\ +\ 1.73 \\ \hline \end{array}$

c) $\begin{array}{r} 546 \\ -\ 174 \\ \hline \end{array}$

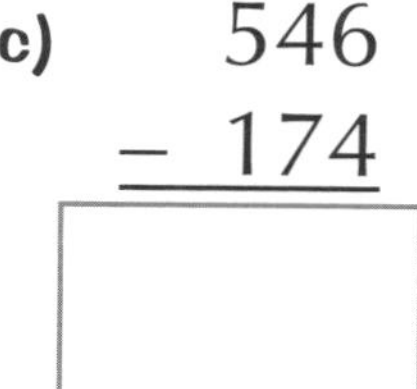

d) $\begin{array}{r} 174.7 \\ -\ 30.8 \\ \hline \end{array}$

2 **Calculate, showing your working clearly:**

a) 1.07 + 2.85

b) 27.8 – 2.5

c) 83.6 + 2.19

3 **Rosie has £27.16 in her piggy bank. She is given the same amount again.**

How much does she now have in her piggy bank?

4 **Mrs Coates is building cupboards. She has a bag of 300 nails. One cupboard will need 84 nails and the other will need 198 nails.**

How many nails will Mrs Coates have left over?

Activity

Put numbers in the boxes to make this sum correct:

☐0 + ☐0 = 1☐0

How many other solutions can you find? Write them down.

Learning Objective:

"I can add and subtract whole numbers and decimals with up to two places."

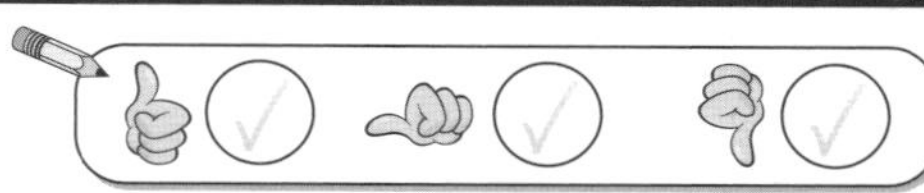

 Name: .... Date: ....

Written Multiplying and Dividing

1 **Circle the two divisions which have the same remainder.**

2 **Solve these problems. Fill in each step of the multiplication in the box.**

a)	$43 \times 6 =$	$40 \times 6 = 240$	+	$3 \times 6 = 18$	=	
b)	$62 \times 4 =$	$60 \times 4 =$	+	$2 \times 4 =$	=	
c)	$28 \times 3 =$	$20 \times 3 =$	+	$8 \times 3 =$	=	

3 **Jake wants to buy a toy car which costs 78p.**

He only has 5 pence coins. How many will he need to buy the toy?

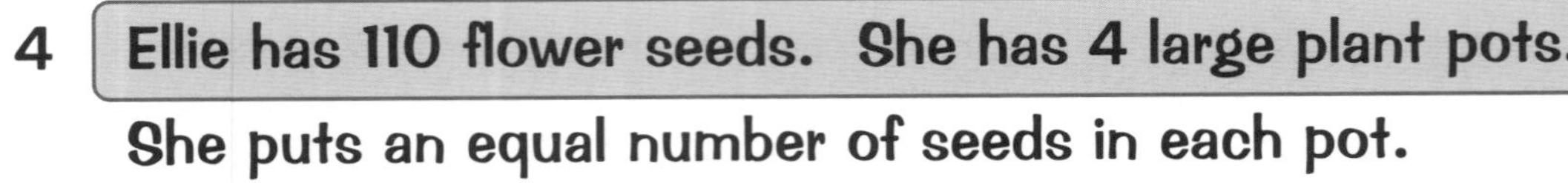

4 **Ellie has 110 flower seeds. She has 4 large plant pots.**

She puts an equal number of seeds in each pot.
How many seeds does she plant in each pot?

Activity Arrange these 3 number cards in the following equation.

What is the highest answer you can make? Or the lowest?

Learning Objective:

"I can multiply and divide with two-digit numbers."

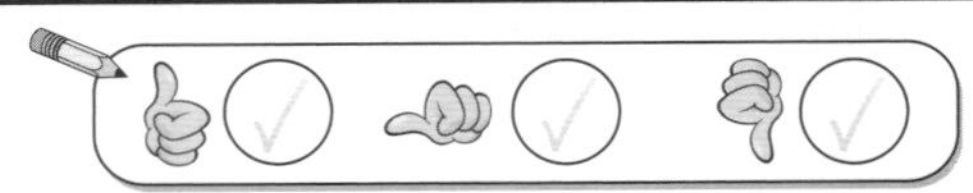

Key Objective

Written Multiplying and Dividing

1 Complete these calculations.

a)
$$\begin{array}{r} 26 \\ \times \quad 4 \\ \hline \end{array}$$
$20 \times 4 =$ ☐
$6 \times 4 =$ ☐ +
☐

b)
$$\begin{array}{r} 74 \\ \times \quad 5 \\ \hline \end{array}$$
$70 \times 5 =$ ☐
$4 \times 5 =$ ☐ +
☐

c)
$$\begin{array}{r} 57 \\ \times \quad 3 \\ \hline \end{array}$$
$50 \times 3 =$ ☐
$7 \times 3 =$ ☐ +
☐

2 Complete these divisions. The final answer goes on the top.

Example: 25 r 2

$3\overline{)77}$

$60 \div 3 = 20$

$17 \div 3 = 5 \text{ r } 2$

a) ☐ r

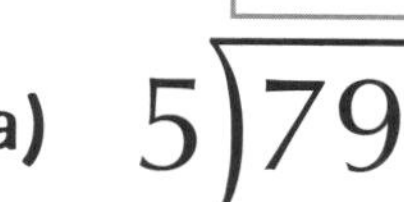

$5\overline{)79}$

$50 \div 5 =$ ☐

$29 \div 5 =$ ☐

b) ☐ r

$6\overline{)81}$

$60 \div 6 =$ ☐

$21 \div 6 =$ ☐

3 Solve these problems. Show your working for each.

a) Billy buys 6 pens for 96p. How much is one pen?

b) Katie swims 9 lengths of a 25 m pool. How far did she swim altogether?

Activity Look at this division: 74 ÷ 8 = 9 r 2. Think up two situations that could be solved with this division. Try to find one where the answer is rounded down to 9 and one where it's rounded up to 10.

Learning Objective:

"I can multiply and divide two-digit numbers and understand how to deal with the remainder."

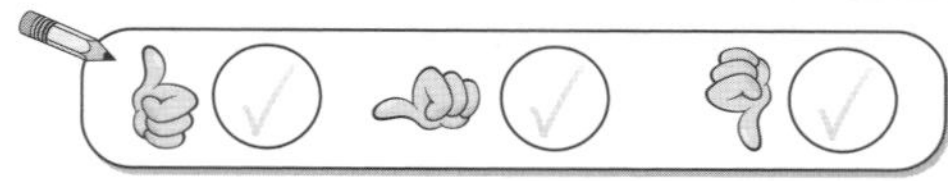

Written Multiplying and Dividing

1 Complete these multiplications. Fill in all the empty boxes.

a) 345×8

$300 \times 8 =$ ☐

$40 \times 8 =$ ☐

$5 \times 8 =$ ☐

☐

b) 14×26

$10 \times 26 =$ ☐

$4 \times 20 =$ ☐

$4 \times 6 =$ ☐

☐

c) 5.3×9

$5 \times 9 =$ ☐

$0.3 \times 9 =$ ☐

☐

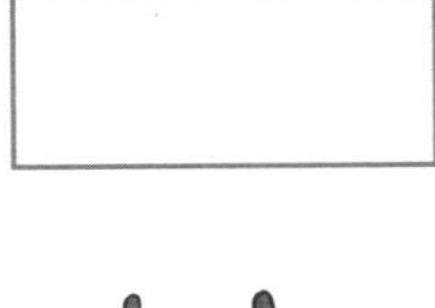

2 Solve the following problems.

a) 928 cakes are put in boxes of 8.
How many complete boxes can be made?

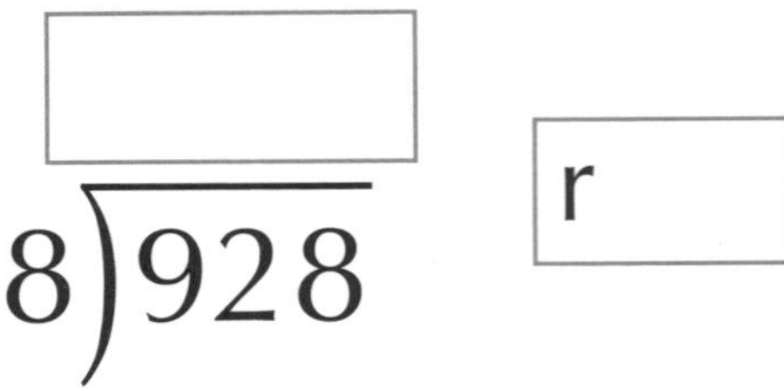

8)928   r ☐

Example:

6)277 = 46 r 1

$2 \div 6 = 0$
Carry over 2: $27 \div 6 = 4$ r 3
Carry over 3: $37 \div 6 = 6$ r 1

b) Four friends win £766 and split it evenly.
How much do they each get, and how much is left? Show your working.

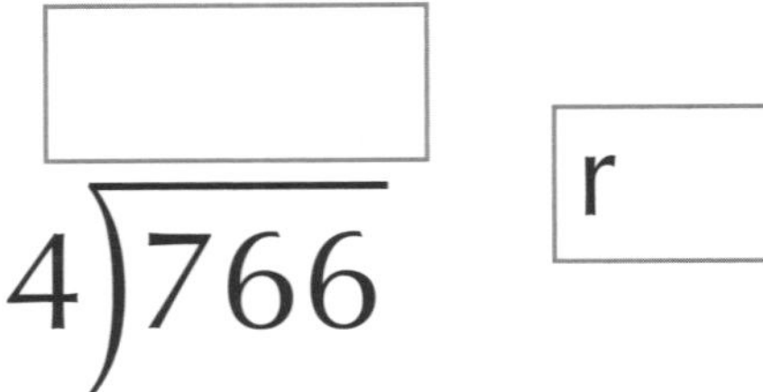

4)766   r ☐

Activity Using only the digits 4, 5 and 6, write multiplications which give an answer that is less than 50. For example, $4.5 \times 6 = 27$.

Learning Objective:

"I can divide and multiply three-digit numbers and decimals."

 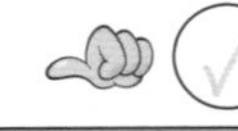 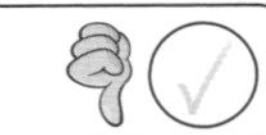

2D Shapes

1 Look at the following 3D shapes and name the 2D shapes that are shaded on them.

a) 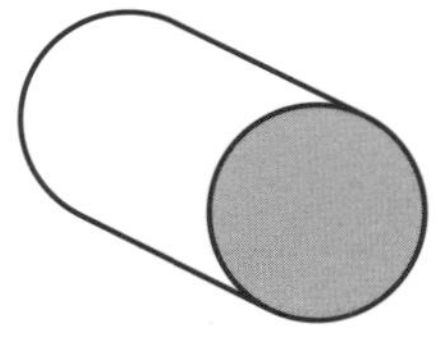

b) 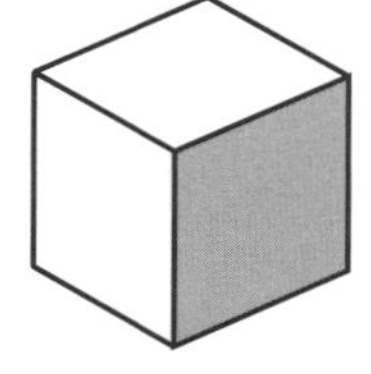

c) 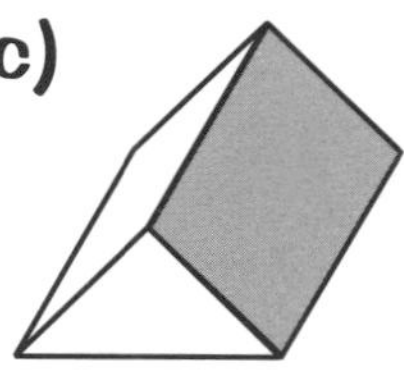

d) 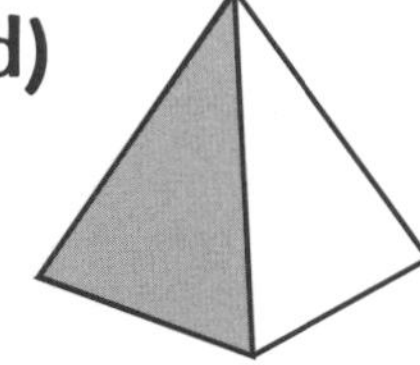

2 Look at the shapes and write their names in the correct place in the table.

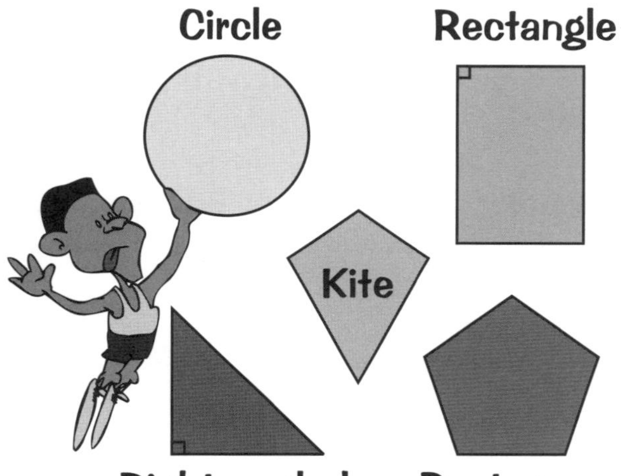

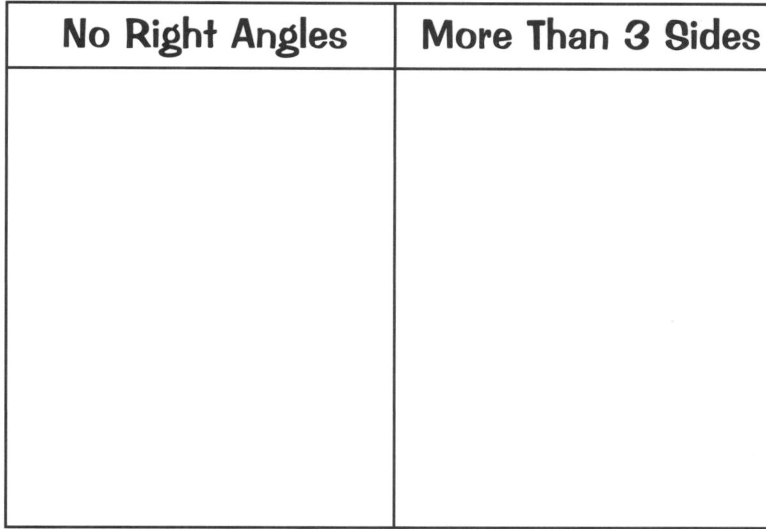

No Right Angles	More Than 3 Sides

Activity Cut out the shapes below. Use 2 or 3 shapes at a time to make new shapes. Draw around them on plain paper.

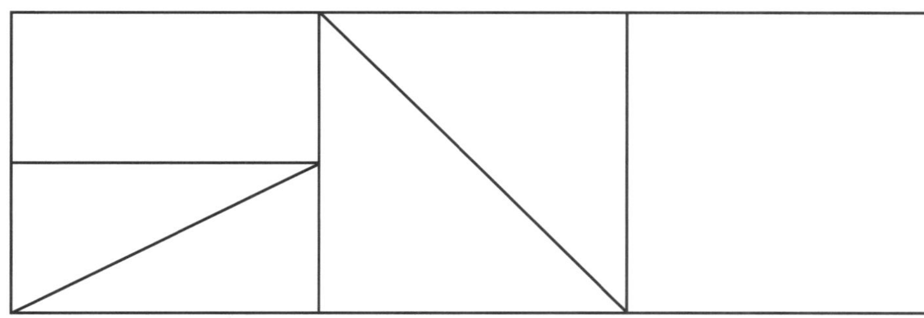

Make as many different shapes as you can.

Learning Objective:

"I can recognise shapes from drawings and describe their properties."

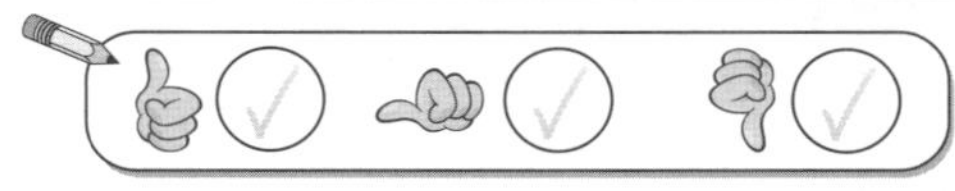

2D Shapes

1 This picture is made from polygons. Count the number of each type of polygon and record it on the chart.

Polygon	Number
Rectangles	
Triangles	
Pentagons	
Circles	

2 For each shape, say how many sides and how many right angles it has:

a) Square

☐ equal sides

☐ right angles

b) Equilateral Triangle

☐ equal sides

☐ right angles

c) Regular Pentagon

☐ equal sides

☐ right angles

3 Draw these shapes on the grids below. Use a ruler.

a) An isosceles triangle (2 equal sides)

b) A pentagon

c) A 4 sided shape with only two right angles

Activity Look at the picture. These hexagons tessellate — they fit together with no gaps. Use squared paper to find three other shapes that tessellate.

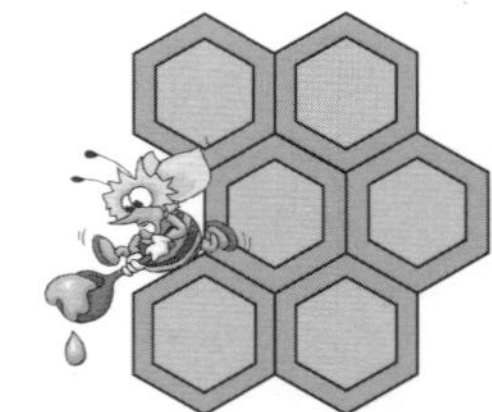

Learning Objective:

"I know facts about regular polygons such as the number of sides and number of angles."

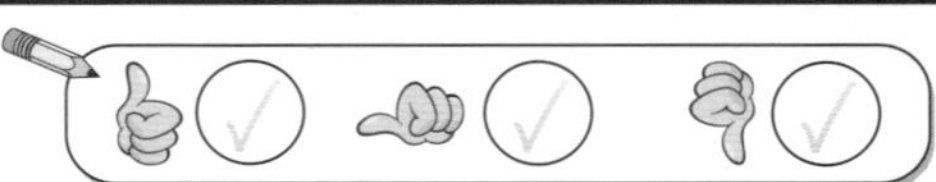

2D Shapes

1 **Draw in the missing sides to create 3 rectangles.**

a) 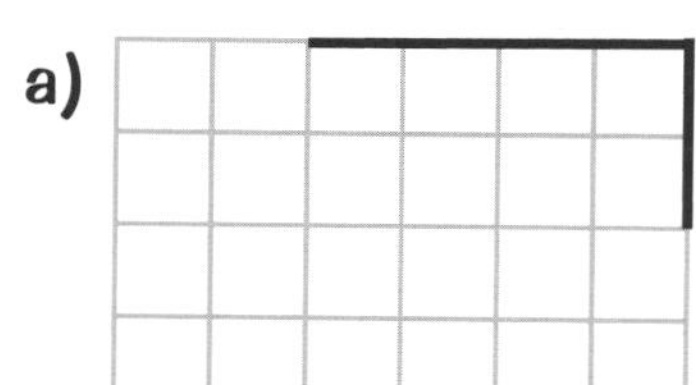

b) 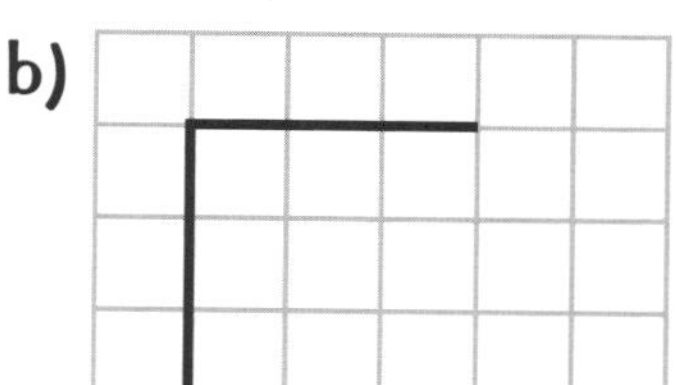

c) 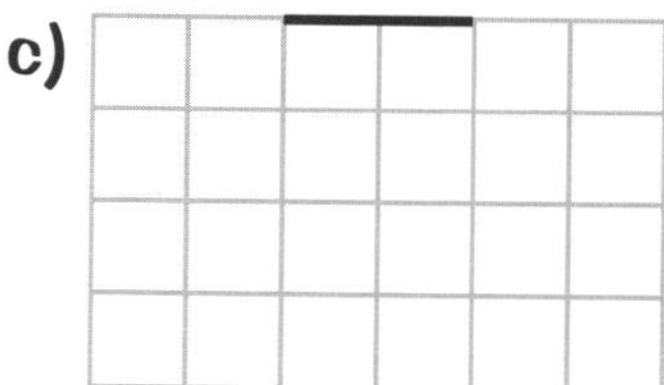

2 **Read the following sets of properties and use them to draw the shape being described.**

a) This shape has 5 lines of symmetry and no right angles.

b) This shape has 2 pairs of equal sides and no right angles.

c) This shape has 8 equal sides and no right angles.

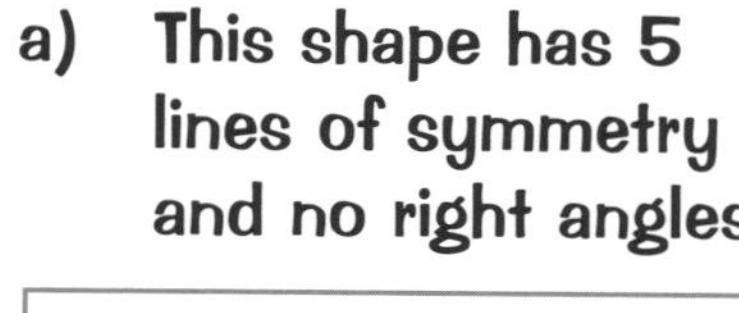

3 **Here are some special types of triangle:**

An equilateral triangle has 3 equal sides and 3 equal angles.

An isosceles triangle has 2 equal sides and 2 equal angles.

A scalene triangle has 3 sides of different lengths.

A right angled triangle has 1 right angle.

Look at the following triangles and name them using the information given above.

a) 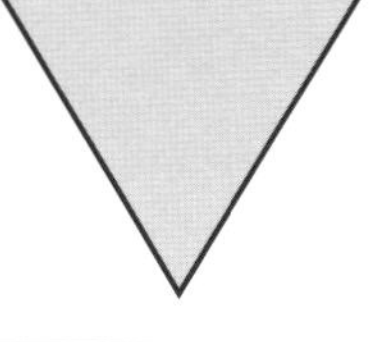

b) 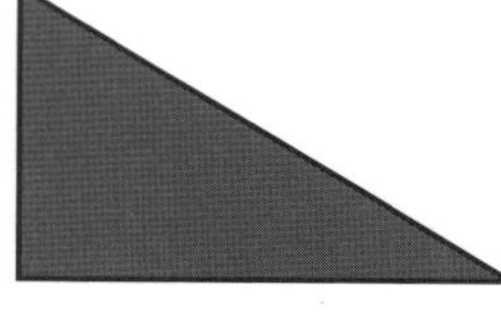

c) 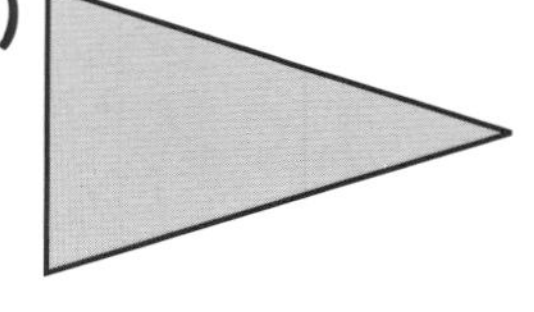

d) 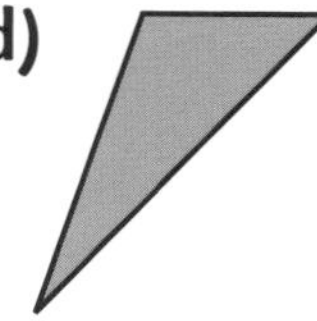

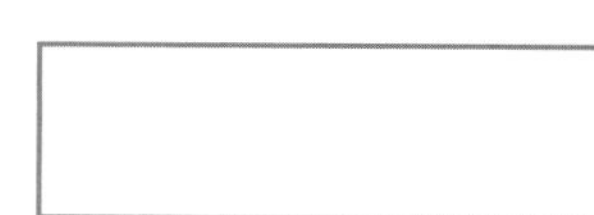

Activity Use a ruler to draw the four different types of triangle — label them with the correct names.

Learning Objective:

"I can describe the important features of 2D shapes."

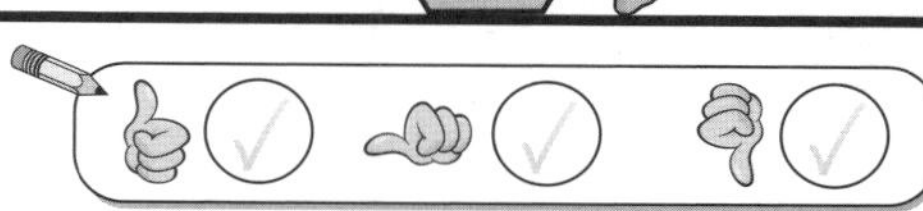

 Name: .... Date: ....

3D Shapes

1 Join each 3D shape to the number of faces it has.

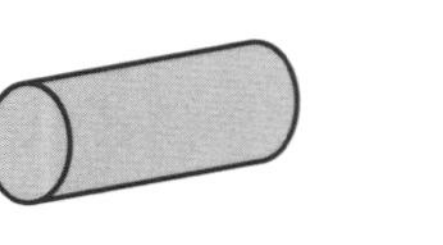   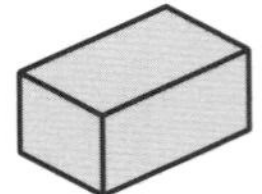

1 face 6 faces 3 faces 2 faces

2 Complete these facts.

a) A CONE has  faces and  curved edge. 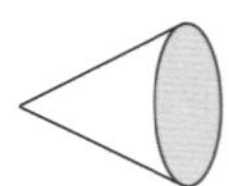

b) A CUBE has 6  and 8 . 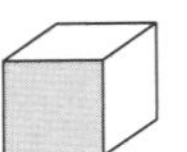

c) A [ ] has 6 vertices and 5 faces. 

3 Draw the 3D shape described and write its name.

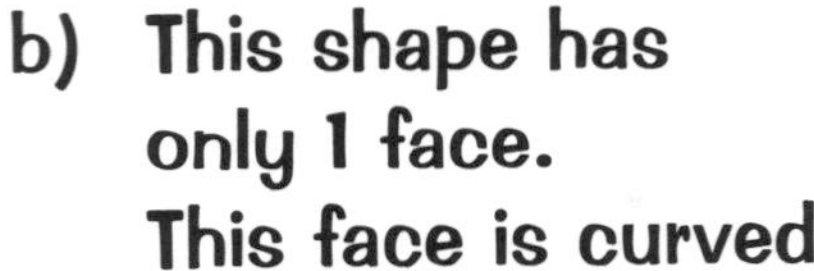

a) This shape has 6 faces. 4 of them are rectangles.

b) This shape has only 1 face. This face is curved.

c) This shape has 2 circular faces and 2 curved edges.

Activity Look for 3D shapes in your home or classroom. Find as many different shapes as you can. Draw the shapes and label them.

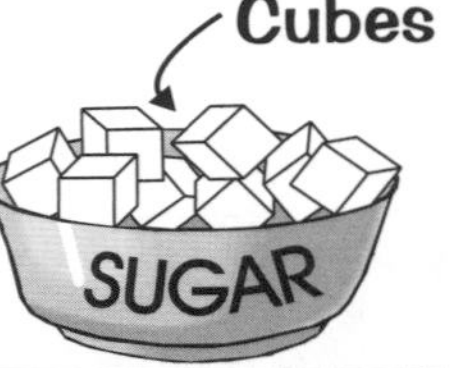

Learning Objective:

"I can name and describe 3D shapes."

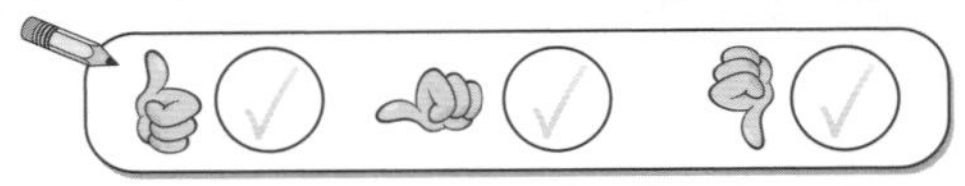

3D Shapes

1 Name the 3D shapes that are made from these nets.

a)

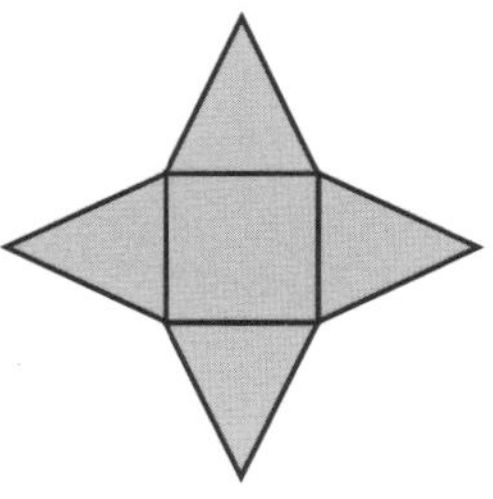

b)

c)

2 Hamish links 5 cubes together.

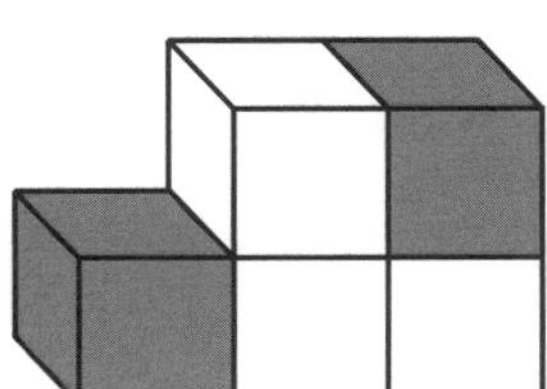

Hamish moves the shape. Shade in the black cubes on the shape in its new position.

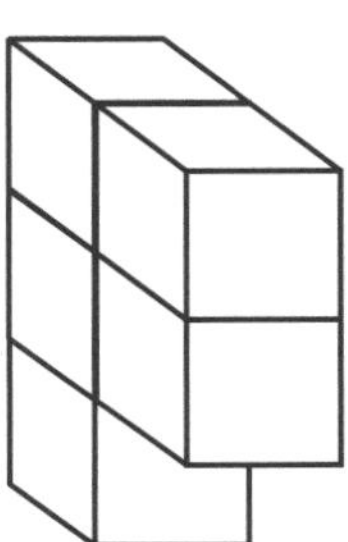

3 Circle the nets that will fold up to make a cube.

a)

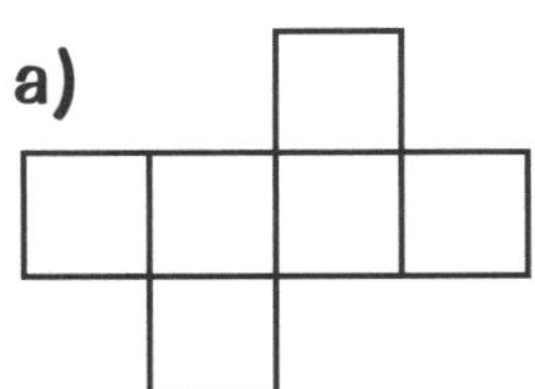

b)

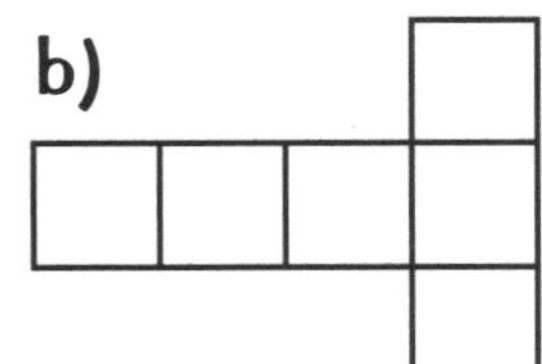

c)

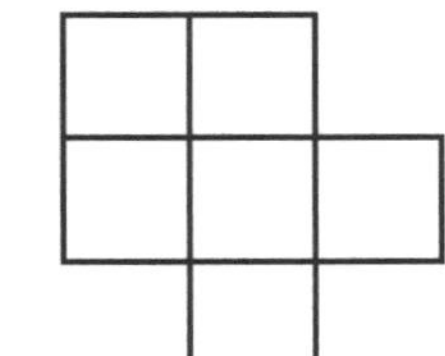

d)

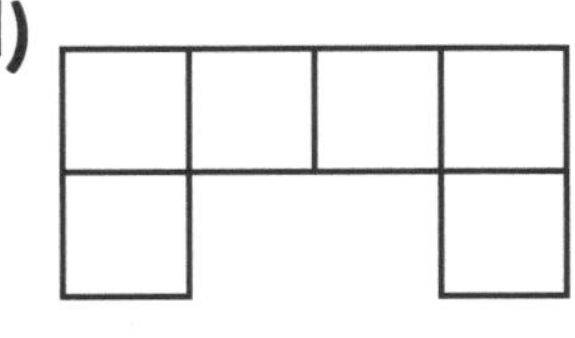

Activity Draw your own net for a cube. Make the sides of each square 5 cm long. Remember to include tabs so that you can stick the edges together. Cut out your net and fold it into a 3D cube.

Learning Objective:

"If I see a drawing of a 3D object I can visualise the solid shape. I recognise nets of 3D shapes."

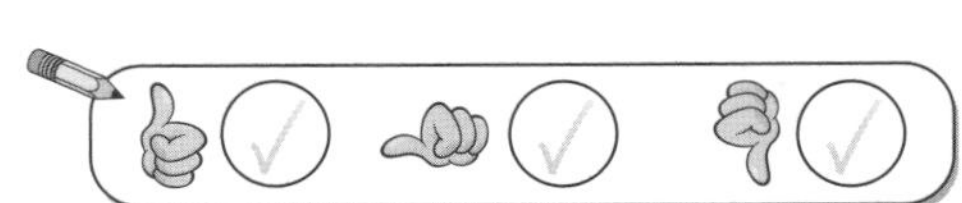

 Name: .... Date: ....

3D Shapes

1 **Circle the diagrams that show the net of a cuboid.**

a) 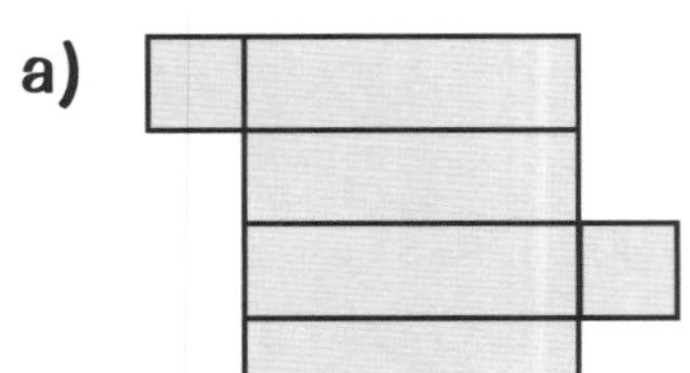

b) 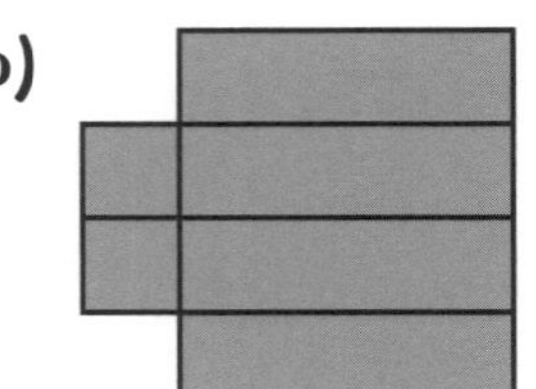

c) 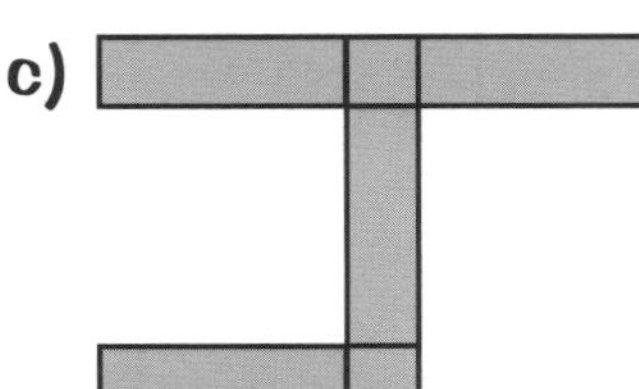

d) 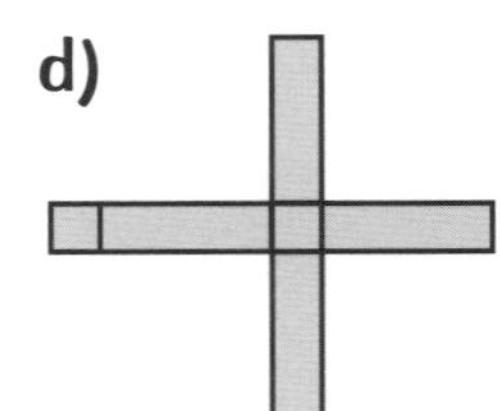

2 **Name the 3D shape, then draw its net.**

a) 4 vertices, 6 edges and 4 faces.

3D shape:

Net:

b) 5 faces, made up of rectangles and triangles.

3D shape:

Net:

3 **A square-based pyramid has 5 faces, 5 vertices and 8 edges.**

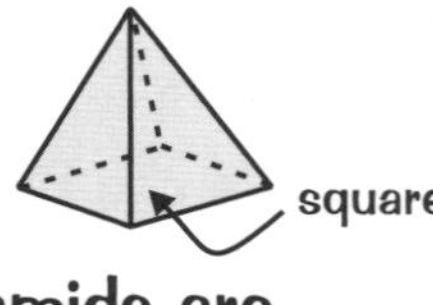

In the diagram below, 2 of these pyramids are joined together. How many faces, edges and vertices are there on the new shape?

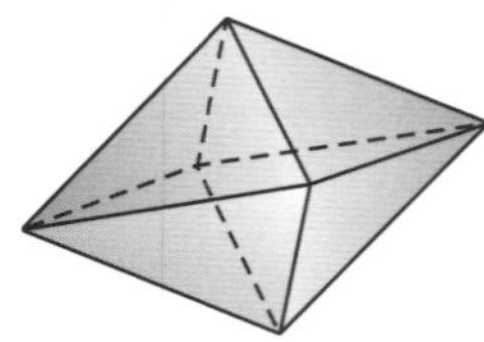

Faces: 

Edges:

Vertices: 

Activity How many different ways can you draw a net for this triangular prism? Draw as many different nets as you can.

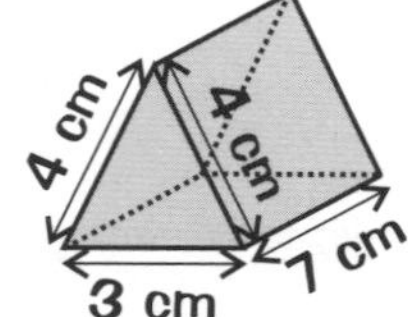

Learning Objective:

"I can identify 3D shapes and draw their nets."

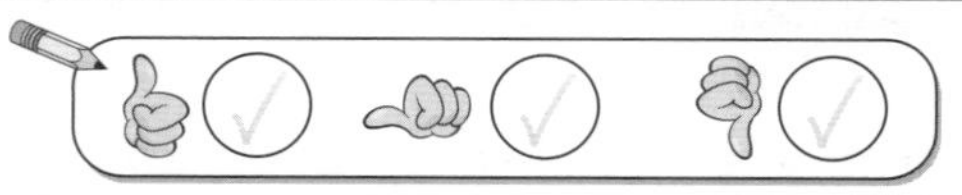

Angles

1 **Look at the shape below and label each angle:**

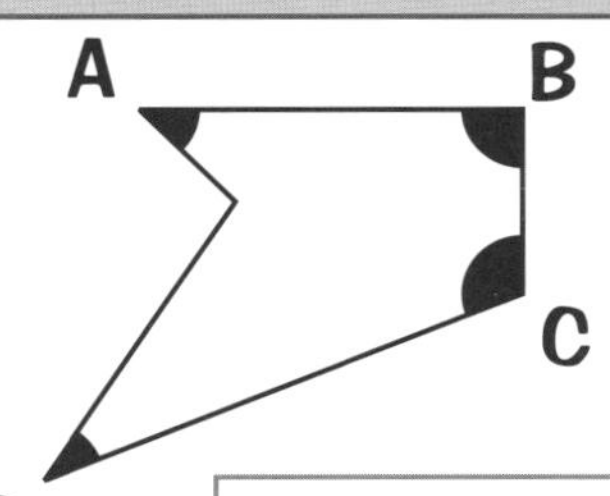

"right angle"
"less than a right angle"
"more than a right angle"

A: ______ B: ______

C: ______ D: ______

2 **Draw squares on the letters where two right angles meet to make a straight line.**

The first one has been done for you.

Circle the letters which have no right angles.

B E A K H T

3 **Two right angles can be put together to make a straight line.**

Circle the 2 pieces of each pizza which will make a straight line.

a) 

b) 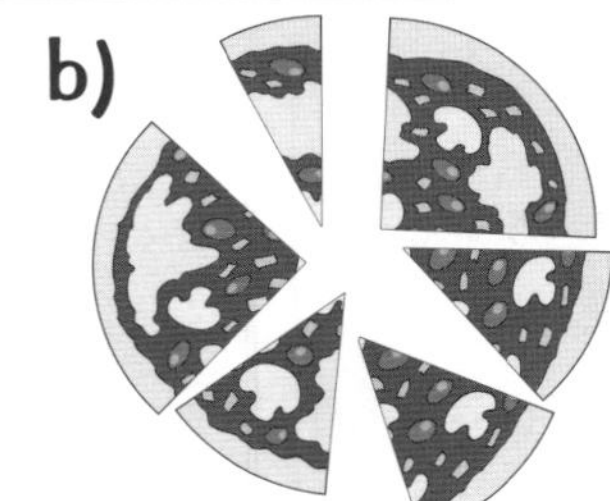

Activity

Draw some pictures of objects you find around the house. Label each angle you find on them "less than a right angle", "more than a right angle" or "right angle".

Learning Objective:

"I can find a right angle.
I know that two right angles make a straight line."

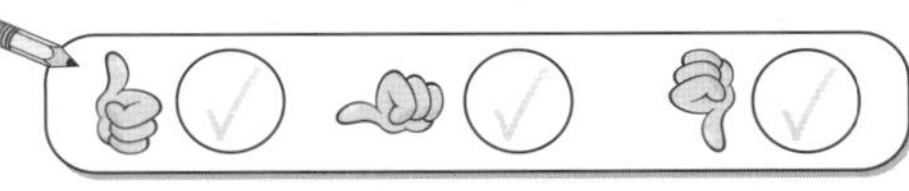

 Name: .... Date: ....

Key Objective

Angles

1 **Add the angles together in each of these diagrams.**

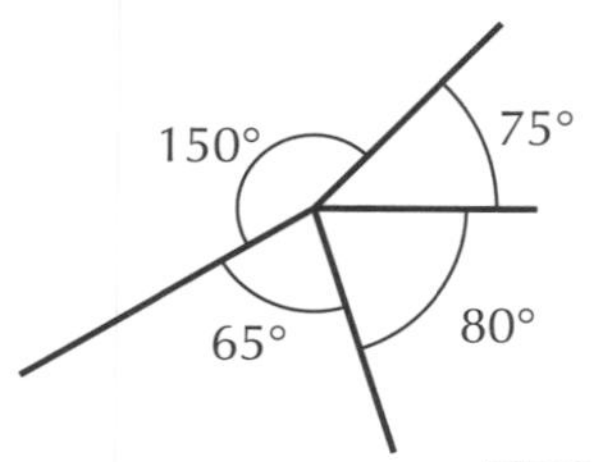

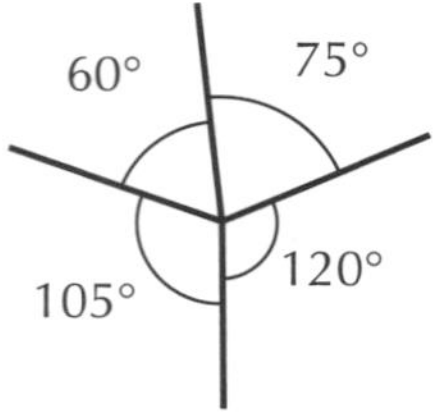

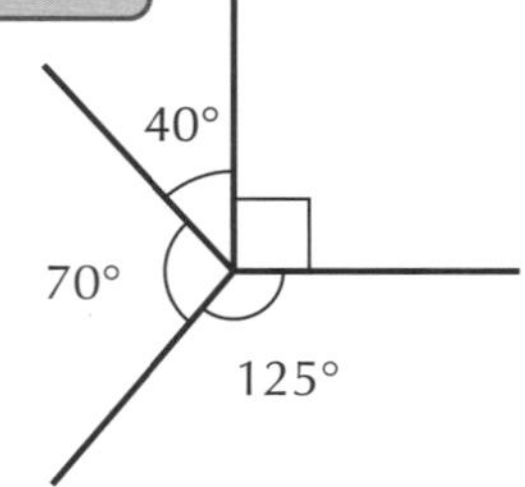

a) Angles add to  ° b) Angles add to  ° c) Angles add to  °

Two of the diagrams are wrong.
Which ones? How do you know?

2 **Circle the greater angle in each pair below.**

a) 

b) 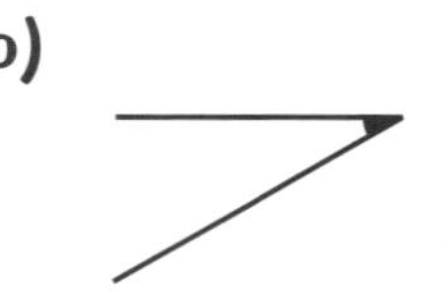 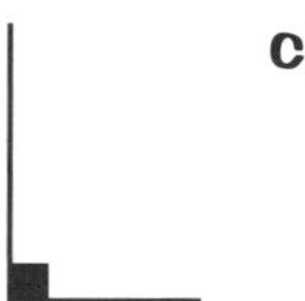

c) 

3 **Put these angles in order of size.**

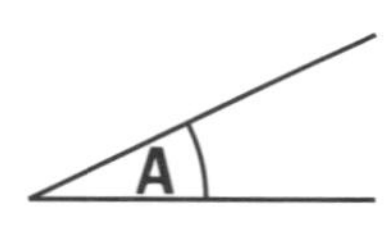

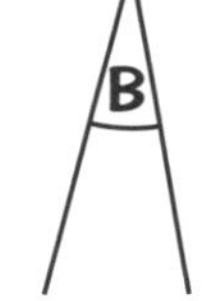

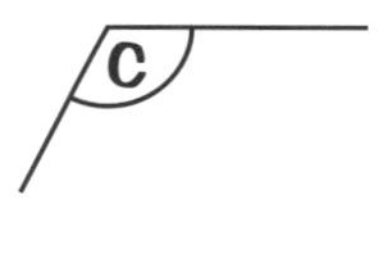

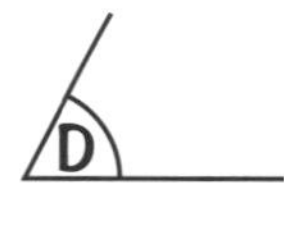

smallest B, , 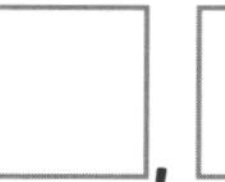, , largest

4 **Look at the following angles:**

Put a circle around the angle closest to 180°.
Put a square around the angle closest to 90°.

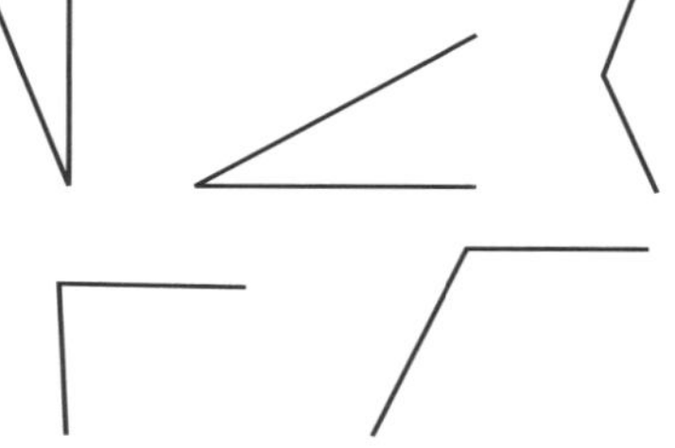

Activity Draw a selection of angles (like in question 3).
Label them with letters, then put them in order of size.

Learning Objective:

"I know that one whole turn is 360°.
I can compare and order angles less than 180°."

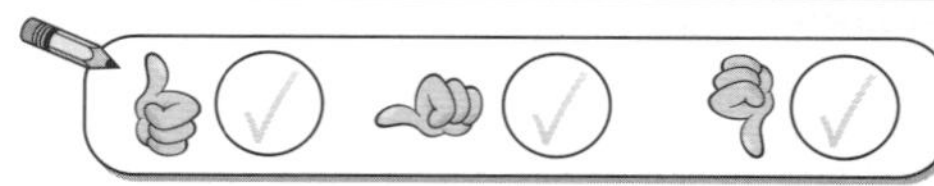

Angles

1 Estimate the following angles to the nearest 10°.

a) 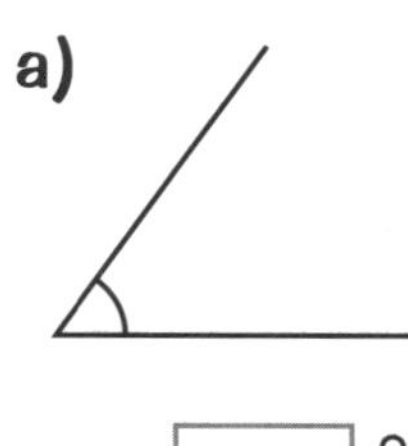

= ☐ °

b) 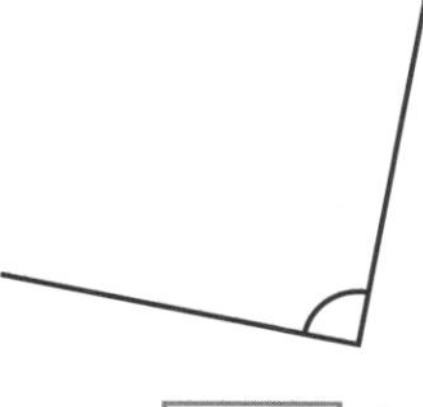

= ☐ °

c) 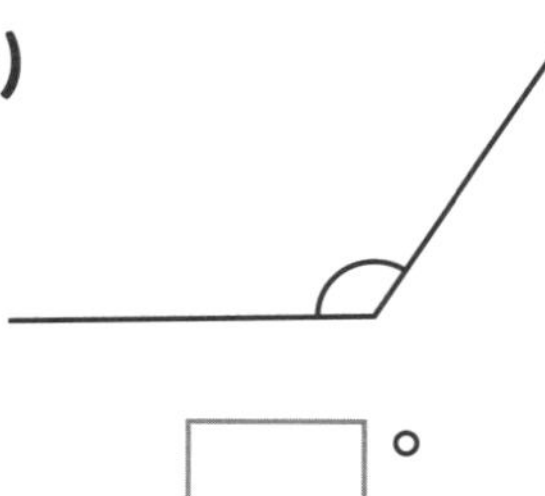

= ☐ °

2 Measure each of the missing angles in the flowers below using a protractor.

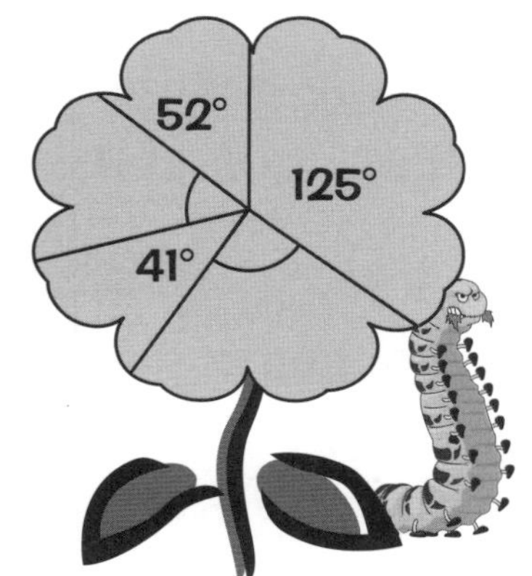

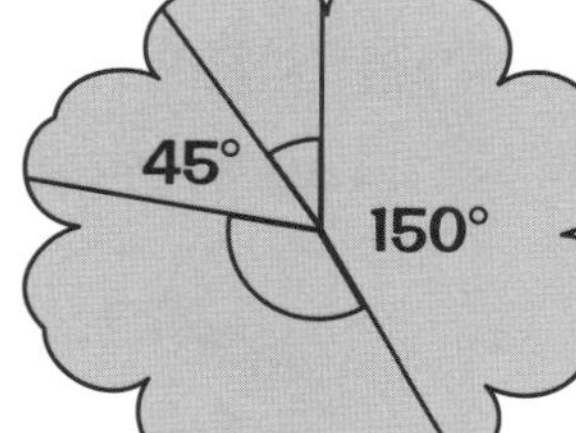

a) ☐ ° and ☐ ° b) ☐ ° and ☐ ° c) ☐ ° and ☐ °

3 Using a protractor, draw the following angles.

65° 22° 137°

Activity Without using a protractor, draw the following angles by estimation. Then, using the protractor, measure each angle you have drawn and see how close you were.

a) 90° b) 45° c) 150° d) 22° e) 178°

Learning Objective:

"I can estimate, draw and measure acute and obtuse angles using a protractor to a suitable degree of accuracy."

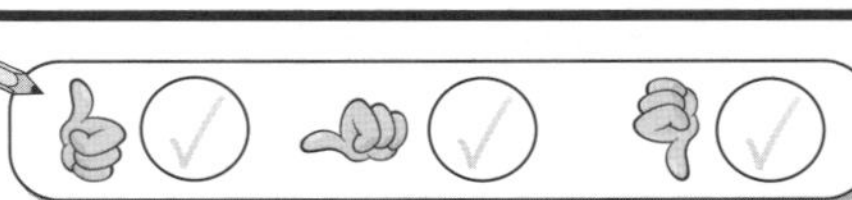

 Name: .... Date: ....

Coordinates

1 **Look at this grid:**

Circle the direction you need to go in to get:

a) from the cat to the food bowl
north south east west

b) from the bird to the worm
north south east west

c) from the mouse to the cheese
north south east west

2 **Here is a map of Hook Island.**

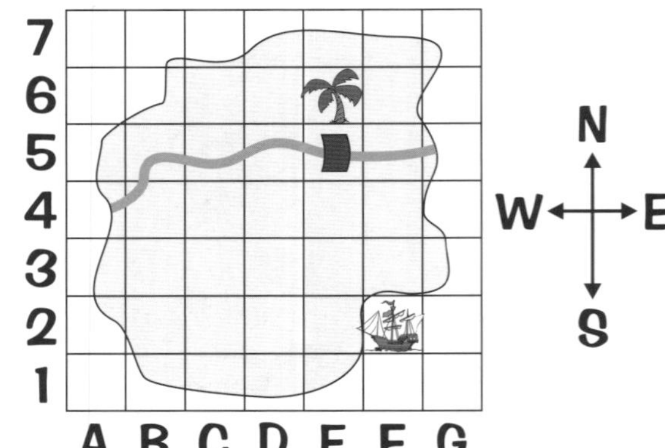

Pirate Bill has buried some gold.
Follow these directions to find it:

Start at the tree
Go south 2 spaces
Go west 3 spaces
Go south 1 space

a) Mark an X on the map where the gold is.

b) The tree is in square E6. Which square is the gold in? ☐

c) Write directions to get from the gold to your boat in square F2.

Activity Draw your own map on squared paper. Mark 4 places on it.
Write directions to get from one place to another.
Use north, south, east and west.

Learning Objective:

"I can use the compass points (north, south, east and west) to describe a direction."

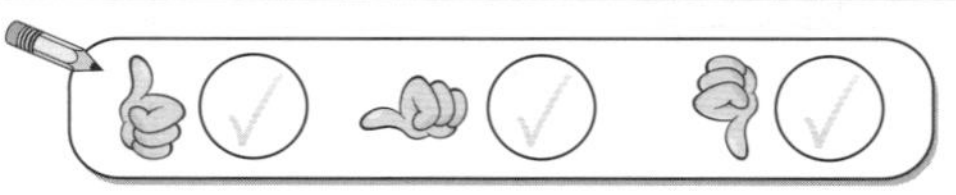

Coordinates

1 **Poppy is facing north-east.**

She turns through a half turn clockwise.
In what direction is she facing now?

2 **Shade these squares on the grid:**

a) Shade C2, E1, C5, F1 and G2.

b) Shade the square half way between A1 and G1.

c) Start at B1. Go 4 squares north and 5 squares east. Shade this square in.

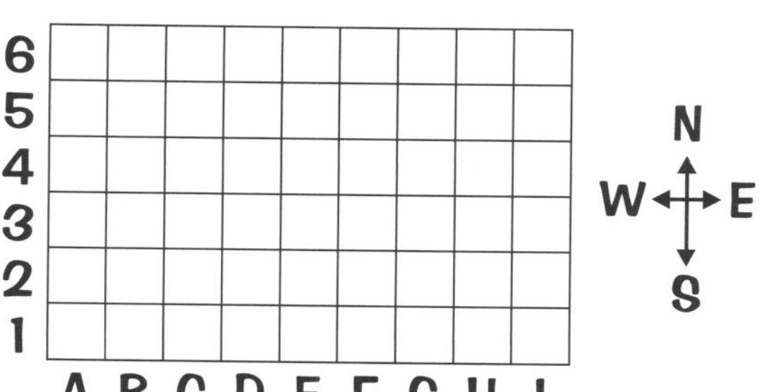

3 **A dragon has kidnapped the princess.**

The knight wants to rescue her and get the dragon's treasure.
First he has to fight the dragon at Fire Mountain (in square C3).

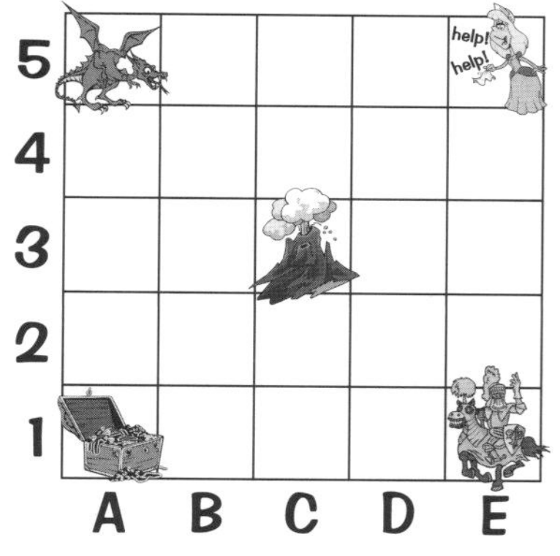

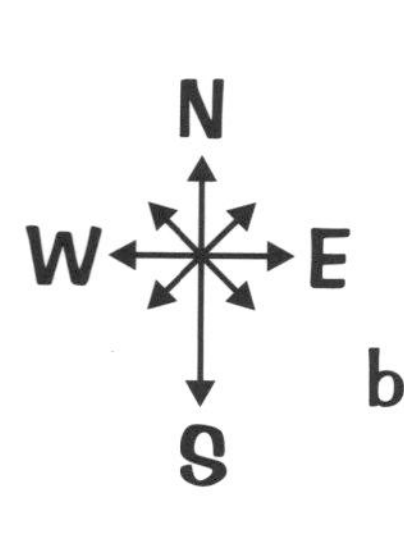

a) In what direction must the knight go to get straight to Fire Mountain?

b) In what direction must he go from Fire Mountain to save the princess?

c) Complete these directions to get from the princess to the treasure.

Go ☐ squares in a ☐ direction.

Activity Make up your own story like the one above.
Draw a map and write some questions to go with it.

Learning Objective:

"I can use the eight compass points."

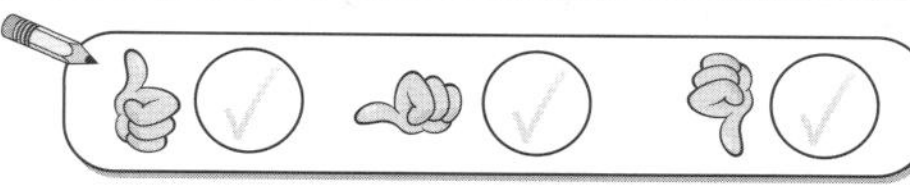

 Name: .... Date: ....

Key Objective

Coordinates

1 **The map shows an island.**

The coordinates of 'Norton' are (10,7).

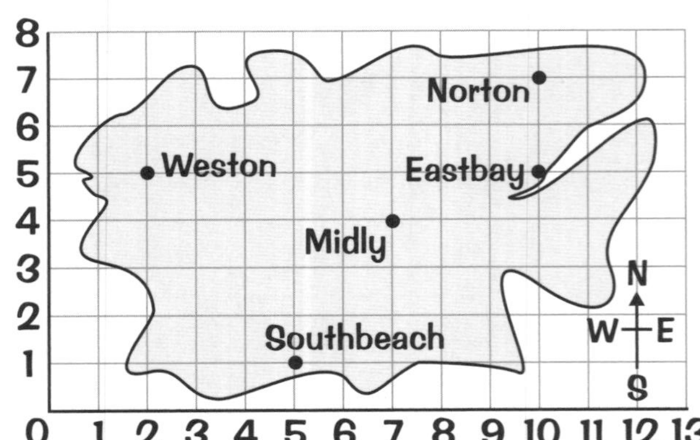

Write the coordinates of:

a) Weston ☐

b) Midly ☐

c) Eastbay ☐

d) Southbeach ☐

2 **Look at the grid below.**

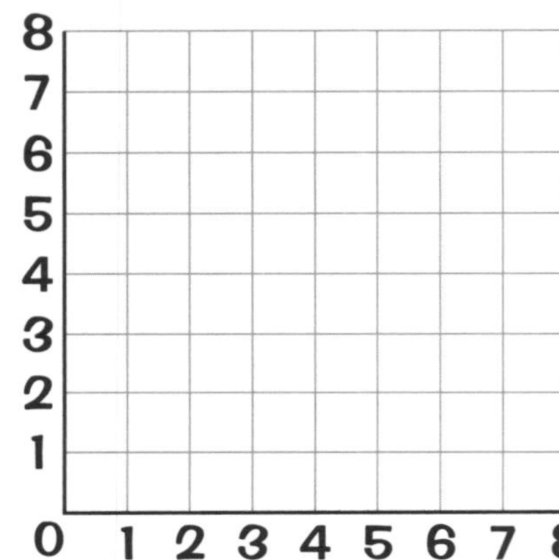

a) Plot these points on the grid:
(1,7), (5,7), (5,2), (1,2).

b) Join the points in order using straight lines.
What shape have you drawn?

☐

Use this grid to help you with question 3.

3 **Danny plots the points (2,6), (8,1) and (2,1) on a grid.**

He joins the points in order using straight lines. What shape has he drawn?

☐

Activity The coordinates (2,5), (5,5), (5,2) and (2,2) are the vertices of a square. Write sets of coordinates that are the vertices of a scalene triangle and an isosceles triangle. Use squared paper to help you.

Learning Objective:

"I can read and plot coordinates to make shapes."

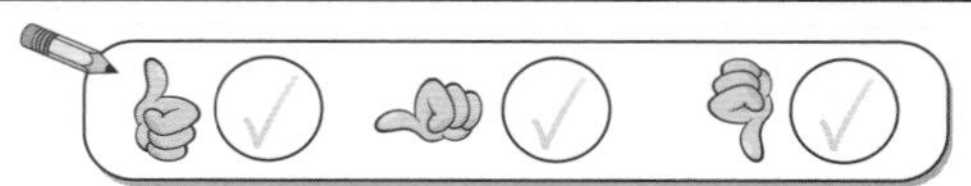

Drawing Shapes

1 **Draw circles round the right angles in these shapes.**

Use a set-square to help you.

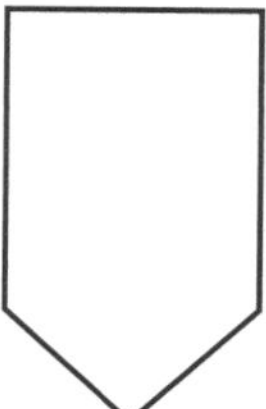 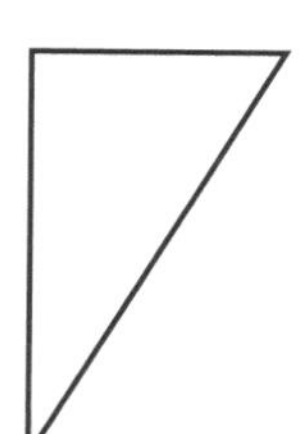  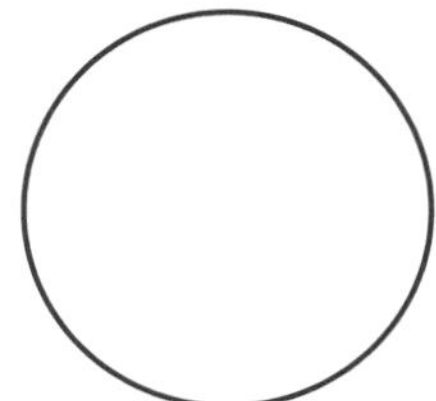

2 **Complete this shape so that it has 3 right angles.**

You need to draw an extra side. You'll end up with a 5-sided shape.

3 **How many right angles are there in this shape?**

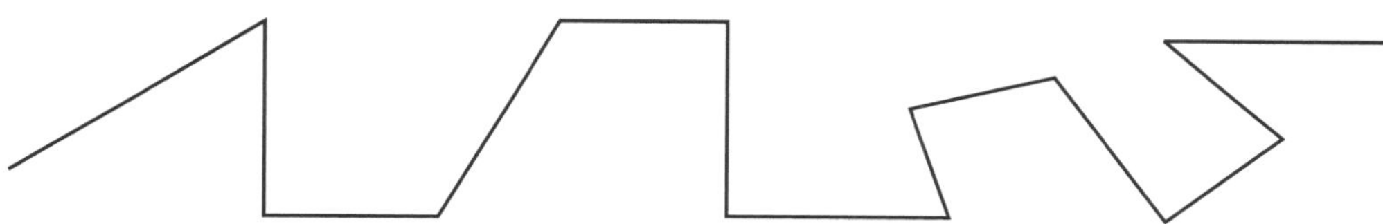

There are  right angles.

Activity It's hard to build things with exact right angles. Can you find any square corners that aren't quite right angles? Use your set-square. Try looking at corners of rooms and window frames.

Learning Objective:

"I can identify right angles in shapes and use a set-square to check."

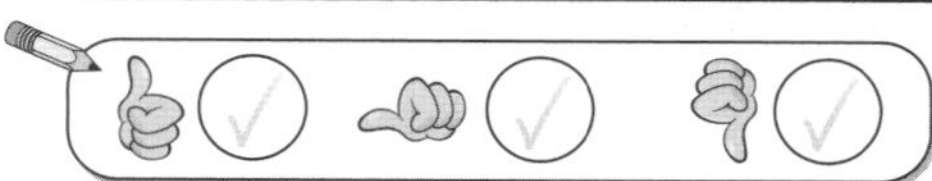

 Name: .... Date: ....

Drawing Shapes

1 **Fill in the gaps in these sentences.**

a) Horizontal lines go [ ] the page.

b) Vertical lines go [ ] the page.

2 **Find all the horizontal lines in the picture below.**

Go over the horizontal lines with a coloured pencil.

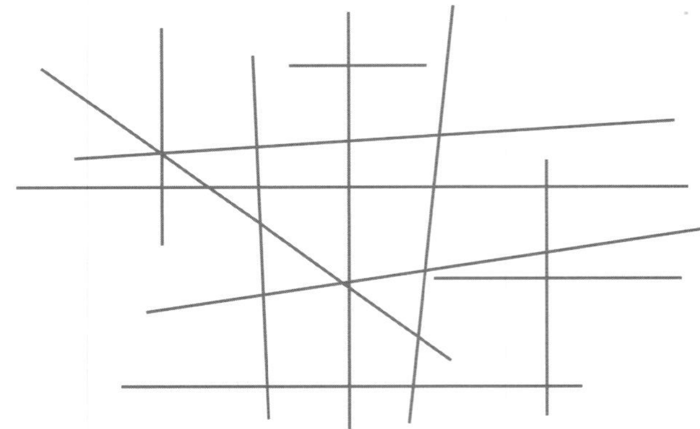

You might find a set-square helpful.

How many horizontal lines are there in the picture?

3 **Now find all the vertical lines in the picture below.**

Go over the vertical lines with a different coloured pencil.

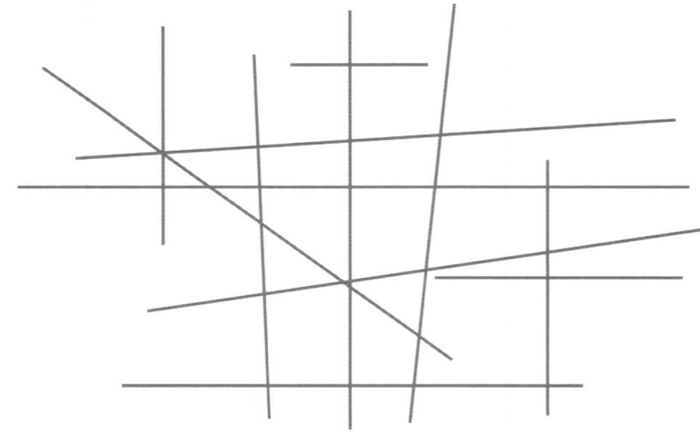

How many vertical lines are there in the picture?

Activity You can draw letters using only vertical and horizontal lines. Try writing your name this way.

Learning Objective:

"I know whether a line is horizontal or vertical."

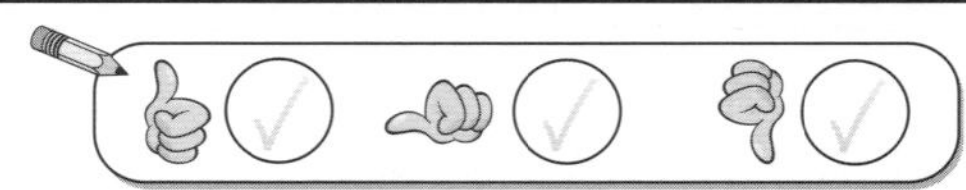

Key Objective

Drawing Shapes

1 Tick the boxes under the sets of lines that are parallel to each other.

a) 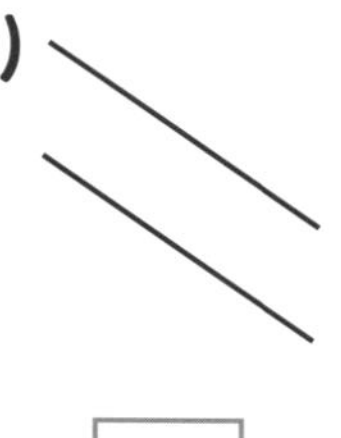

b) 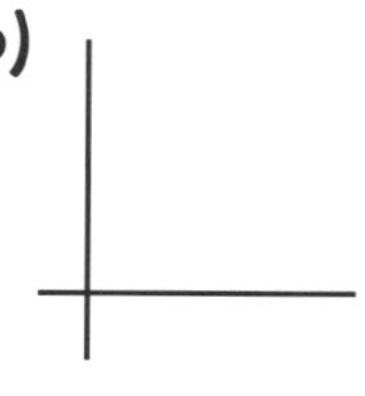

c) 

d) 

e)

2 Which of these shapes have exactly two right angles?

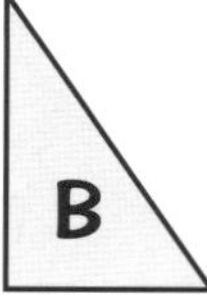

E

3 Use a set-square and ruler to complete these shapes.

Start with the perpendicular lines.

a) A right-angled triangle with its two shorter sides both 4 cm long.

b) A square with 4 cm sides.

Activity Plumb lines show if something is perpendicular to the ground. To make one you need a long piece of string (more than 50 cm) and a lump of Plasticine. Tie one end of the string to the Plasticine and make a loop for your finger at the other end. Hang the plumb line near a vertical line in your home, like a doorframe. If the frame is parallel to the string, then it is perpendicular to the ground.

Learning Objective:

"I can use a set-square and ruler to draw shapes with parallel and perpendicular sides."

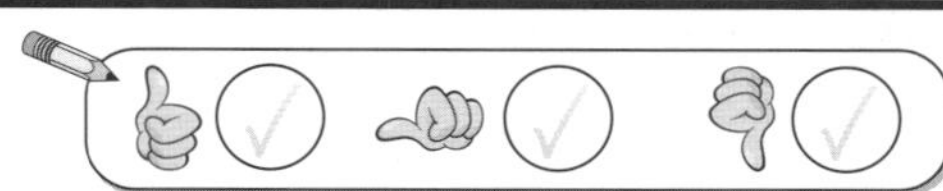

 Name: .... Date: ....

Key Objective

Symmetry

1 **Draw the reflections to complete these symmetrical shapes. Write the names of the shapes in the boxes below.**

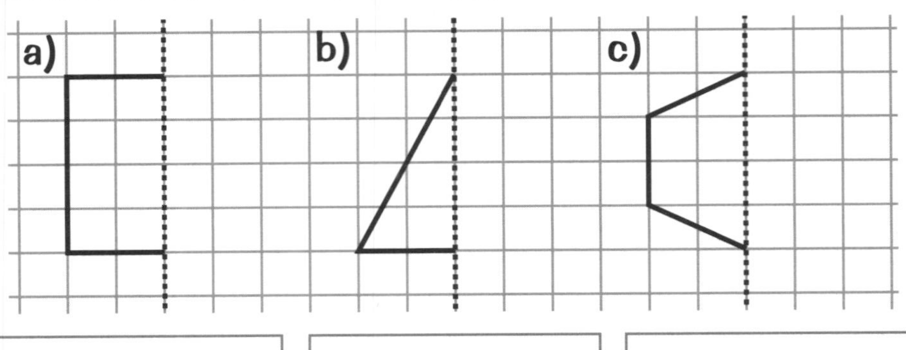

2 **Complete these symmetrical letters. What word do they spell?**

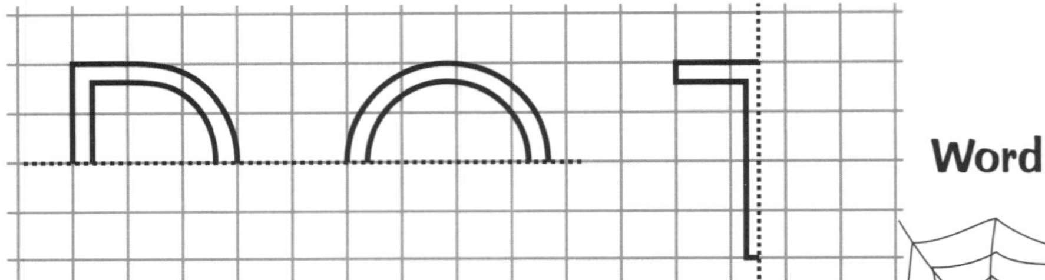

Word:

3 **Draw the reflections of these shapes:**

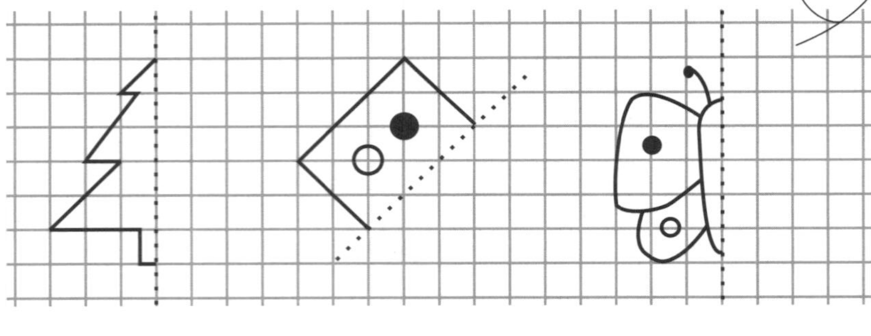

Activity Draw some more capital letters at home. Try and find out which are symmetrical by drawing mirror lines on them. Can you find an entire word that is symmetrical?

Learning Objective:

"I can draw the reflection of a shape."

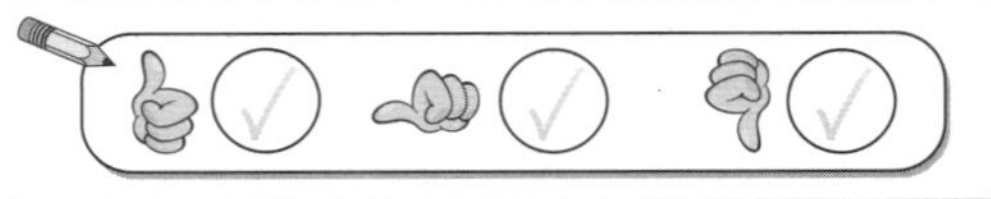

Symmetry

1 Draw 2 lines of symmetry on each of these polygons.

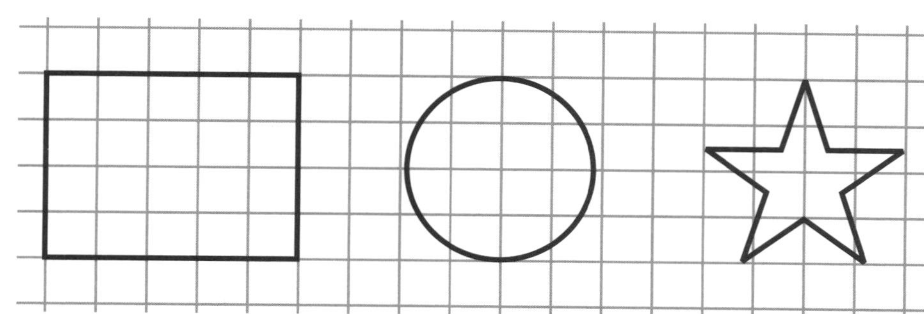

Use a mirror to help you spot lines of symmetry.

2 Complete the polygons below by filling in the other side of the line of symmetry.

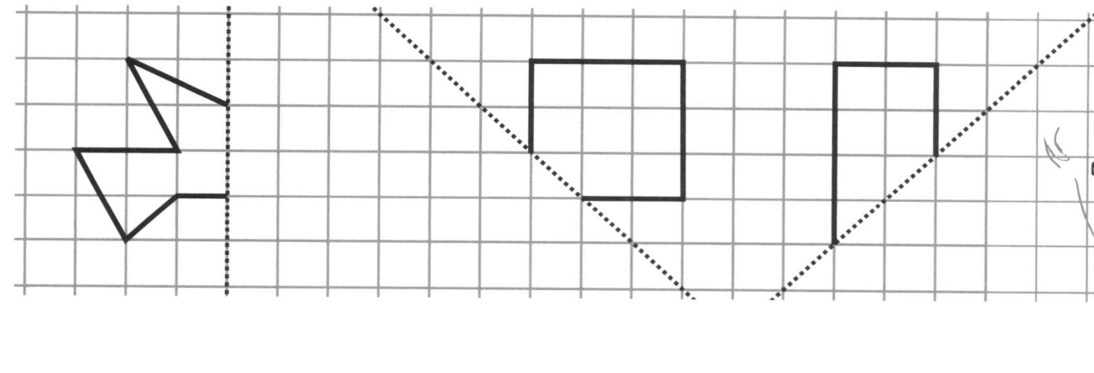

3 Draw lines of symmetry on these irregular polygons.

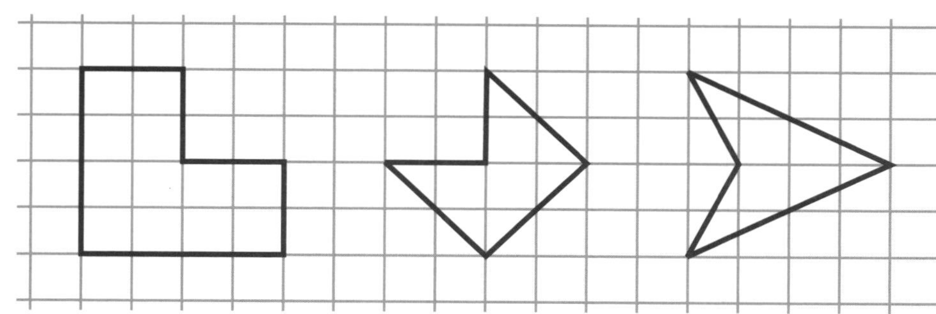

Activity Draw three irregular shapes on some squared paper. If you draw a line of symmetry along one of the sides, can you fill in the other side to make a symmetrical shape?

Learning Objective:

"I can recognise and draw symmetrical polygons."

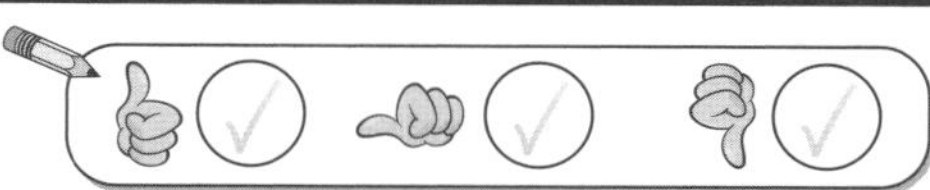

Symmetry

1 Draw two lines of symmetry on each of these patterns.

2 Shade in the squares to make the patterns symmetrical about their lines of symmetry.

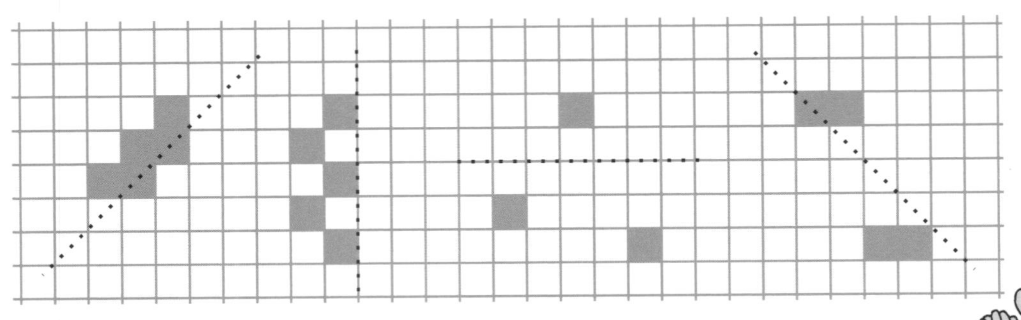

3 Complete these patterns so that they are symmetrical about both lines of symmetry.

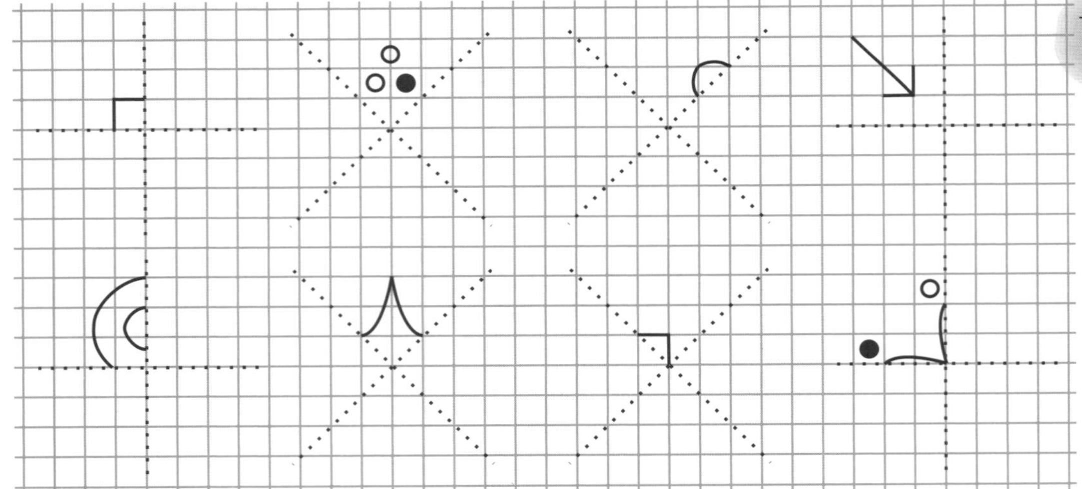

Activity Using some squared paper to help, draw three patterns that all have at least two lines of symmetry.

Learning Objective:

"I can draw patterns with two lines of symmetry."

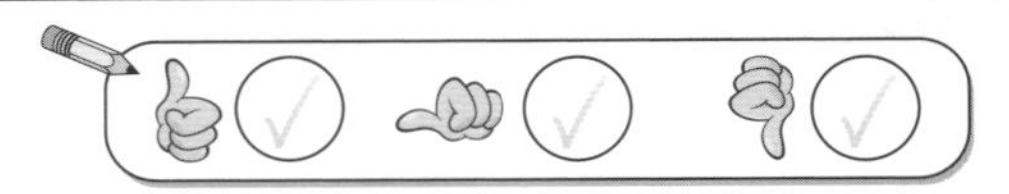

Calculating Perimeters and Areas

1 **What are the perimeters of these rectangles?**

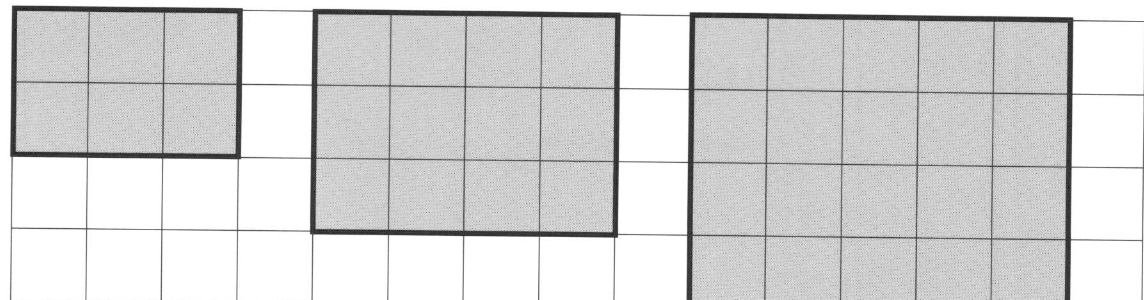

cm cm cm

2 **Draw two rectangles with perimeters of 8 cm. One edge of each has been drawn for you.**

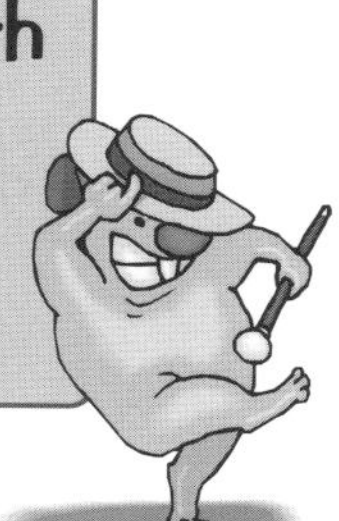

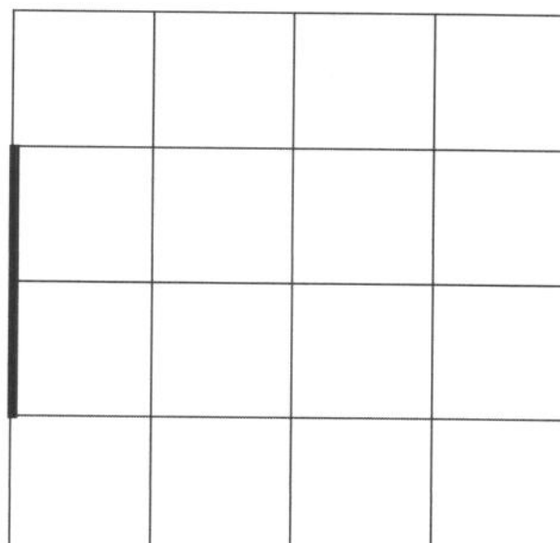

3 **Find the areas of these shapes:**

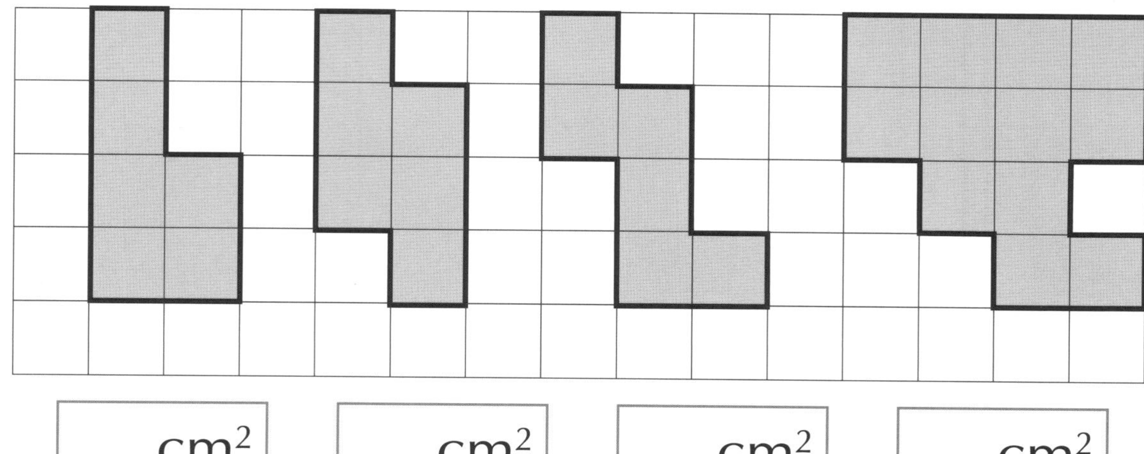

cm^2 cm^2 cm^2 cm^2

Activity Draw some shapes with a perimeter of 14 cm. How many different shapes can you draw?

Use squared paper.

Learning Objective:

"I can draw a rectangle and work out its perimeter.
I can find the area of shapes by counting squares."

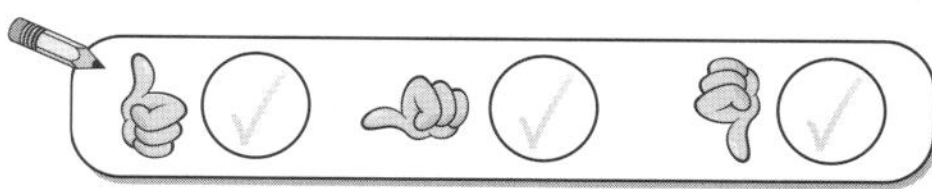

 Name: .... Date: ....

Calculating Perimeters and Areas

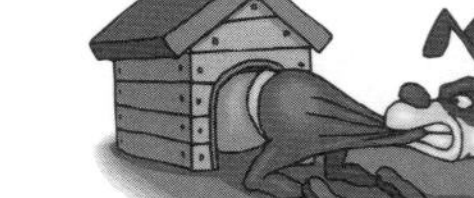

1 **Draw rectangles with these perimeters:**

a) 12 cm

b) 16 cm

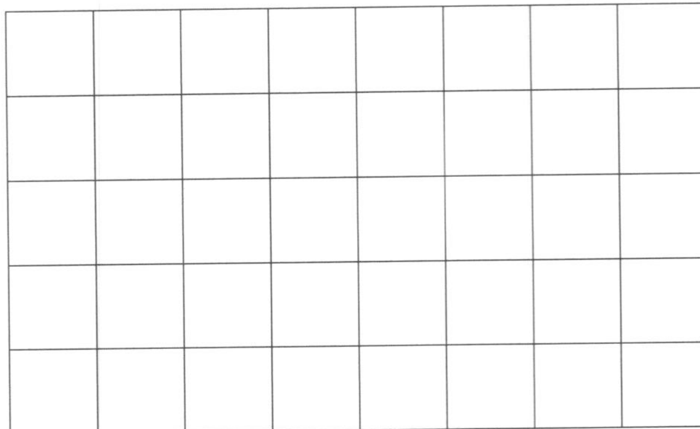

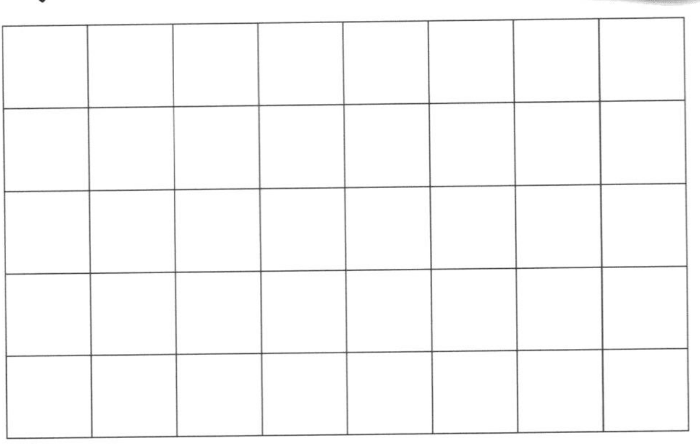

2 **Find the perimeter of these posters. They aren't drawn to scale.**

a)

30 cm

40 cm

[ ] cm

b)

90 cm

50 cm

[ ] cm

3 **Find the areas of these shapes.**

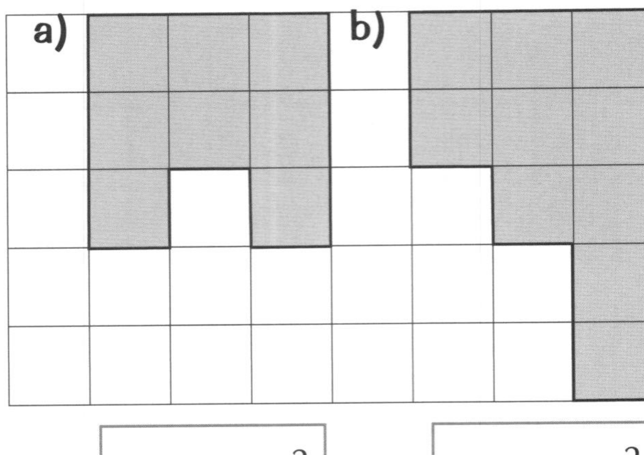

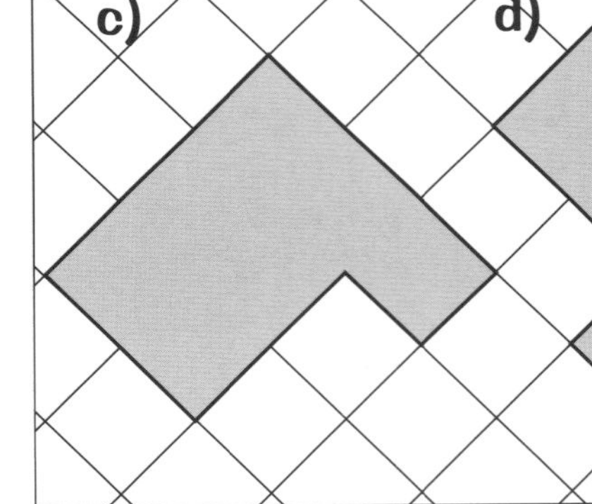

[ ] cm^2 [ ] cm^2 [ ] cm^2 [ ] cm^2

Activity Draw three different shapes that have the same area.

Learning Objective:

"I can draw a rectangle and work out its perimeter.
I can find the area of shapes by counting squares."

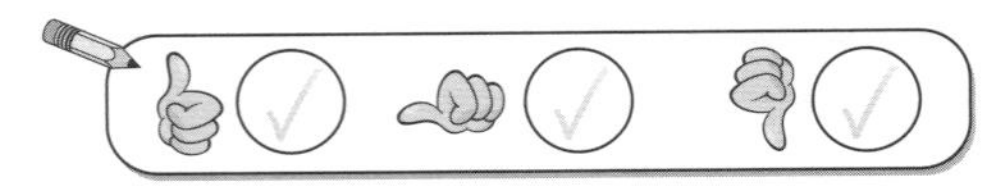

Key Objective

Calculating Perimeters and Areas

1 Measure the perimeters of these shapes:

a)   cm

b) 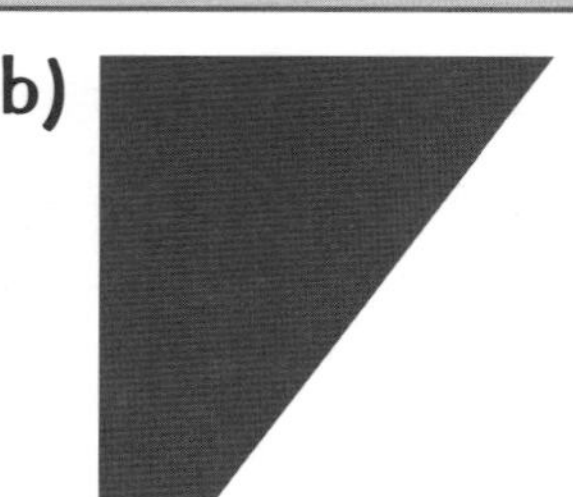  cm

c)  cm

d)  cm

2 Calculate the perimeters of these regular polygons:

a) 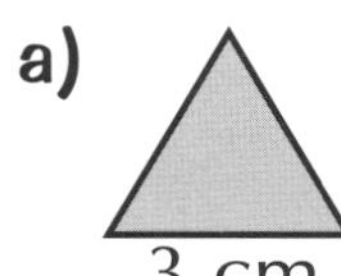 3 cm  cm

b) 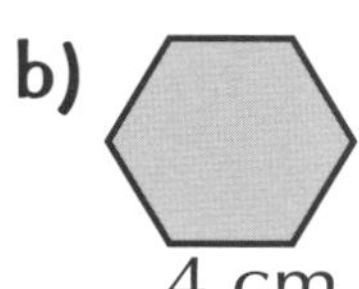 4 cm cm

c) 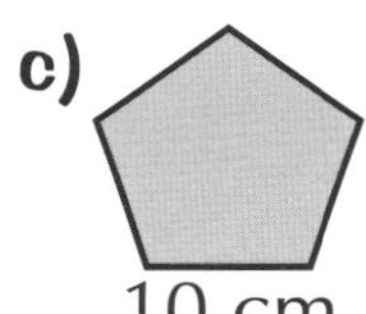 10 cm  cm

d) 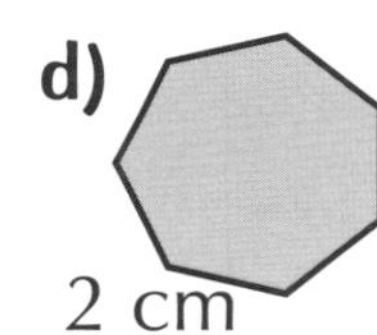 2 cm cm

3 Use the formula area = length × width to calculate the areas of these rectangles:

a) 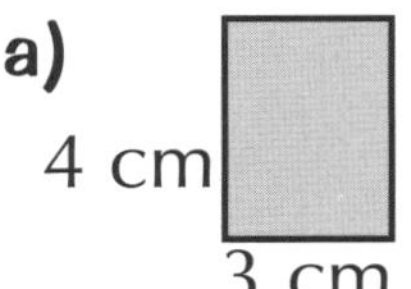 4 cm, 3 cm cm^2

b) 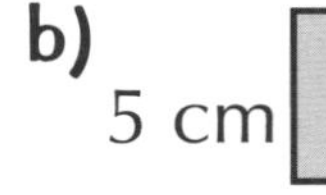 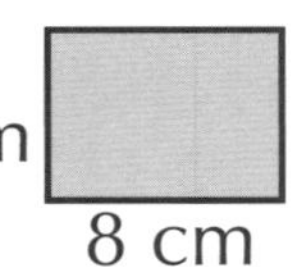 5 cm, 8 cm cm^2

c) 9 cm, 7 cm cm^2

d) 2 cm, 4 cm cm^2

Activity Draw four different rectangles with a perimeter of 20 cm. Calculate their areas. Are they all the same?

Learning Objective:

"I can measure the sides of polygons and find the perimeter.
I can find the area of a rectangle using the formula."

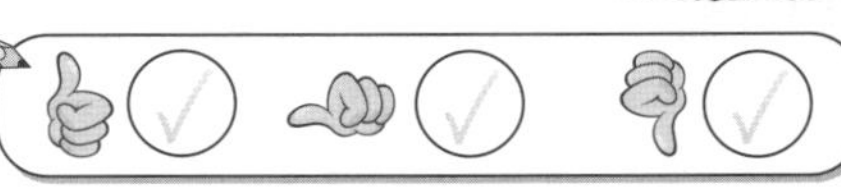

 Name: .... Date: ....

Key Objective

Drawing and Measuring

1 Write the masses shown by the arrows.

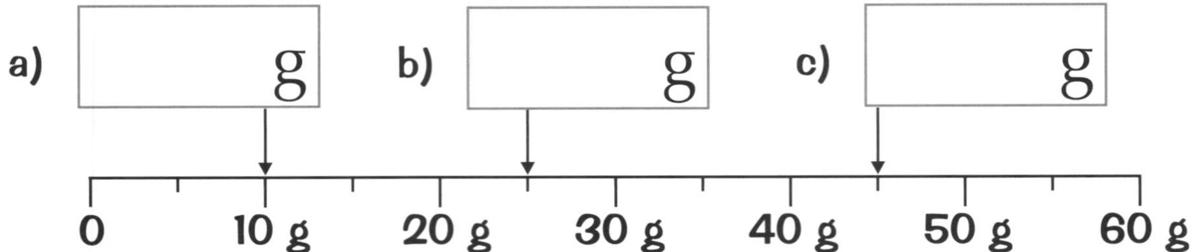

2 Measure the length of each of the ship's masts.

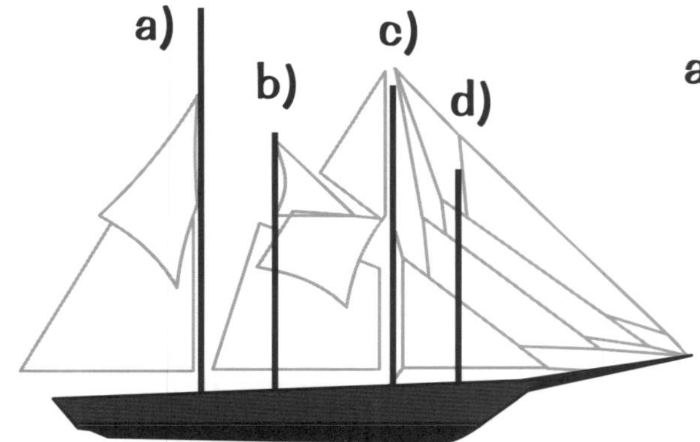

a) cm b) cm

c) cm d) cm

3 The masts on this ship are not finished. They need to be 1.5 cm shorter than the masts on the ship in question 2.

Finish drawing the masts. Use a ruler.

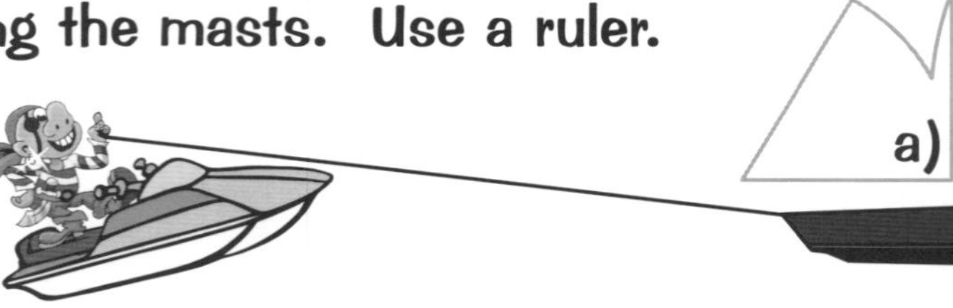

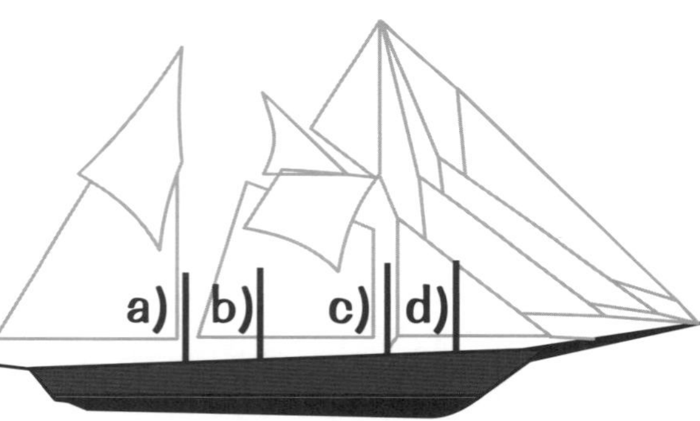

Activity Find the masses of five fruits or vegetables.
Write their masses in order starting with the lightest.
Find items that are about 100 g heavier than each fruit or vegetable and record their masses.

Learning Objective:

"I can use a ruler or a scale to measure a value to the nearest ½ unit."

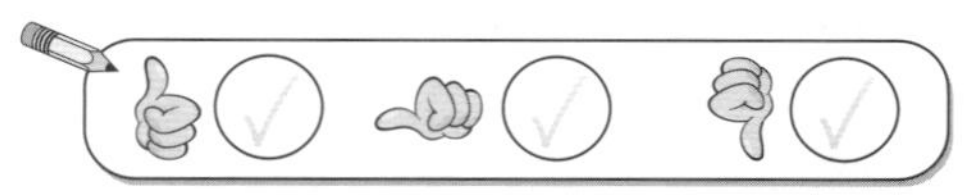

Drawing and Measuring

1 **Complete the diagrams so that they become rectangles. Measure the perimeter of each rectangle.**

a)  

b)

c)

Perimeter = cm

Perimeter = cm

Perimeter = cm

2 **Draw rectangles of the correct sizes around the clowns. One corner has been drawn for you. Measure the perimeter of your rectangles.**

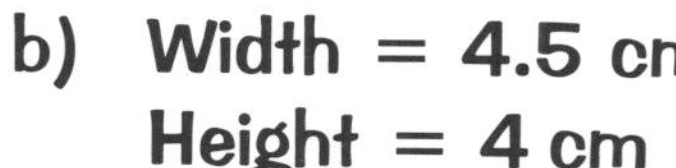

a) Width = 4 cm
Height = 3.5 cm

b) Width = 4.5 cm
Height = 4 cm

c) Width = 3.5 cm
Height = 3 cm

Perimeter = cm

Perimeter = cm

Perimeter = cm

Activity

Draw as many rectangles as you can that have a perimeter of 20 cm. The lengths of the sides can be whole or half centimetres.
For example: Width 7 cm, length 3 cm.
The perimeter is
3 cm + 7 cm + 3 cm + 7 cm = 20 cm.

7 cm

3 cm

Learning Objective:

"I can draw a rectangle accurately and measure its perimeter."

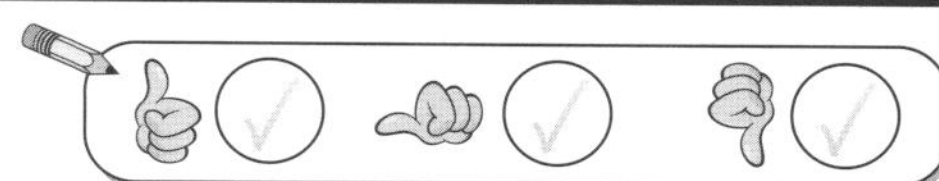

 Name: .... Date: ....

Key Objective

Drawing and Measuring

1 Measure these to the nearest millimetre.

a)

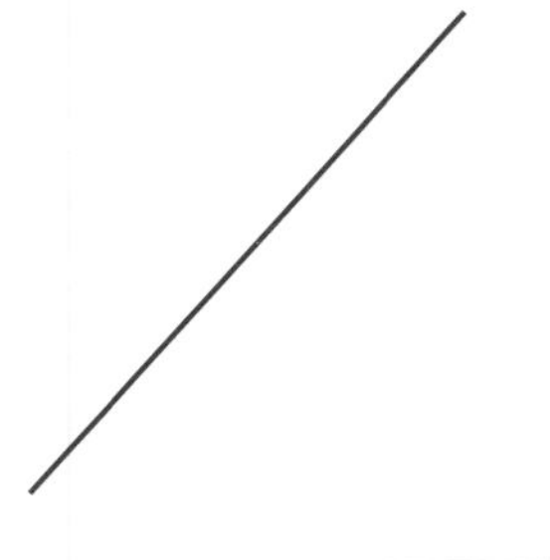

Length = mm

b)

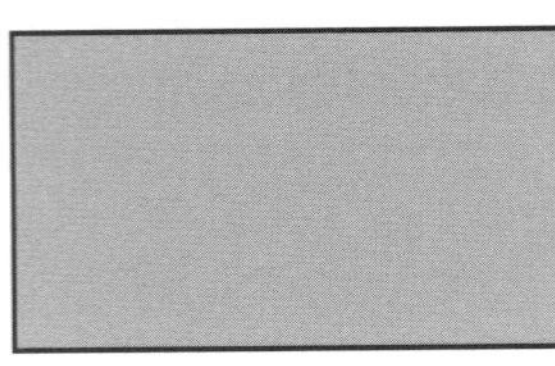

Width = mm

Length = mm

c)

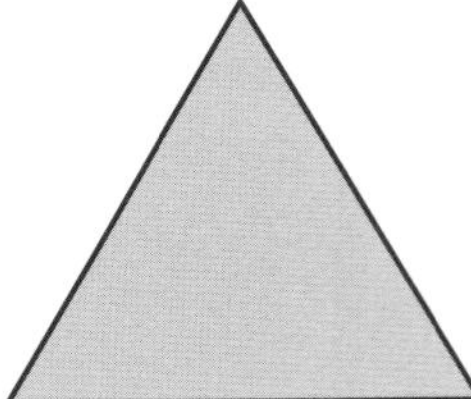

Length of each side = mm

2 James the ant has to carry leaves to six different places.

His paths are shown by the dotted lines. Draw lines of the exact lengths given to show how far he has to walk.

a) 42 mm

b) 27 mm

c) 35 mm

d) 1.8 cm

e) 5.1 cm

f) 4.9 cm

Start from here

3 Meera has 2 identical boxes on her shelf.

Draw a new box between these 2 boxes so that there is a 4 mm space between each box. The new box should be half the height of the other 2.

Activity Identify at least three things around your home that measure between 221 mm and 247 mm. Record the items and their measurements in a table.

Learning Objective:

"I can draw and measure lines to the nearest millimetre."

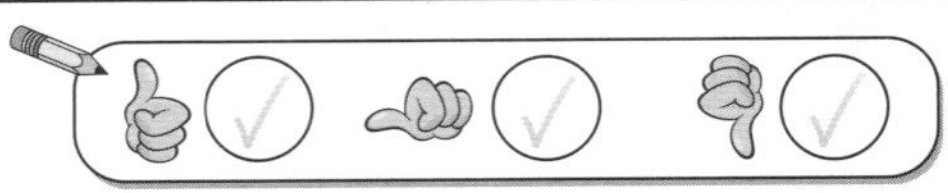

Key Objective

Reading Scales

1 **This bar chart shows how long it takes some children to get to school.**

How long does it take each child to get to school?

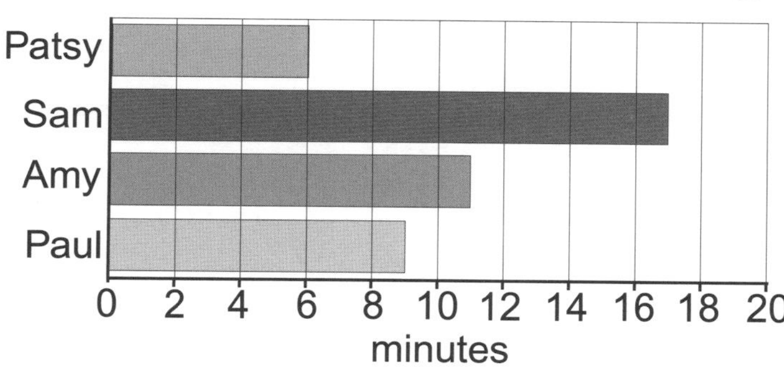

Patsy = mins

Sam = mins

Amy = mins

Paul = mins

2 **Write the correct number in each box.**

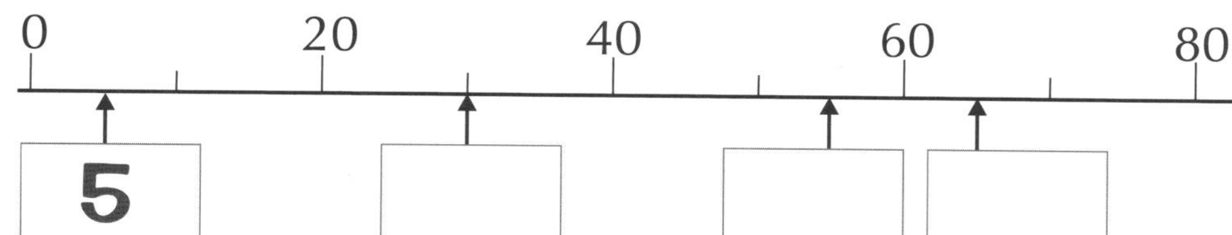

3 **Label 8, 14, 27 and 35 on this scale.**

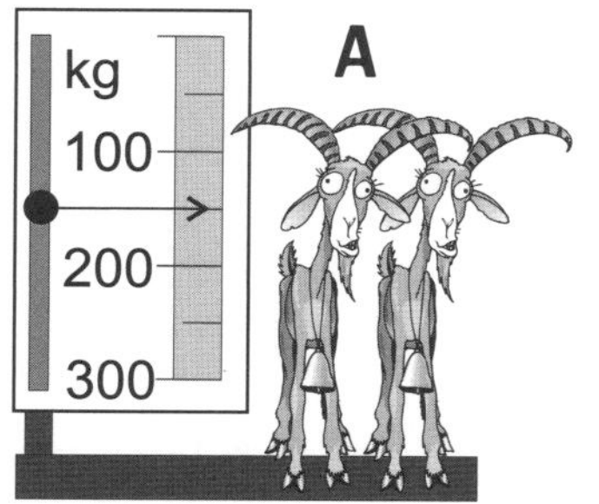

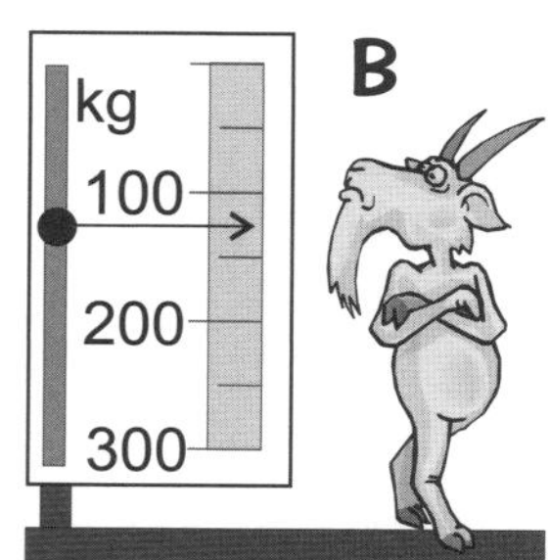

4 **What does each scale read?**

A = kg

B = kg

Activity Ask your family or friends how many hours of TV they watch each week. Create a bar chart of the information. Use a scale where some values aren't labelled (e.g. 0, 2, 4).

Learning Objective:

"I can read a scale to the nearest division or half-division."

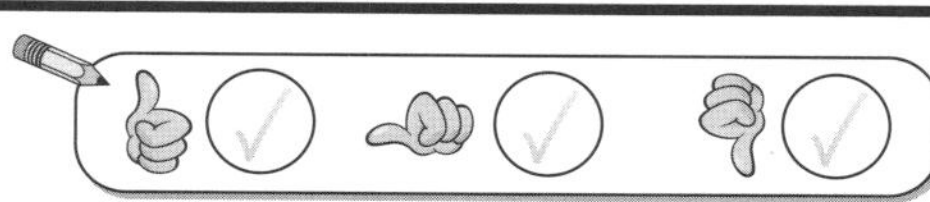

 Name: .... Date: ....

Reading Scales

1 **Draw the pointers on the scales to show each alien's mass.**

a)
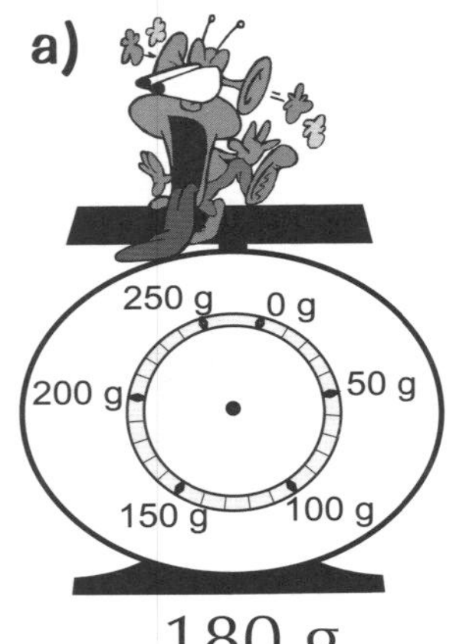

180 g

b)
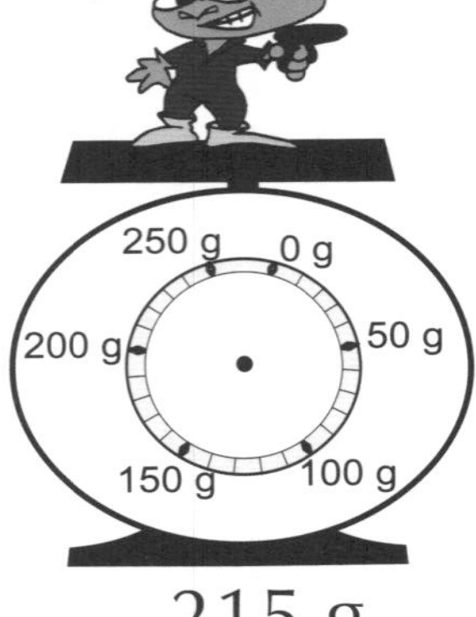

215 g

c)
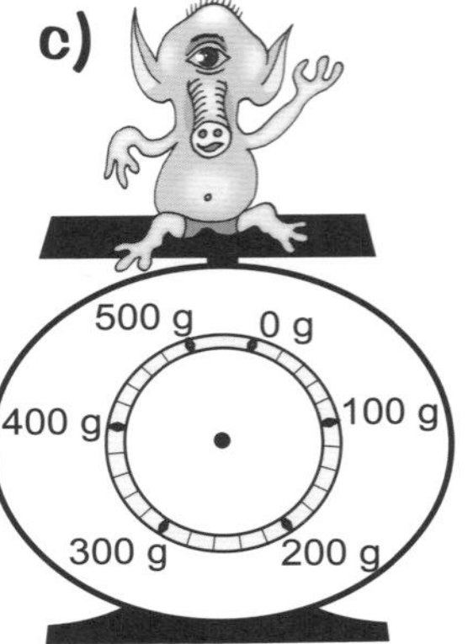

180 g

d)
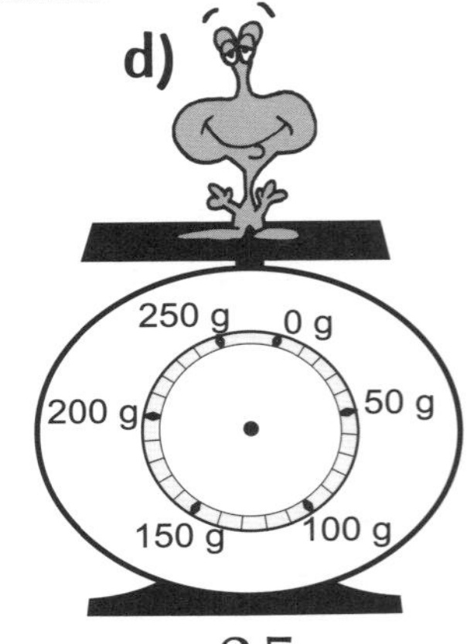

25 g

2 **Write the correct number in each box. One is done for you.**

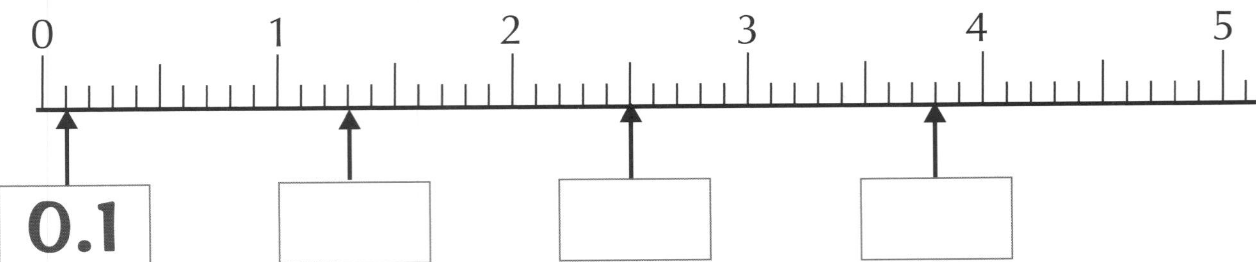

3 **Label 0.8, 2.5 and 3.7 on this scale.**

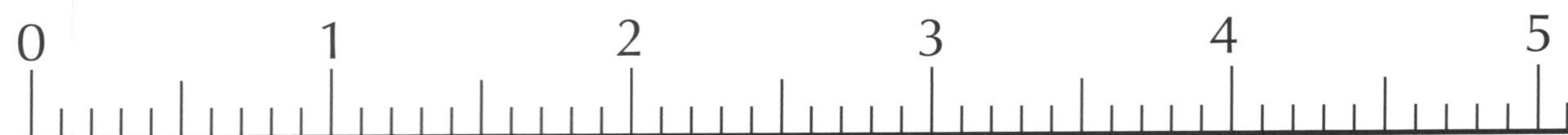

4 **Read the temperature on each thermometer.**

a)

b)
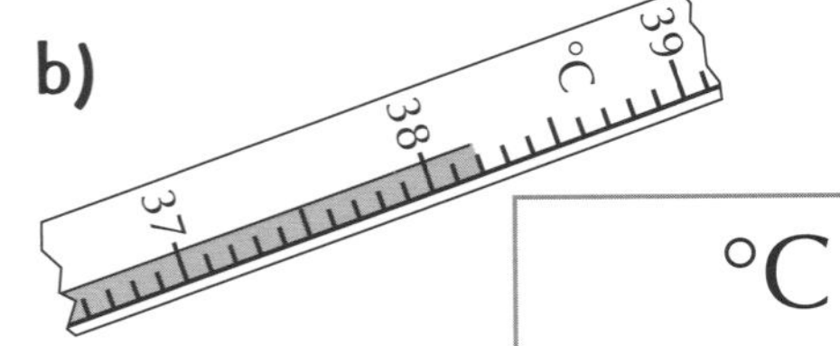

Activity Use a ruler to measure the lengths of some objects in centimetres. Give the measurements to the nearest tenth of a centimetre.

Learning Objective:

"I can read a scale to the nearest tenth of a unit."

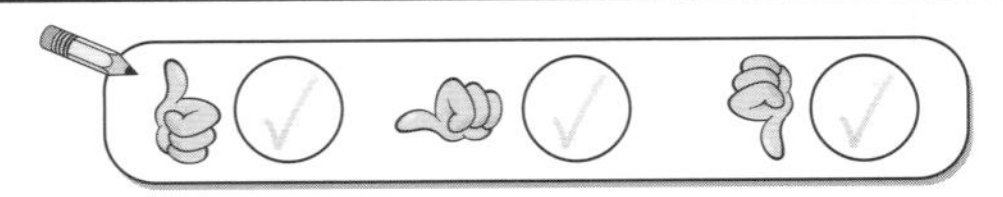

Reading Scales

1 What temperature is shown on each of these thermometers?

a) 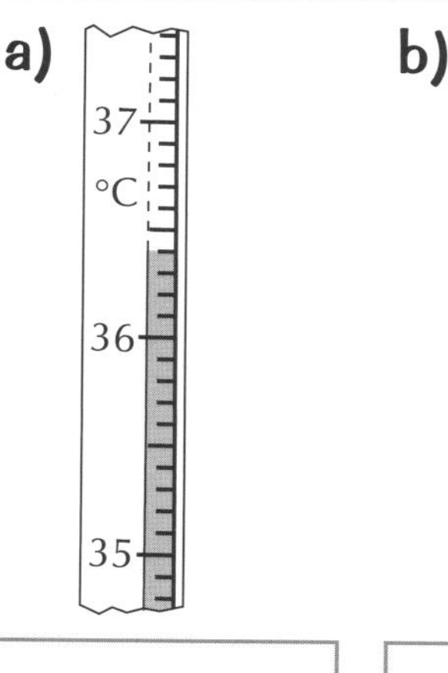
b) 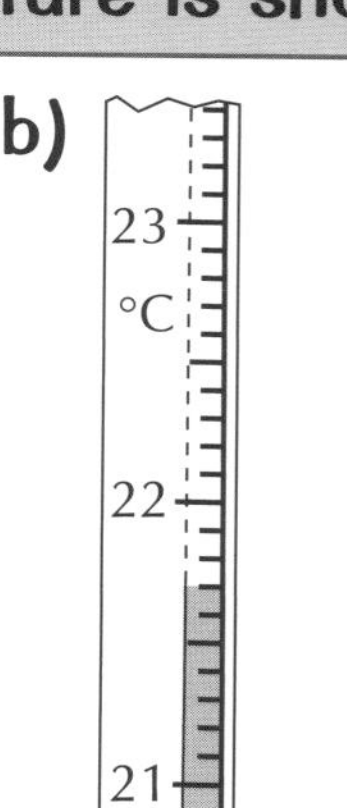
c) 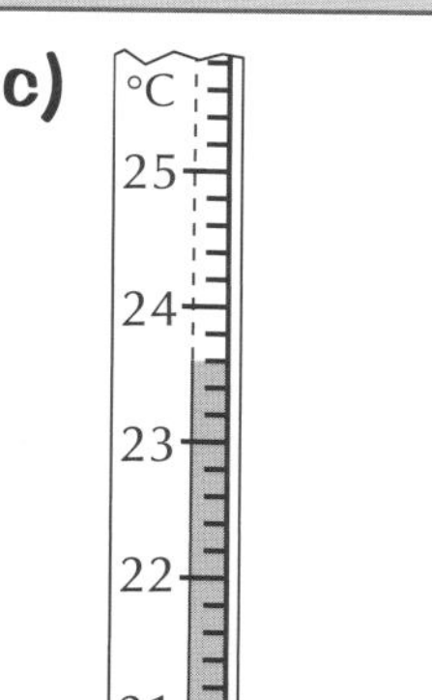
d) 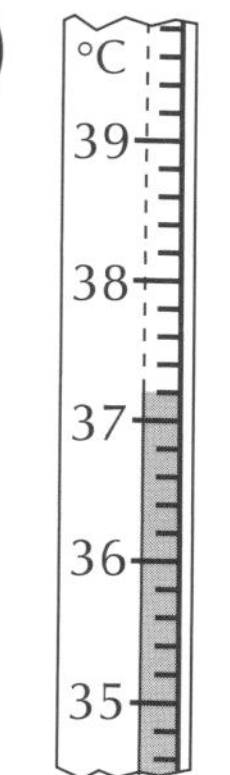

Watch out. c) and d) have a trickier scale.

a) °C b) °C c) °C d) °C

2 How much camel spit is in each jug?

a) 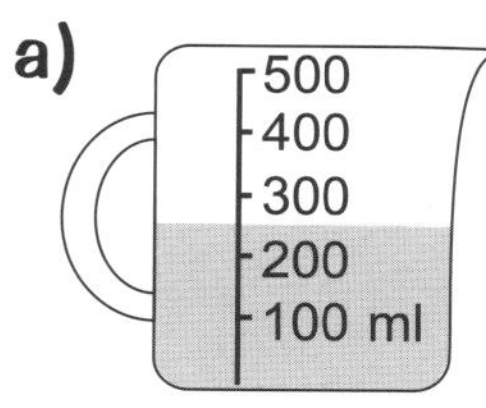
b) 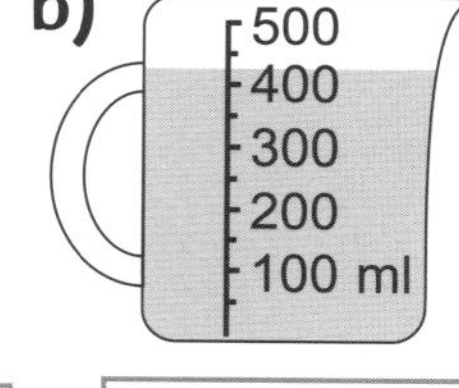

c) 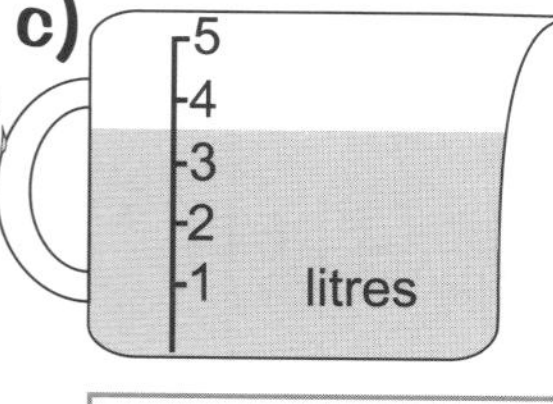
d) 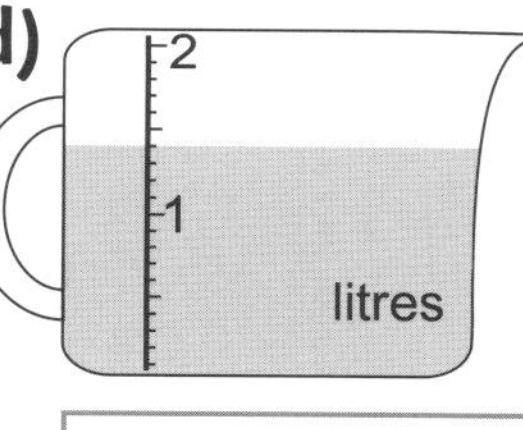

a) ml b) ml c) litres d) litres

3 Work out the mass of each dog.

a) 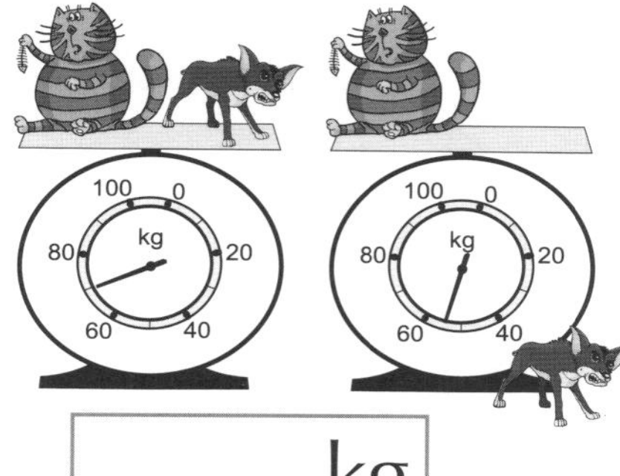

kg

b) 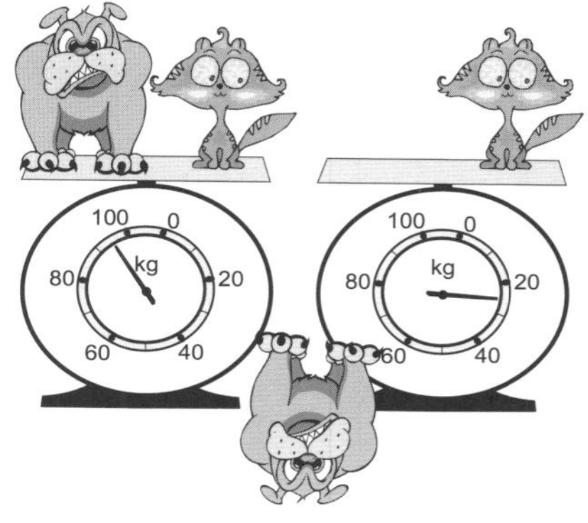

kg

Activity Find four small containers, such as yoghurt pots and cups. Fill one of the containers with water, tip it into a measuring jug and read the scale. Do this with the other containers.

Learning Objective:

"I can read a scale to the nearest tenth of a unit."

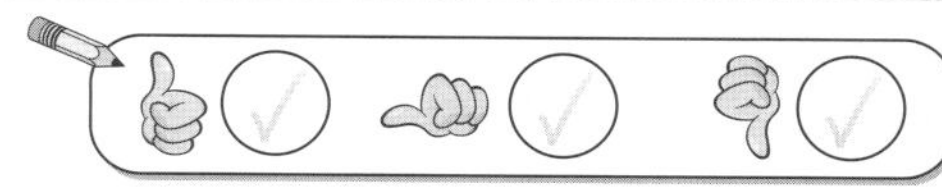

Reading Scales

1 **Write the correct number in each box.**

a) 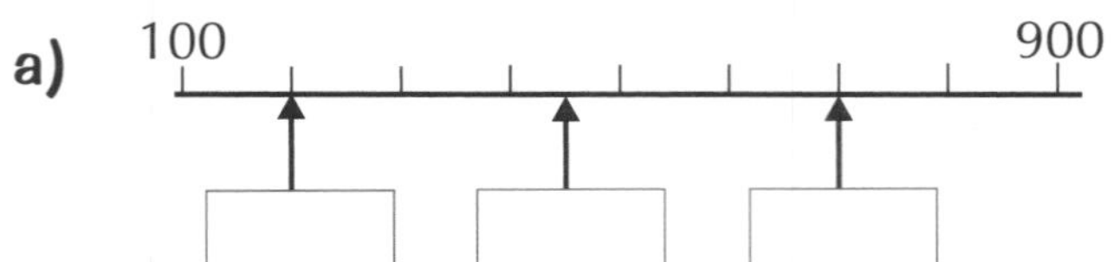

b) 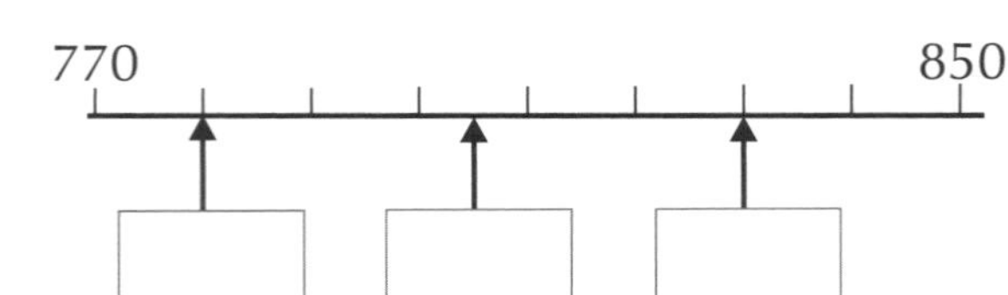

c) d) 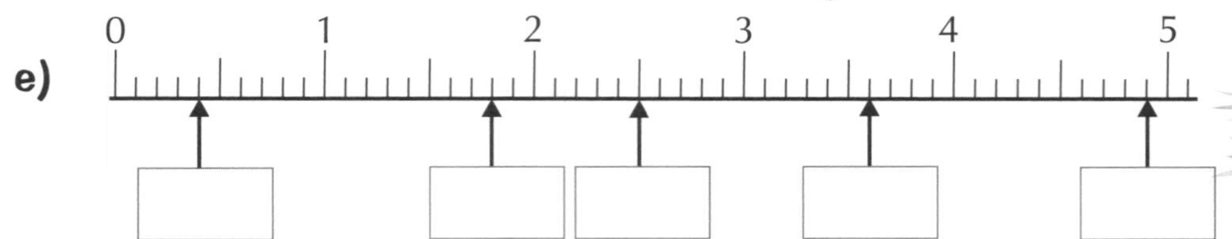

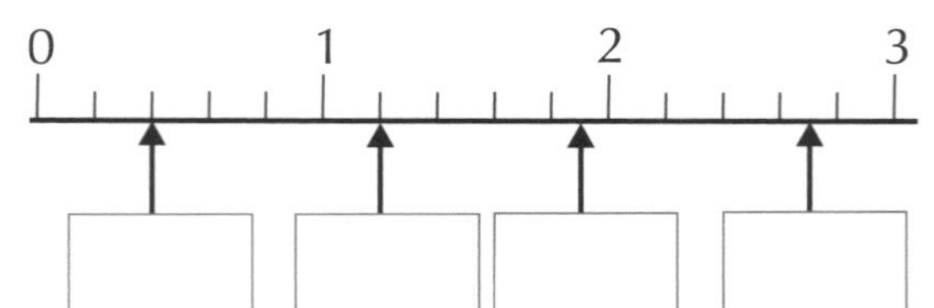

e) 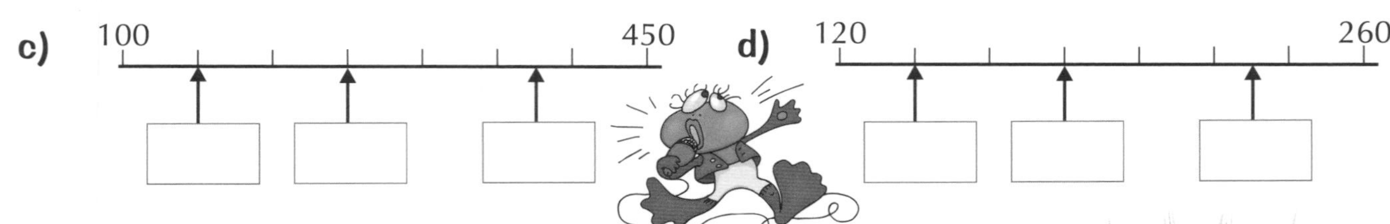

Watch out. These scales are all different.

f) 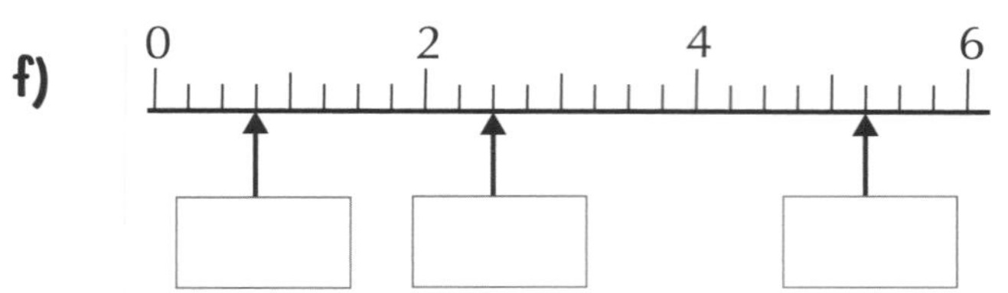

g)
0 1 2 3

2 **How much liquidised frog is in each jug?**

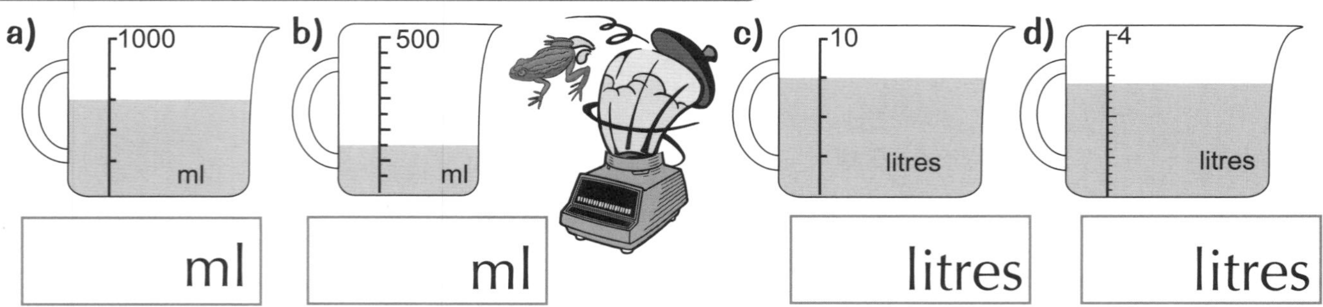

ml ml litres litres

Activity Measure your height, mass and hand span. You'll need to make sure you choose the right measuring device and read the scale correctly.

Learning Objective:

"I can find the value of each interval on a scale so that I can read measurements accurately."

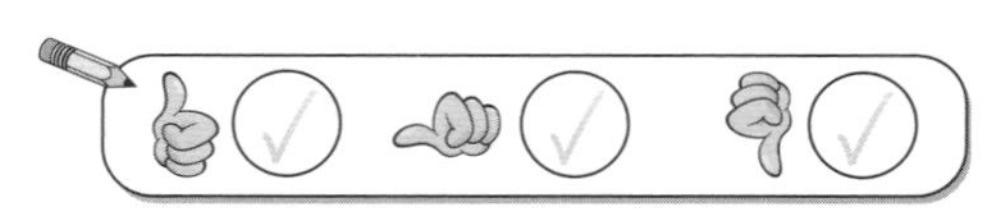

Time

1 Match the digital times to the clock faces below.

One has been done for you.

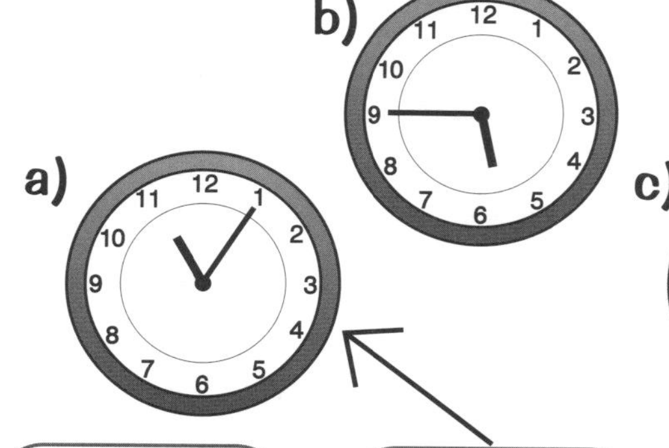

08:35 | 11:05 | 05:45 | 07:25 | 12:15

2 Look at the TV guide on the right.

a) How long is The Telebutties on for?

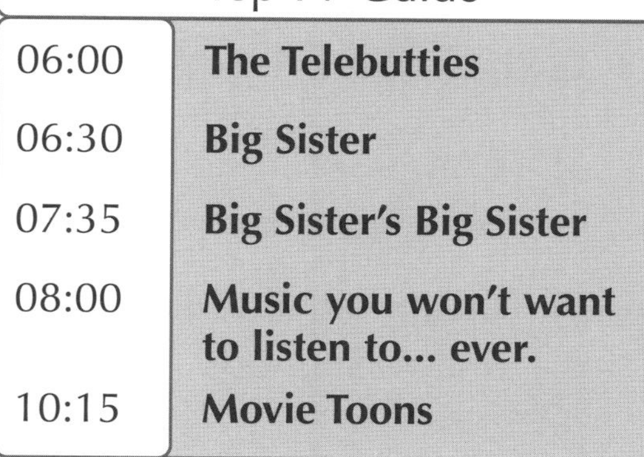

Top TV Guide	
06:00	The Telebutties
06:30	Big Sister
07:35	Big Sister's Big Sister
08:00	Music you won't want to listen to... ever.
10:15	Movie Toons

b) How long is the music programme on for?

minutes

c) Movie Toons is on for 45 minutes. When will the next programme start?

:

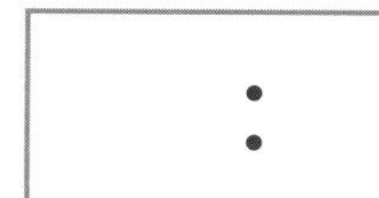

d) Wildlife Wonders is on before The Telebutties and is 75 minutes long. What time does it start?

:

Activity Write a timetable of your school day. Put on the start and end times for the different parts of your day. Add some after-school activities too.

Learning Objective:

"I can tell the time on clocks and I can work out when things will start or finish."

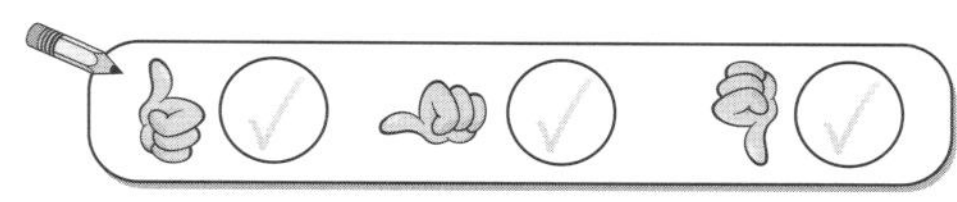

 Name: .... Date: ....

Time

1 **Fill in the missing times below.**

a) 

12:17

b) 

10:56

c) 

11:13

d) 

 :

2 **What time will the watches below show in 47 minutes time? Write whether the time is am or pm.**

a) 11:23 am

 :

b) 11:48 pm

 :

c) 6:13 pm

 :

3 **Answer the questions below using the best unit of time.**

a) Ellen's birthday is on November 28th. How long does she have to wait until Christmas?

b) Dwain leaves Maths at 11.30 and 10 seconds. He gets to English at 11.31 and 4 seconds. How long did it take to get there?

4 **Use the train timetable to answer the questions below.**

London King's Cross	10.50 am
Taunton	12.40 pm
Exeter St Davids	1.13 pm

a) How long does it take to travel from London King's Cross to Exeter St Davids?

b) Rachel arrives in Taunton at 11.55 am. How long does she have to wait for the train to Exeter St Davids?

Activity Find a train or bus timetable at home. Pick two places and try to work out the length of time between each stop.

Learning Objective:

"I can use am and pm, and work out time intervals."

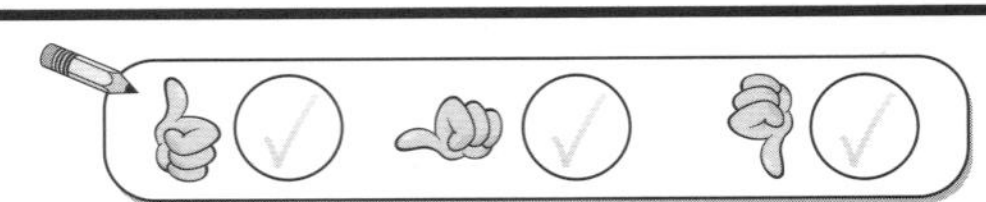

Time

1 Joe gets a digital watch for his birthday which uses a 24 hour clock. He gets home from school at a quarter to five. Write how his new watch displays this time.

a) 

b) He eats his tea an hour and a half later. How does his watch display this time?

2 Write these 24 hour clock times using a 12 hour clock and am or pm.

a) 23:50   ___ : ___

b) 17:31   ___ : ___

c) 0:11   ___ : ___

3 Look at the swimming pool timetable.

a) Write the start and finish times for the sessions when the pool is open to the public.

b) For how long is the pool open to the public on Monday?

c) Dan is catching the bus to play canoe polo. It takes 27 minutes. He catches it at 18.34. What time will he get to the swimming pool? Will he be early or late?

Time	Monday
7.00 – 9.00	Open to the public
9.00 – 12.00	School booking
12.00 – 17.30	Open to the public
17.30 – 19.00	Aquafit
19.00 – 20.00	Canoe polo
20.00 – 22.00	Lifesaving club

Activity Try setting a timer to record a TV programme or a film at home in the evening. What time will you need to <u>start</u> the timer? How <u>long</u> will it record for and when will it <u>finish</u>?

Learning Objective:

"I can use a 24 hour clock."

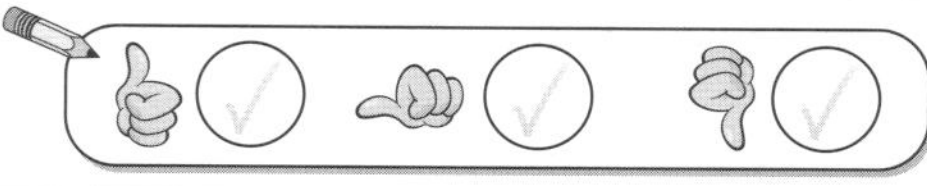

Units and Measures

1 **Draw an arrow on each of the scales to show the mass.**

a) 350 g

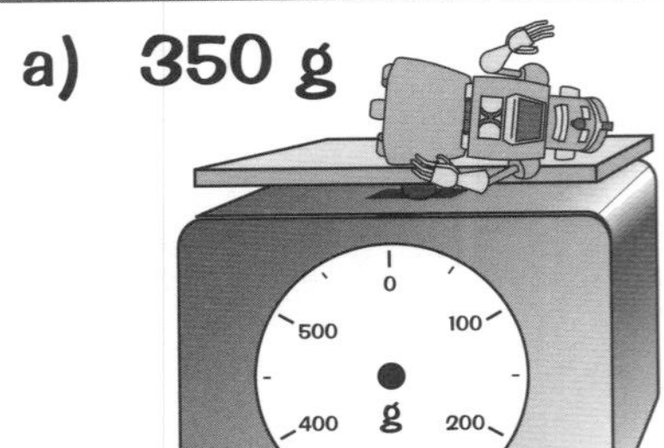

b) 475 g

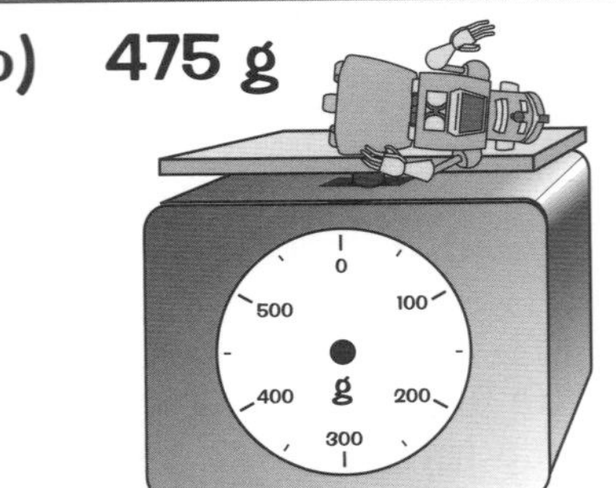

c) 525 g

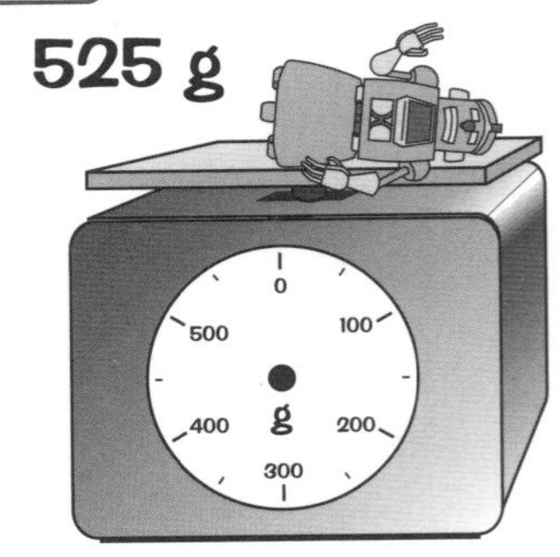

2 **Write the masses in grams.**

a) 1 kg [ ]

b) 1.5 kg 

c) 2 kg [ ]

d) 10 kg [ ]

3 **Circle the units you would use to measure:**

a) the mass of an orange. grams kilograms

b) a glass of lemonade. millilitres litres

c) the length of the whiteboard. metres kilometres

4 **Circle one length to complete each sentence.**

a) The length of a paperclip is about: 3 cm 30 cm 300 cm

b) The height of a door is about: 2 cm 20 cm 200 cm

Activity Estimate some distances, such as the distance from your elbow to your hand, or how far it is to school. Try estimating them using different units. What's the best unit to use for each distance?

Learning Objective:

"I can suggest sensible units to measure lengths and masses."

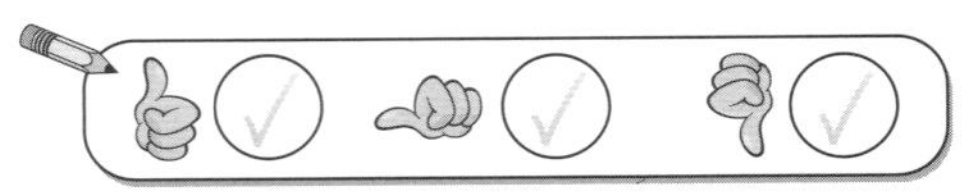

Key Objective

Units and Measures

1 Write the masses as kilograms.

a) 1200 g ☐ b) 2300 g ☐

c) 3575 g ☐ d) 1609 g ☐

2 Kate has bought a can of cherryade.

Circle the most likely capacity of the can.

30 ml 300 ml 3 litres 30 litres

3 Two of the sentences below are true.

Put a tick next to the true sentences.

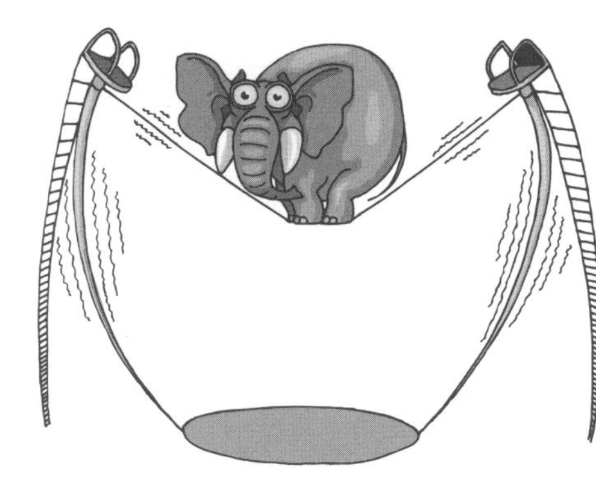

☐ Dan's mug holds 3 litres of tea.

☐ Pete is just over 1 metre tall.

☐ Amy's chocolate bar has a mass of 40 grams.

☐ Sarah's pet hamster is 80 cm long.

4 Which is heavier? Circle the correct answer.

30 000 g

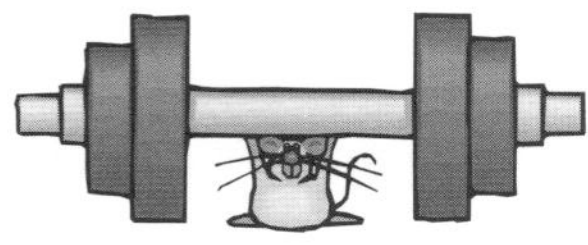

40 kg

Activity Find three objects with a mass of less than 1 kg. Arrange them in order from lightest to heaviest.

Learning Objective:

"I can use units for length, mass and capacity."

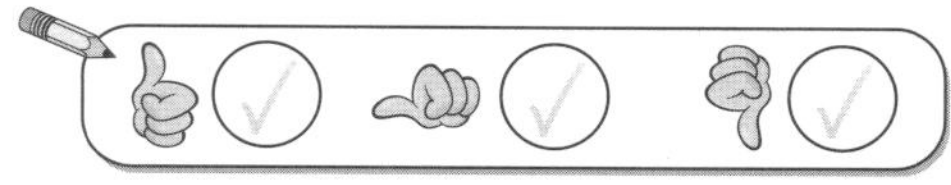

 Name: .... Date: ....

Key Objective

Units and Measures

1 **Write three and a half kilometres using these different units.**

metres [ ] centimetres [ ]

2 **Circle the correct amount to complete the sentences.**

a) Cardiff to London is about: 240 cm 240 m 240 km

b) An apple is likely to have a mass of about: 14 g 140 g 1400 g

c) The capacity of a saucepan is likely to be about: 2.5 ml 25 ml 2.5 l

d) The height of a room is likely to be about: 250 mm 250 cm 250 m

3 **Write these distances in order from smallest to largest.**

2 m 250 cm 20 cm 200 m 2 km 2.6 m

[ ] [ ] [ ] [ ] [ ] [ ]

4 **Estimate the length of the lines below.**

Check your estimate by measuring the lines and writing the answer to the nearest half centimetre.

a) ——————— Estimate [ ] Length [ ]

b) ————————————— Estimate [ ] Length [ ]

Activity Find some pencils and estimate their lengths in centimetres. Then check your estimates by measuring the pencils. Round your answers to the nearest half centimetre.

Learning Objective:

"I can estimate and measure a length using metres, centimetres or millimetres."

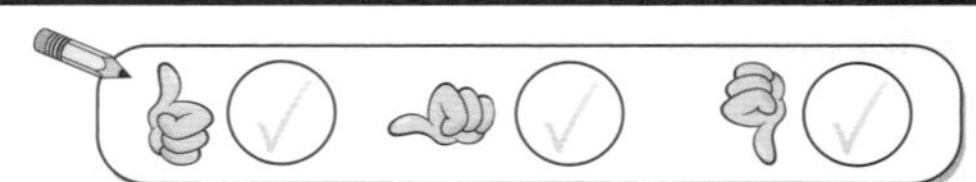

Units and Measures

1 **Estimate the length of the vulture's perch in cm.**

cm

Check your estimate by measuring the perch to the nearest centimetre.

cm

2 **One alien has a mass of 125 g. What is the mass of 6 aliens?**

Tick the scale which shows the correct reading.

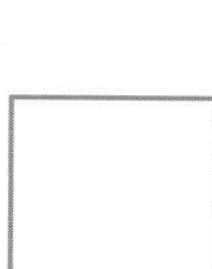

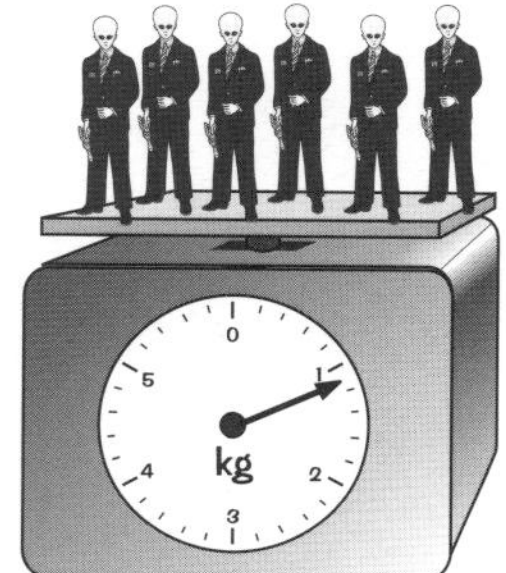

3 **Joanne has 2 vases.**

The first vase is full and contains 2.8 litres of water.
The second vase is half the capacity of the first and is half filled with water.

How much water does the second vase contain in ml?

Activity Find a bag with lots of the same item in, such as a bag of apples, and find the mass of one of them. Count the items in the bag and estimate the mass of the contents of the whole bag. Then find the mass of the whole bag. How close was your estimate to the real mass?

Learning Objective:

"I can estimate and measure length, mass and capacity."

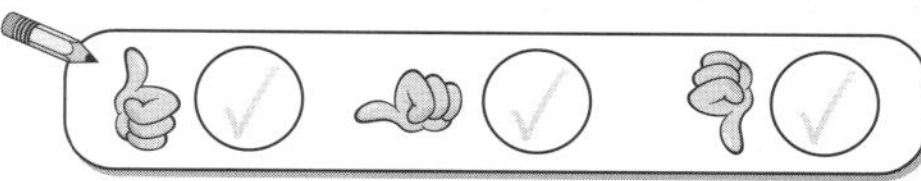

 Name: .... Date: ....

Data

1 **You are going to collect data to answer this question:**

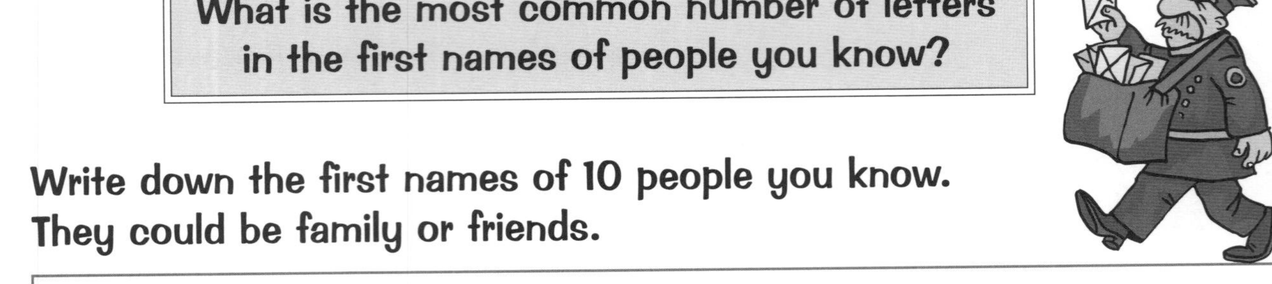

What is the most common number of letters in the first names of people you know?

a) Write down the first names of 10 people you know.
They could be family or friends.

b) Count the number of letters in each name.
Record your results in this frequency table:

Only use as much of the table as you need

Number of letters										
Tally										
Frequency										

c) On squared paper, draw a bar chart of your results.
Put frequency on the vertical axis.
Put number of letters on the horizontal axis.

d) What is the most common number of letters?

Activity Find the results of some football matches. Look in newspapers or on the internet. Make a frequency table to show the total number of goals scored in each match.

Learning Objective:

"I can collect and organise data using tally charts and frequency tables."

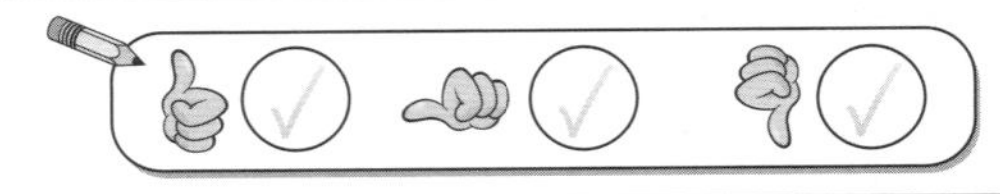

Key Objective

Data

1 You are helping to plan a party for a Year 2 class.

You need to decide:

- How to decorate the hall.
- What games to play.
- What food and drink to have at the party.

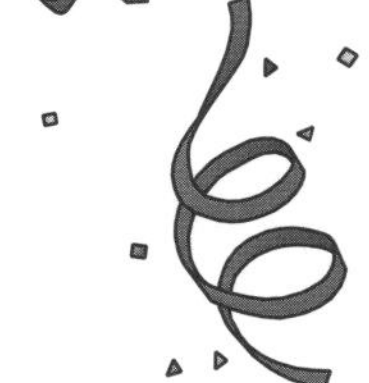

You will need a questionnaire to find out what the children would like.

a) You decide to decorate the hall with balloons.
Write a question to help you choose what colours to use.

b) Think of five different games you could play at the party.
Draw a table that you could use to find the most popular games.

c) Write three questions to help you decide what food and drink to have.
In your questions, give options to choose from.

Activity Answer this question: "Which word comes up most on a page of my reading book?" Count the common words "a", "the", "in", "is", "to" and "of". Make a tally chart.

Learning Objective:

"I can decide what data I need to collect and put it into a table to help me answer questions."

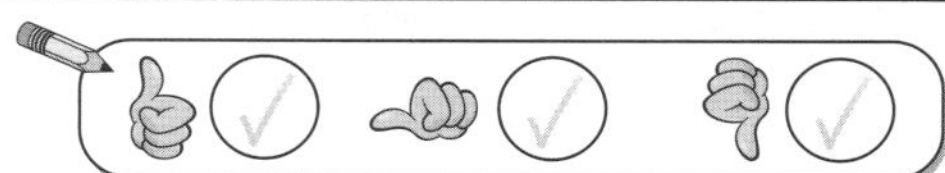

 Name: .... Date: ....

Data

1 **Jane works in a shop that sells school clothes by age.**

She recorded the sizes of all the pairs of trousers she sold over a week.

	Trousers sold by size					
Monday	9	9	11	13		
Tuesday	12	8	10	13		
Wednesday	8	11	10	10	10	
Thursday	9	8	8	8	14	
Friday	9	9	13	8	10	
Saturday	14	14	14	9	12	8

a) Fill in this frequency table to show how many pairs of trousers of each size she sold over the week.

Size							
Tally							
Frequency							

b) Which size of trousers did Jane sell the most of?

2 **You want to answer this question:**   

"What is the most common colour of car in your area?"

Describe how you would collect information to answer this question. Think about <u>where</u> and <u>for how long</u> you would collect the data.

Activity You will need an ordinary 6-sided dice. Roll the dice 50 times. Record your score on each roll in a frequency table. Do you notice any numbers coming up more than others?

Learning Objective:

"I can decide what information needs to be collected to answer a question and how best to collect it."

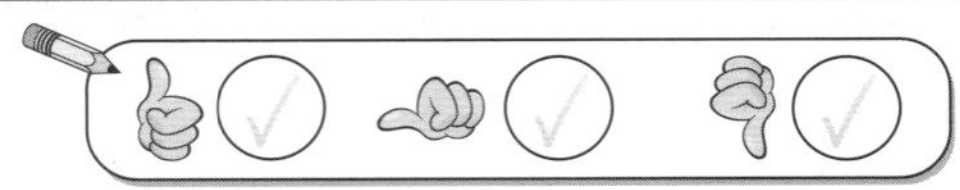

Tables and Charts

1 **This pictogram shows the number of ice lollies of each colour in a box.**

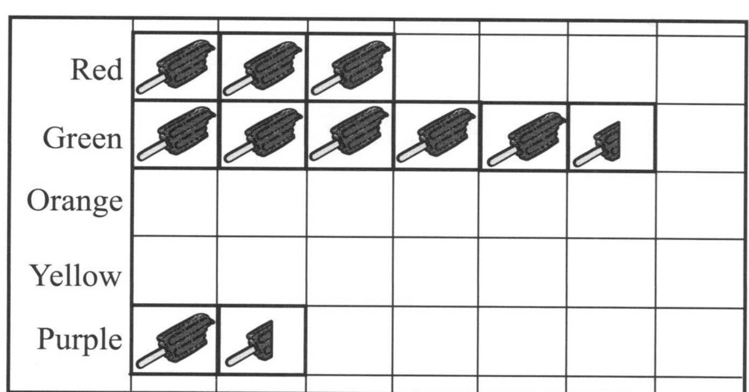

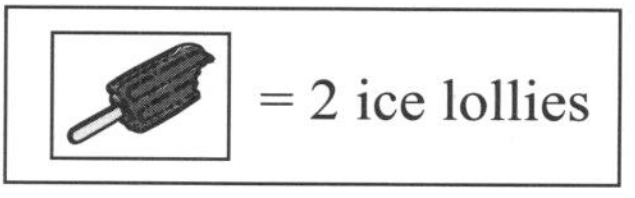

a) How many green lollies were there?

b) There were 4 orange lollies and 1 yellow lolly. Finish the pictogram.

2 **Count how many times each vowel appears in this rhyme. Complete the tally chart and bar chart. The a's are done for you.**

My weeds grew and grew,
right out of the blue,
and now they're as tall as the trees.

Vowel	Tally
a	𝍸
e	
i	
o	
u	

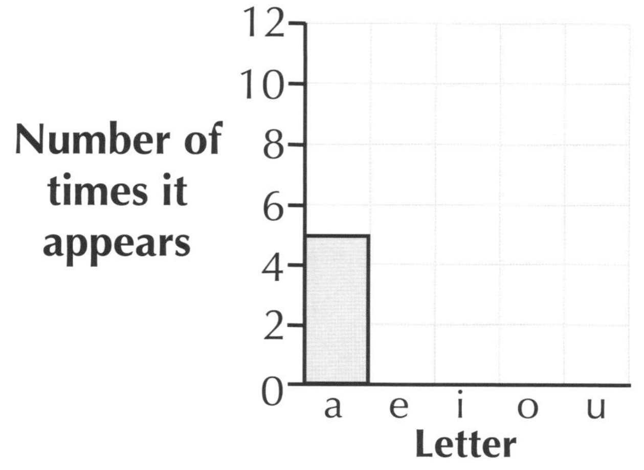

Activity Throw a dice 35 times. Draw a tally chart to show each throw. Use this information to draw your own bar chart.

Learning Objective:

"I can show information in a tally chart, pictogram or bar chart."

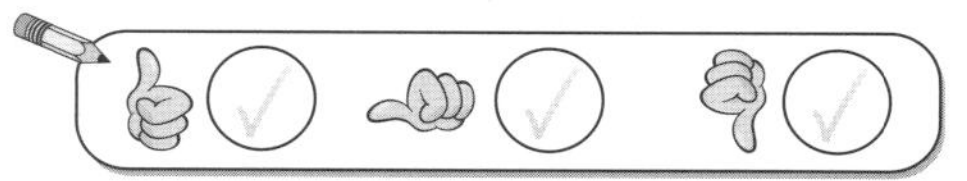

 Name: .... Date: ....

Key Objective

Tables and Charts

1 Jo counted how many books were borrowed from the library each hour.

Time	Tally	Total
9 am - 10 am	𝍸 𝍸 𝍸 ||	17
10 am - 11 am	𝍸 |||	8
11 am - 12 noon		2
12 noon - 1 pm	𝍸 𝍸 𝍸 𝍸 |||	
1 pm - 2 pm		14
2 pm - 3 pm	𝍸 𝍸 𝍸	
3 pm - 4 pm		5

a) Complete this frequency table.

b) How many books were borrowed between 9 am and 11 am?

c) Were more books borrowed in the morning or the afternoon?

d) On a sheet of squared paper, draw a pictogram of this information.

Use: 📖 = 2 books

2 These bar charts show how many books Kim read each month this year.

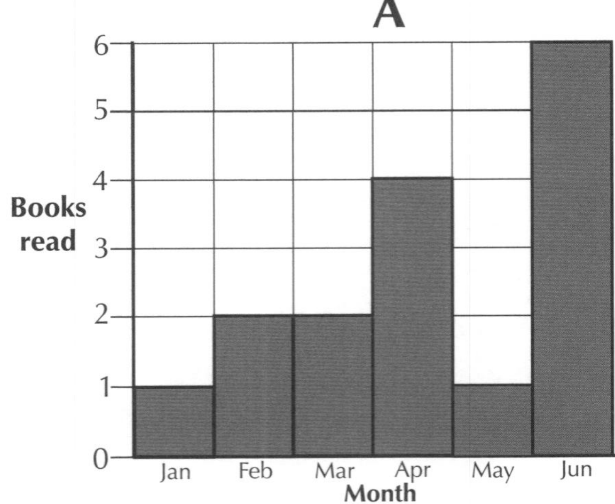

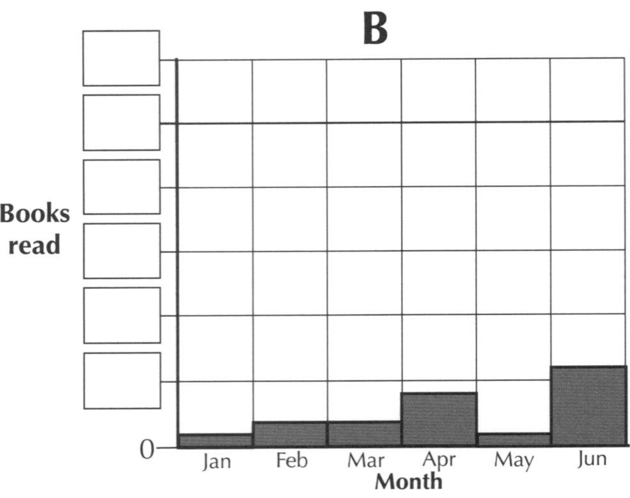

a) Complete the missing numbers on the scale of bar chart B.

b) Which bar chart makes it look like Kim reads lots of books?

Activity Deal 30 cards from a shuffled pack.
Draw a frequency table to show how many you dealt of each suit.

Learning Objective:

"I can use tables, tally charts, pictograms and bar charts."

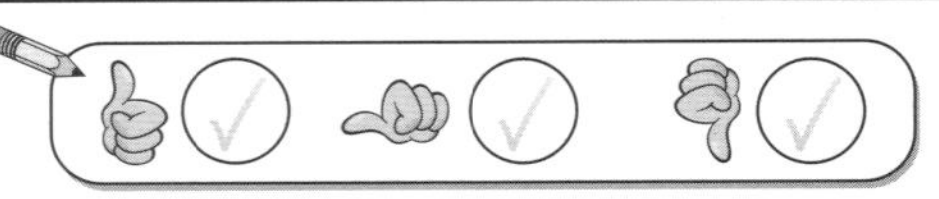

Key Objective

Tables and Charts

1 Kath's Cafe sells coffees, cakes and cookies.
The chart shows how many of each were sold on Wednesday.

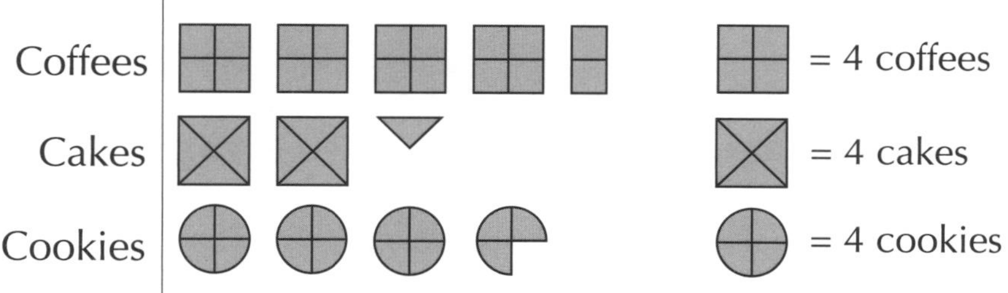

a) The cafe had 16 slices of cake at the beginning of the day.
How many slices did the cafe have left at the end of the day?

b) On Thursday the cafe sold twice as many coffees as on Wednesday.
How many coffees did the cafe sell on Thursday?

c) On some squared paper, draw a bar chart to show what the cafe sold on Wednesday.

2 This chart shows how many people went to a hairdresser each day one week.

= 5 people

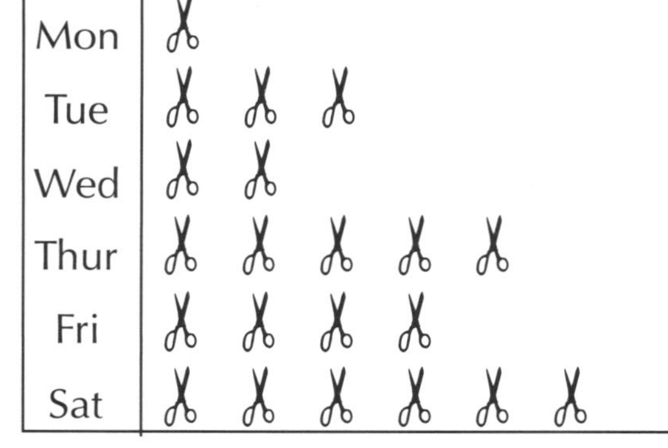

a) How many more people went to the hairdresser on Thursday than on Tuesday?

b) How many people went to the hairdresser in total that week?

c) On a separate piece of paper make a frequency table of this data.

Activity Count how many cups, plates, bowls and pans are in your kitchen cupboards at home.
Make a frequency table and a pictogram of this data.
Think of three questions that you could use your pictogram to answer.

Learning Objective:

"I can make and understand pictograms, bar charts and frequency tables."

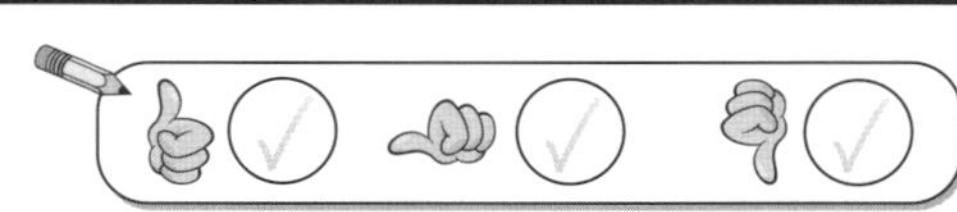

Answers

Page 1 — Explaining Problem Solving, Sheet 2

Q1 **9** of the children are boys.
$26 - 17 = 9$

Q2 a) Louise has **30 slices of cake**.
$5 \times 6 = 30$
Possible diagram:

b) There are **3 whole cakes** left. You could colour in the eaten slices on your picture.

Q3 b) $54 + 27 = 54 + 30 - 3$
$= 84 - 3 = \mathbf{81}$

c) $148 - 95 = 148 - 100 + 5$
$= 48 + 5 = \mathbf{53}$

Activity:
Joshua starts with 44 stickers and keeps 23. He has 44 – 23 = 21 to share between Ruth and David.
If Ruth has **5** stickers, David has 21 – 5 = **16**.
If Ruth has **6** stickers, David has 21 – 6 = **15**.
In the same way:
If Ruth has **7** stickers, David has **14**.
If Ruth has **8** stickers, David has **13**.
If Ruth has **9** stickers, David has **12**.
If Ruth has **10** stickers, David has **11**.
If Ruth has **11** stickers, David has **10**.
If Ruth has **12** stickers, David has **9**.
If Ruth has **13** stickers, David has **8**.
David has at least 8 stickers, so these are all the possible ways of sharing.

Page 2 — Explaining Problem Solving, Sheet 3

Q1 a) 18 **÷** 3 = 6
b) 24 **–** 9 = 15
c) 42 **+** 12 **=** 54

Q2 £4.30 + £2.45 = **£6.75**

Q3 **Offer 1** is cheaper.
Offer 1 costs 40p, but offer 2 costs 45p.

Activity:
Many possible answers. For example:
Stavros the cheetah catches four mice every day. How many does he catch in a week?
There are 7 days in a week, so the answer is 4 × 7 = 28.

Page 3 — Explaining Problem Solving, Sheet 4

Q1 a) Rosie is most likely to pull out a **mint chocolate**. There are 4 mint chocolates, but only 2 orange chocolates and 1 plain chocolate.

b) Rosie is now most likely to pull out an **orange chocolate**. There are five orange chocolates altogether, but only 4 mint chocolates and 1 plain chocolate.

Q2 A square number is found by multiplying another number by itself. 25 = 5 × 5, so 25 is a square number.
Possible diagram:

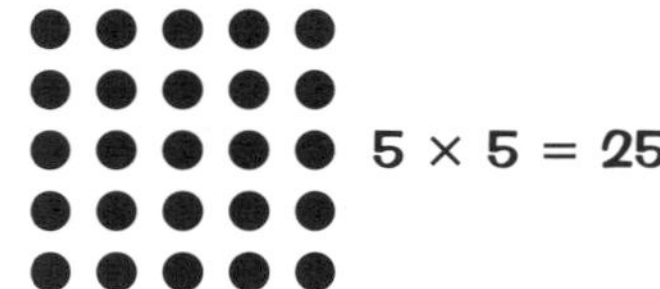

Q3 The perimeter is **48 m**.

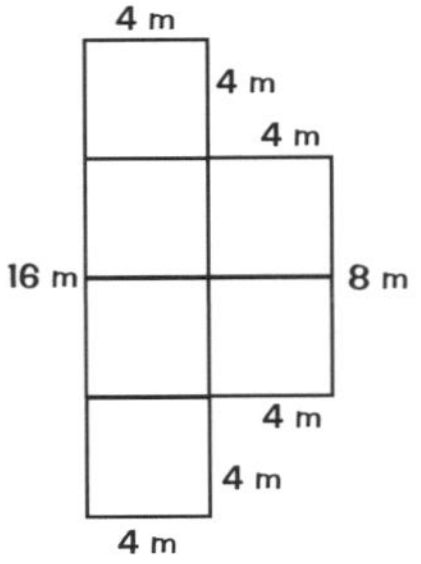

4 m + 4 m + 4 m + 8 m
+ 4 m + 4 m + 4 m + 16 m
= 48 m

Activity:
The number combinations are:

Score	Combinations
3	2 + 1
5	1 + 4, 2 + 3
6	1 + 5, 2 + 4, 3 + 3
8	2 + 6, 3 + 5, 4 + 4
10	4 + 6, 5 + 5
11	5 + 6
12	6 + 6

Page 4 — Number Patterns, Sheet 3

Q1 a) 70, 60, **50**, **40**, 30, **20**, **10**
b) 4,6, **8**, 10, **12**, **14**, **16** — rule is **add 2**.
c) 8, 11, **14**, **17**, 20, **23**, **26** — rule is **add 3**.
d) 35, 30, 25, **20**, **15**, **10**, **5** — rule is **subtract 5**.

Q2 a) **16, 32, 64**
b) **No. If you double an even number, it always produces an even number.**

Q3 a) **11 matches**
b) **The number of matches goes up by 2 each time.**

Activity:
Here are some examples:

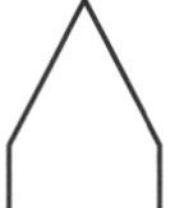

Answers

Page 5 — Number Patterns, Sheet 4

Q1 a) 32, 36, 40, **44**, **48**, **52** — rule is **add 4**.
b) 450, 400, 350, **300**, **250**, **200** — rule is **subtract 50**.
c) 0, 20, 40, 60, **80**, **100**, **120** — rule is **add 20**.

Q2 Any of the following are correct for a) and b):
23 + 74
34 + 27
43 + 72
32 + 47
c) **odd + even** or **even + odd**

Q3
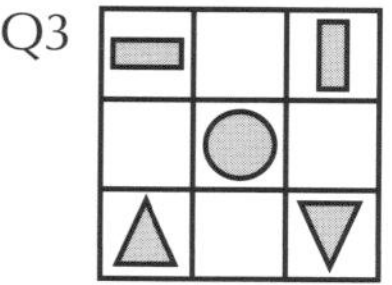

Activity:
3p (2p + 1p), 4p (2p + 2p), 6p (5p + 1p), 7p (5p + 2p), 11p (10p + 1p), 12p (10p + 2p), 15p (10p + 5p).

Page 6 — Number Patterns, Sheet 5

Q1 a) 63, 51, **39**, **27**, **15**, **3** — rule is **subtract 12.**
b) 80, 105, **130**, **155**, **180**, **205** — rule is **add 25.**
c) 3, 6, 12, 24, 48, 96 — rule is **double the previous number**.

Q2 **Yes, Jane is correct. If you can divide the last 2 digits of a number by 4, you can divide the whole number by 4 and 28 ÷ 4 = 7.**

Q3 My number was **12.** You can prove this by reversing the calculation:
31 – 7 = 24
24 ÷ 2 = 12

Q4 a) **False**
True
b) **Possible answers: Shape A has 2 right angles, Shape A has 2 acute angles (angles less than 90°), Shape A has 2 reflex angles (angles greater than 180°)**
c) **Possible answer: Shape B has 2 lines of symmetry.**

Activity:
3, 9, 15, 21, 27, 33, 39, 45

Page 7 — Planning Problem Solving, Sheet 3

Q1

	Odd number of sides	Even number of sides
Grey		
White		

Q2

Boys		Girls	
Name	Has brother	Name	Has brother
Ajay	✗	Anita	✓
Harry	✗	Jenny	✗
Jamie	✓	Kerry	✓
Paul	✓	Milly	✗

Q3 a) **Friday** (£53)
b) **34**
c) 42 – 27 = **15**

Activity:
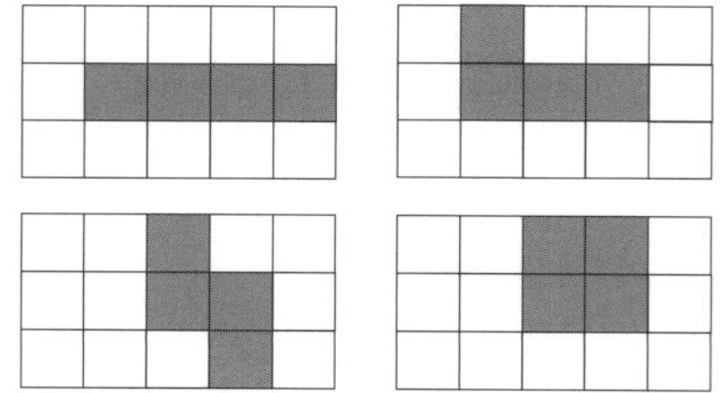

Page 8 — Planning Problem Solving, Sheet 4

Q1

	Only straight lines	Only curved lines	Straight and curved lines
No lines of symmetry	N	S	G
One or more lines of symmetry	A	C	D

Q2 a) **11** should be written in the table (shown below).
b) 11 + 1 = **12**
c) 7 + 11 + 12 = 30
32 – 30 = **2**

Type of newt	Tally	Total
Smooth	~~IIII~~ II	7
Palmate	~~IIII~~ ~~IIII~~ I	11
Crested	~~IIII~~ ~~IIII~~ II	12
Banded	II	2

Q3 a) 5 cherry buns cost 5 × 15p = 75p.
If Charlotte buys 5 cherry buns, she'll have 200p (£2) – 75p = 125p.
5 iced buns cost 5 × 25p = 125p.
So Charlotte **can** afford to buy 5 cherry buns and 5 iced buns.
b) 4 cream buns cost 4 × 20p = 80p.
4 cherry buns = 4 × 15p = 60p.
2 iced buns = 2 × 25p = 50p.
Total = 80p + 60p + 50p = 190p.
200p – 190p = 10p.
Charlotte's change from £2 is **10p.**

Activity:
Many possible answers, e.g. "In my name / Not in my name", "Vowel / Consonant", "Has a gap in it / Is a closed shape", etc.

Page 9 — Planning Problem Solving, Sheet 5

Q1 a)

Height: 0, 50, 100, 150, 200
Name: Lily, Kim, Azir, Simon, Tom

Age: 0, 2, 4, 6, 8, 10, 12
Name: Lily, Kim, Azir, Simon, Tom

Answers

b)

	Shorter than 150 cm	150 cm or taller
10 or older	**Simon**	**Lily**
Younger than 10	**Azir** **Kim**	**Tom**

Q2 a) **Amy**
b) **Charlie**
c) Many possible answers, e.g. "Who owns a cat but not a fish?" (Ella), "How many children own a rabbit?" (1), etc.

Activity:
There are **eight** different possibilities:
Vanilla ice cream, chocolate sauce, marshmallows.
Vanilla ice cream, chocolate sauce, jelly beans.
Vanilla ice cream, toffee sauce, marshmallows.
Vanilla ice cream, toffee sauce, jelly beans.
Strawberry ice cream, chocolate sauce, marshmallows.
Strawberry ice cream, chocolate sauce, jelly beans.
Strawberry ice cream, toffee sauce, marshmallows.
Strawberry ice cream, toffee sauce, jelly beans.

Page 10 — Problem Solving, Sheet 3

Q1 a) 160p + 95p = **£2.55**
b) **£2 + 20p + 20p + 5p**

Q2 a) **10:58**
b) **12:08**

Q3 (30 cm × 10) = 300 cm
300 cm + 30 cm = 330 cm
So, **11 chairs**

Q4 8 + 2 = 10 hours
10 × 7 = **70 hours**

Activity:
E.g. if 6 hours are spent at school each day, the total number of hours spent at school each week = 6 × 5 = 30 hours a week.

Page 11 — Problem Solving, Sheet 4

Q1 a) £15.75 + £17.23 = **£32.98**
b) £34.99 – £32.98 = **£2.01**

Q2 a) 17.4 – 16.6 = **0.8 s**
b) **118.8 s**

Q3 2nd prize = £167 × 2 = **£334**
1st prize = £334 + £167
= **£501**

Activity:
E.g. If the times taken to get to school are: 25 minutes, 7 minutes, 12 minutes, 3 minutes and 37 minutes, the difference between the shortest and longest times is: 37 – 3 = 34 minutes.

Page 12 — Problem Solving, Sheet 5

Q1 215.3 – 87.4 = **127.9** m

Q2 a) 39 + 31 + 23 + 16 = **109**
b) 31 – 14 = **17**
c) 23 + 16 = **39**

Q3 Shop A: £179.99 + £39.99
= £219.98

Shop B: £189.95 + £36.50
= £226.45

Difference: £226.45 – £219.98
= **£6.47**

Activity:
E.g. If petrol costs £1.16 per litre, and it costs £40 to fill up the tank, then 40 ÷ 1.16 = about 34 litres.

Page 13 — Problem Solving, Sheet 6

Q1 1.5 ÷ 12 = **0.125 l** or **125 ml**

Q2 a) 6 ÷ 0.86 = 6.98
= **6 loaves**
b) 6 × £0.86 = £5.16.
£6.00 – £5.16 = **£0.84** or **84p**

Q3 a) (0.42 × 1.5) + (0.39 × 1.5) + (0.87 × 1.5)
= **£2.52**
b) (0.42 × 2) + (0.87 × 3) + (0.39 × 2) = £4.23.
£4.23 ÷ 10 = **£0.42**

Activity:
E.g. 2.6 kg of apples would cost 2.6 × 0.29 = **£0.75**.

Page 14 — Write and Draw to Solve Problems, Sheet 2

Q1 a) **5, ... 11, 13**
b) **9, ... 21**

Q2 a) Four small squares should be shaded.
b) **£1.60**
c) **80p**

Q3 a) **863**
b) **368**
c) **683** or **863**

Activity:
E.g. if pocket money = £2 per week

Week	Amount (£)
1	2
2	4
3	6
4	8
5	10
6	12
7	14

and so on...

Page 15 — Write and Draw to Solve Problems, Sheet 3

Q1 a)

b) **12**

Q2 a) **12 – 5**
b) **22 – 5**

Q3 a) **50p**
b) **75p**
c) 7 × 25p (= 175p or £1.75) or 25p + 25p + 25p + 25p + 25p + 25p + 25p (= 175p or £1.75)

EXERCISE 7c

Re-arrange in order in your mind the five things in each line below. When you have done so, write down the name of the middle one.

Father, boy, youth, grandfather, infant. 2. House, town, street, county, country.
Lake, sea, ocean, puddle, pond. 4. Foot, head, knee, chest, neck.
Minute, hour, second, day, week. 6. Chapter, page, letter, word, book.
Shirt, overcoat, jacket, vest, waistcoat. 8. Kennel, nest, house, castle, mansion.
Australia, China, Great Britain, Monaco, France.
Canoe, battleship, yacht, liner, rowing-boat.

EXERCISE 7d

You will find below some sets of words that are used in describing things. Arrange them in order and write down the name of the middle one.

Huge, enormous, minute, small, large.
Never, sometimes, generally, seldom, always.
Evil, naughty, wicked, good, virtuous.
Interested, keen, apathetic, indifferent, enthusiastic.
Fond, harsh, loving, hateful, friendly.
Black, white, dark, grey, light.
Cold, boiling, hot, tepid, warm.
Some, all, none, most, few.
Better, worse, bad, good, best.
Quick, slow, swift, leisurely, lightning-like.

EXERCISE 7e

You will find four things named in each line below. They are followed by the names of four other things, one of which can be fitted in to a place among the first four. Pick it out and write down both its name and the order in which it should come.

Example

Basement, ground floor, first floor, attic . . . cellar, second floor, storeroom, kitchen.

Answer : Second floor (4).

Semi-quaver, quaver, crotchet, semi-breve . . . rest, breve, bar, minim.
Stroke, pat, smack, clout . . . crush, slap, blow, thrust.

3. Creep, walk, march, run . . . stroll, rise, relax, scuttle.
4. March, May, July, September . . . February, November, December, October.
5. Silent, quiet, sounding, loud . . . full, deafening, hoarse, inaudible.
6. Solo, duet, quartet, quintet . . . sonata, sextet, trio, symphony.
7. Pink, rose-red, vermilion, crimson . . . scarlet, buff, orange, green.
8. North, north-east, east, south . . . west, south-west, south-east, north-west.
9. Rare, infrequent, frequent, constant . . . daily, perpetual, often, common.
10. Wallet, attaché-case, suit-case, trunk . . . despatch-case, canister, crate, haversack.

EXERCISE 7f

Think of the order in which you would place the following and then write the number of the one that comes in the middle.

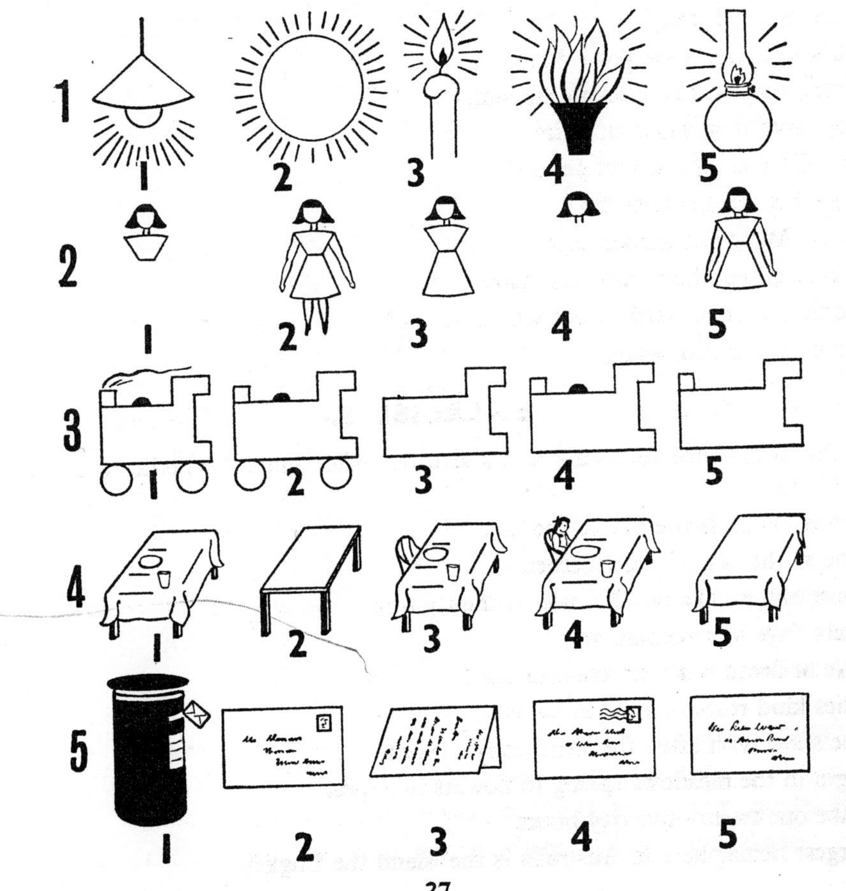

Angles

1 Estimate the following angles to the nearest 10°.

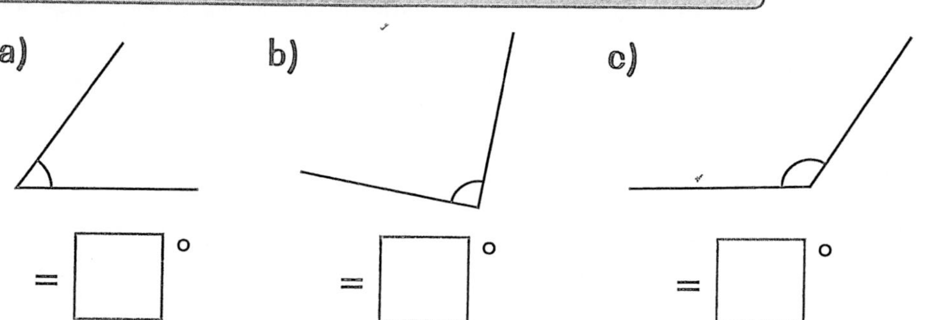

a) = □° b) = □° c) = □°

2 Measure each of the missing angles in the flowers below using a protractor.

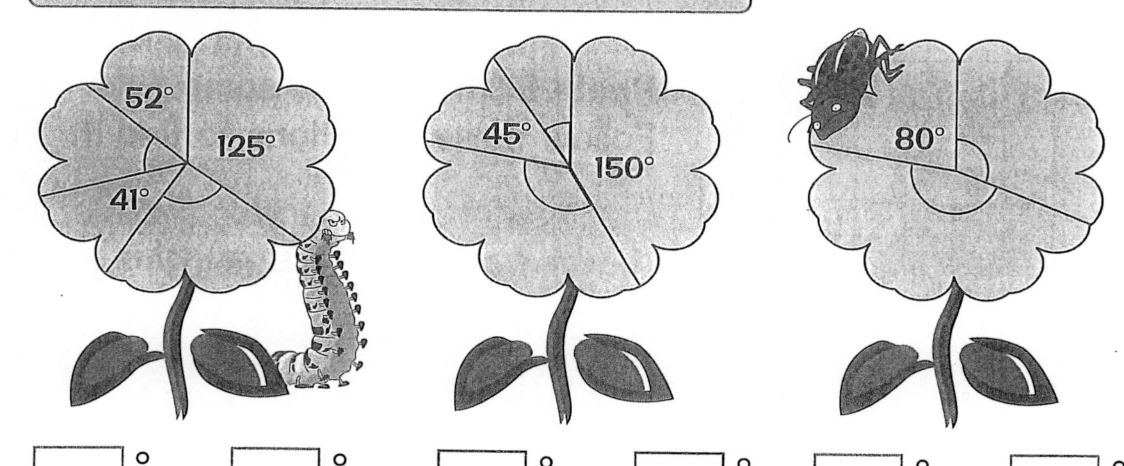

a) □° and □° b) □° and □° c) □° and □°

3 Using a protractor, draw the following angles.

65° 22° 137°

Activity

Without using a protractor, draw the following angles by estimation. Then, using the protractor, measure each angle you have drawn and see how close you were.

a) 90° b) 45° c) 150° d) 22° e) 178°

Learning Objective:

"I can estimate, draw and measure acute and obtuse angles using a protractor to a suitable degree of accuracy."

Answers

Activity:
You need 2 more matchsticks/pens and pencils each time.

Page 16 — Write and Draw to Solve Problems, Sheet 4

Q1 220 + 12 = 232 seats needed. 4 coaches have 212 seats, which is too few. 5 coaches have 265 seats, which is enough. They will need **5** coaches.

Q2 a)

Number of nights	1	2	3	4	5	6
Total cost	£35	£70	**£105**	**£140**	**£175**	**£210**

b) 6 × £5 = **£30**

c) Breakfast at hotel costs £45 – £35 = £10. This is £5 more expensive per day than cafe, so saving is 6 × £5 = **£30**.

Activity:
7 jumps are needed for 5 steps. And, e.g. 11 steps are needed for 7 steps.

Page 17 — Counting and Sequences, Sheet 2

Q1 **8**, **24**, **31**, **111**
12, **21**, **102**, **112**

Q2 a) **100**, **300**, **800**
b) **510**, **540**, **590**

Q3 a) **764**
b) **246**
c) **762** or **764**

Activity:
138, 183, 318, 381, 813, 831

Page 18 — Counting and Sequences, Sheet 3

Q1 a) **64**, **68**, **72**
b) **800**, **825**, **850**

Q2 a) **81**, **91**, **101**
b) **0**, **30**, **60**

Q3 a) +20, +20, +20 (35 40 45 50 55 60 65 70 75 80 85 90 95 100)
b) +10, +10, +10, +10, +10, +10 (35 40 45 50 55 60 65 70 75 80 85 90 95 100)
c) +15, +15, +15, +15 (35 40 45 50 55 60 65 70 75 80 85 90 95 100)

Activity:
Jumping along from 0 in steps of 2 means you always land on even numbers.
Steps of 3 mean you alternate between odd and even numbers.

Page 19 — Counting and Sequences, Sheet 4

Q1 a) **–7**, **–5**, **–3**
b) **–7**, **–4**, ... **11**
c) **12**, **12.6**, **13.2**
d) **2.4**, **2.1**, **1.8**

Q2 15 °C, **12 °C**, **9 °C**, **6 °C**, **3 °C**, **0 °C**, **–3 °C**

Q3 **–20**, **–11**

Q4 0.6 kg, **1.2 kg**, **1.8 kg**, **2.4 kg**, **3.0 kg**

Activity:
5.6, 4.2, 2.8, 1.4, 0
So, 4 times as tall.

Page 20 — Decimals, Sheet 1

Q1 a) **3 units**
b) **3 tenths**
c) **3 hundredths**
d) **3 tens**

Q2 

Q3 **£6.04**, **£6.11**, **£6.14**, **£6.40**, **£6.44**

Q4 **1.04 m**, **1.40 m**, **1.42 m**, **143 cm**, **146 cm**

Activity:
E.g. chocolate bar 30 g, can of tuna 200 g, can of beans 250 g, bag of pasta 400 g, bag of rice 500 g.

Page 21 — Decimals, Sheet 2

Q1 **24**

Q2 **21p**, **£1.02**, **120p**, **£1.21**, **£1.22**

Q3 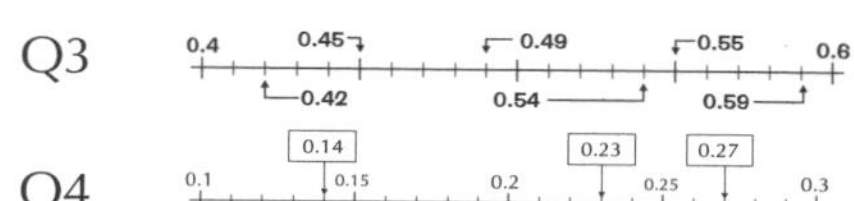

Q4 0.1, **0.14**, 0.15, 0.2, **0.23**, 0.25, **0.27**, 0.3

Activity:
E.g. crisps 35p, pepper 69p, soup 99p, bread £1.08, jam £1.19, apples £1.36, potatoes £1.55, cake £1.99, box of chocolates £3.99, chicken £5.99.

Page 22 — Decimals, Sheet 3

Q1 a) **2.23 m**, **2.19 m**, **2.16 m**, **2.05 m**, **1.96 m**, **1.85 m**.
b) **Rob**

Q2 a) 6.82 = **6 + 0.8 + 0.02**
b) 9.16 = **9 + 0.1 + 0.06**

Q3 a) **3 hundreds**
b) **2 thousands**
c) **4 units**
d) **8 tenths**
e) **5 hundredths**
f) **3 tens**

Activity:
Partition the price of 3 items on a shopping list. E.g. £3.49 = 3.0 + 0.4 + 0.09.

Page 23 — Fractions, Sheet 2

Q1 a) $\frac{1}{2}$ or $\frac{2}{4}$ b) $\frac{3}{4}$ c) $\frac{3}{5}$

Q2 $\frac{1}{4}$

Q3

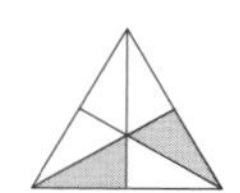

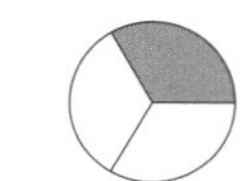

Q4

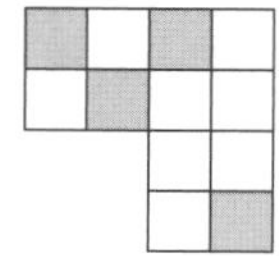

Answers

Activity:
Draw a rectangle and divide it into 10 equal parts. Shade 3 parts of each rectangle.

E.g. 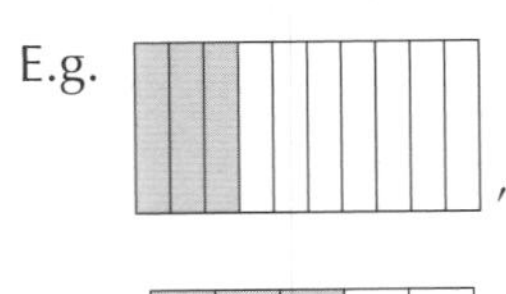

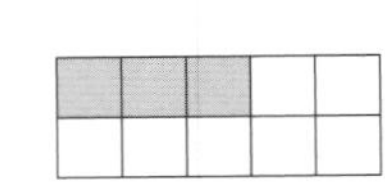

Page 24 — Fractions, Sheet 3

Q1 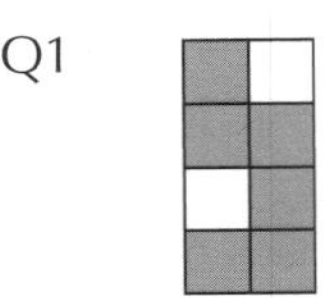

Q2 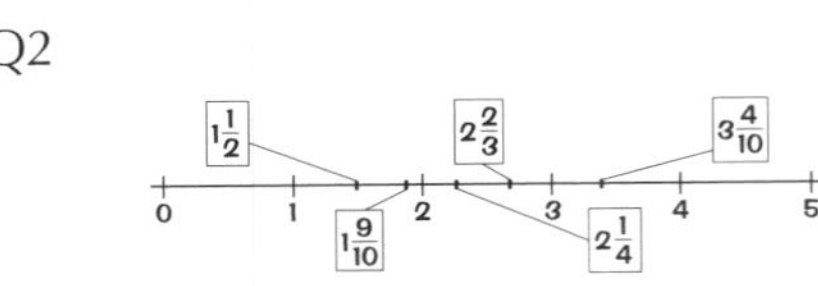

Q3 $1\frac{3}{4}$ $2\frac{1}{4}$ $2\frac{3}{10}$ $2\frac{4}{10}$ $3\frac{1}{2}$

Q4 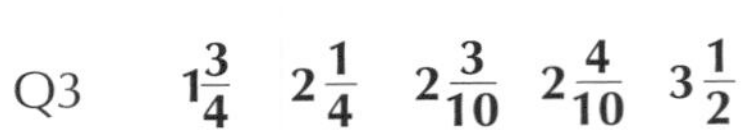

Activity:
E.g.

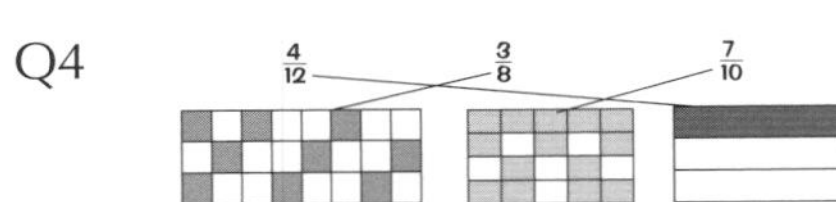

$\frac{3}{4}$ $\frac{1}{4}$ $\frac{1}{3}$ $\frac{1}{2}$

Page 25 — Fractions, Sheet 4

Q1 a) $\mathbf{\frac{5}{8}}$ b) $\mathbf{\frac{3}{8}}$

Q2 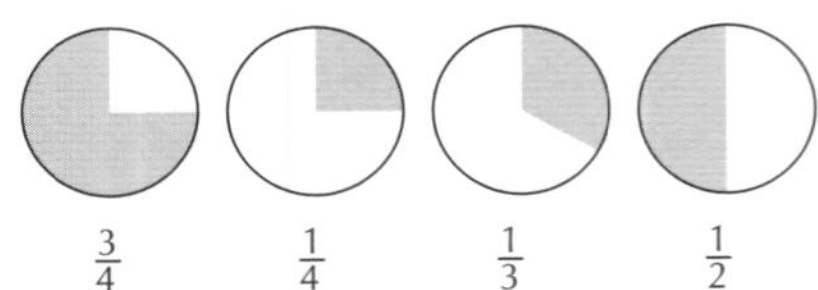

Q3 $\mathbf{\frac{2}{3}}$ $\mathbf{\frac{10}{15}}$

Q4 a) **6**
b) **25**
c) **20**
d) **10**

Activity:
Find equivalent fractions by multiplying the numerator and denominator by the same number.

Page 26 — Fractions and Decimals, Sheet 1

Q1 a) **0.5** b) **0.1** c) **0.04**

Q2 a) **0.7** b) **0.75**
c) $\mathbf{\frac{5}{100}}$ or $\mathbf{\frac{1}{20}}$ d) **0.25**

Q3 a) E.g. $\mathbf{\frac{6}{10}}$
b) E.g. $\mathbf{\frac{35}{100}}$
c) E.g. $\mathbf{\frac{8}{100}}$

Q4 E.g. $\mathbf{\frac{4}{10}}$, $\mathbf{\frac{8}{20}}$, $\mathbf{\frac{12}{30}}$

Activity:
$\mathbf{\frac{3}{10} = 0.3}$, $\mathbf{\frac{1}{2} = 0.5}$, $\mathbf{\frac{1}{4} = 0.25}$,
$\mathbf{\frac{3}{4} = 0.75}$, $\mathbf{\frac{6}{10} = 0.6}$, $\mathbf{\frac{1}{100} = 0.01}$,
$\mathbf{\frac{8}{100} = 0.08}$, $\mathbf{\frac{1}{10} = 0.1}$.

Page 27 — Fractions and Decimals, Sheet 2

Q1 a) $\mathbf{\frac{4}{100}}$ or $\mathbf{\frac{1}{25}}$
b) $\mathbf{\frac{75}{100}}$ or $\mathbf{\frac{3}{4}}$
c) $\mathbf{\frac{6}{10}}$ or $\mathbf{\frac{3}{5}}$
d) $\mathbf{\frac{25}{100}}$ or $\mathbf{\frac{1}{4}}$

Q2 $\mathbf{\frac{2}{10}}$ = 0.2, $\mathbf{\frac{3}{4}}$ = 0.75,
$\mathbf{\frac{10}{100}}$ = 0.1, $\mathbf{\frac{5}{100}}$ = 0.05

Q3 a) $\mathbf{\frac{1}{4}}$ b) $\mathbf{\frac{2}{100}}$

Q4 a) **0.6** b) **0.04**
c) **0.75** d) **0.12**

Activity:
The 3rd decimal place is the thousandths place.
0.009 = $\mathbf{\frac{9}{1000}}$, 0.023 = $\mathbf{\frac{23}{1000}}$.

Page 28 — Fractions and Decimals, Sheet 3

Q1

$\frac{1}{2}$	$\mathbf{\frac{95}{100}}$	$\frac{6}{10}$
$\mathbf{\frac{7}{10}}$	$\frac{2}{10}$	$\mathbf{\frac{1}{4}}$
$\frac{5}{20}$	$\mathbf{\frac{35}{100}}$	$\frac{15}{100}$
$\mathbf{\frac{8}{10}}$	$\frac{3}{4}$	$\mathbf{\frac{4}{10}}$

0.5	0.95	**0.6**
0.7	**0.2**	0.25
0.25	0.35	**0.15**
0.8	**0.75**	0.4

Q2 a) Any **12 squares** shaded, e.g.

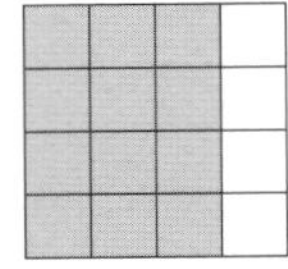

b) Any **12 squares** shaded, e.g.

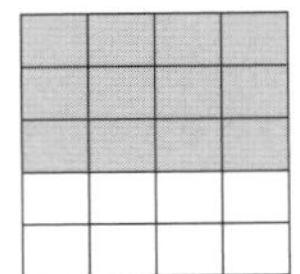

c) Any **4 squares** shaded, e.g.

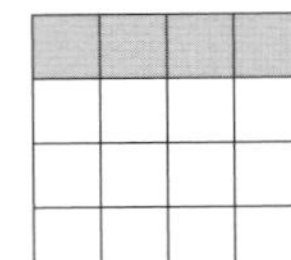

Q3 a) **0.5** b) **0.25**

Activity:
a) **0.23** b) **0.30769...**
c) **0.7888...** d) **0.308181...**

Page 29 — Numbers and Number Lines, Sheet 2

Q1 a) **Nine hundred and sixty**
b) **Seven hundred and thirty seven**

Q2 a) **845** b) **297**

Q3 **9632**

Q4 a) **1011, 901, 316, 251, 198, 18**
b) **125, 217, 220, 601, 611, 1040**

Q5

740 830 890 990

700 750 800 850 900 950 1000

Activity:
For example, the numbers might be:
210, 158, 309, 76, 112
In order (smallest first):
76, 112, 158, 210, 309

Answers

Page 30 — Numbers and Number Lines, Sheet 3

Q1 **–4**, **–2**, **0**, **2**, **6**, **10**

Q2 Left to right:
–1, **3**, **11**

Q3 a) –3 **<** 2 b) –1 **>** –4
c) 0 **<** 10 d) 0 **>** –10

Q4 Left to right:
–8, **2**, **18**
a) **–10** < –5 b) 0 > **–1**

Activity:

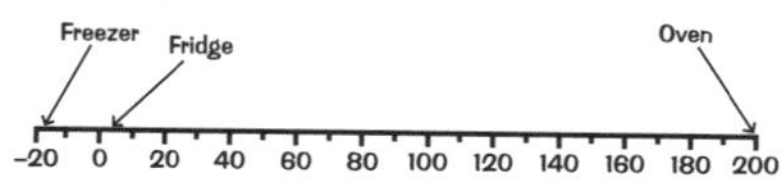

Page 31 — Numbers and Number Lines, Sheet 4

Q1 **5.2**, **5.4**, **5.6**, **6.1**, **6.3**

Q2 a) **8.1**, **8.7**, **9.0**
b) **27.8**, **26.6**
c) **–11**, **–16**
d) **–0.3**, **–0.8**

Q3 Left to right, above and belowline:
–1.6, **–0.8**, **–0.3**, **0.6**, **1.8**

Activity:
For example, a number sequence might be:

-0.8, -0.2, 0.4, 1.0, 1.6

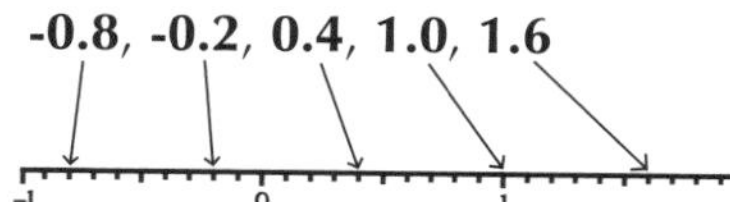

Page 32 — Partitioning, Sheet 2

Q1 a) **200**
b) **35**
c) **3**
d) Several answers possible, for example: **50** + **50** + **50** + **50**+ **20** + **10** + **5** or **200** + **10** + **10** + **10** + **5**.

Q2 In order, left to right:
100, **20**, **8**.
The number shown is **128**.

Q3 a) **50**
b) **400**
c) **9**
d) Several answers possible, for example: **4** + **4** or **3** + **5**.

Activity:
For example, using the number 415 some answers might be:
400 + **10** + **5** or
200 + **150** + **59** + **6** or
100 + **100** + **190** + **16** + **9**.

Page 33 — Partitioning, Sheet 3

Q1 a) **5426** b) **6339**
c) **9871**

Q2 a) **50** b) **20**
c) **2000** d) **7**

Q3 The biggest number is:
6521.
The smallest number is:
1256.

Q4 a), b) and c) Several answers possible, for example:
7000 + **400** + **80** + **2** or
7400 + **82** or
5500 + **1800** + **140** + **39** + **3**.

Activity:
For example, the year might be 1983.
A bigger number might be: **9831**.
A smaller number might be: **1389**.

Page 34 — Partitioning, Sheet 4

Q1 a) **300** b) **20**
c) **200** d) **3**

Q2 10p pieces = 40 × 10 = 400p
£1 coins = 15 × 100 = 1500p
5p pieces = 3 × 5 = 15p
Total in pence =
400 + 1500 + 15 = **1915p**

Q3 a) 19 m = 19 × 100 = 1900 cm
26 + 1900 = **1926** cm
b) 100 in 1900 = 19
100 in 26 = 0
19 + 0 = **19**
c) 10s in 1000 = 100
10s in 900 = 90
10s in 20 = 2
10s in 6 = 0
100 + 90 + 2 = **192**

Activity:
For example, the number might be 4789. Many answers are possible, 3, 4 and 5 number partitions might be:
4000 + **700** + **89** or
4000 + **700** + **80** + **9** or
3000 + **1500** + **200** + **80** + **9**

Page 35 — Proportion and Ratio, Sheet 1

Q1 a) 1 in every 3 shapes is a **triangle.**
There is 1 triangle for every **2** squares.
b) Possible pattern:

□ △ △ △ □ △ △ △

Your pattern should have 2 squares and 6 triangles.

Q2 a) 34 km × 2 = **68 km**
b) 12 × 4 = **48 pens**
c) 18 ÷ 3 = **6 cakes**
d) **120** is the best estimate.

Activity:
Possible pattern could be:

Possible sentences include:
"1 shape in every 5 is a circle.", "There are 4 squares for every circle."

Page 36 — Proportion and Ratio, Sheet 2

Q1 a) $\frac{1}{3}$ or $\frac{3}{9}$
b) 15 windows should be shaded.

Q2 a) 56p × 3 = **£1.68**
b) **Martha will fill about $\frac{1}{4}$ of the bucket with her shells.**

Q3 a) 6 ÷ 2 = 3
3 × 3 = **9 yachts**
b) 10 ÷ 2 = 5
5 × 3 = **15 yachts**

Answers

Activity:
E.g. 3 people liked banana milkshake to 2 people who didn't. Using this ratio, in a group of 20, 12 people would like banana milkshake and 8 wouldn't (multiply number of people by 4). Or, in a group of 100, 60 would like banana milkshake and 40 wouldn't (multiply number of people by 20).

Page 37 — Proportion and Ratio, Sheet 3

Q1 a) There should be 6 blue stripes and 9 yellow stripes in the scarf.
b) 2 in every 5 stripes are coloured **blue**.
3 in every 5 stripes are coloured yellow.

Q2 a)

Away	Home	Total
3	5	**8**
6	10	**16**
9	**15**	**24**
12	**20**	**32**
15	**25**	40

b) **There are 30 away fans.** Using the table to help, double 40 total fans is 80, and double 15 away fans is 30.

Q3 a) 150 g × 2 = **300 g**
b) 600 ml × 2 = **1200 ml**

Activity:

Hotdogs	Onions
4	**1**
8	**2**
12	**3**
16	**4**
20	**5**

Page 38 — Rounding, Sheet 2

Q1 a) **30** b) **80** c) **30**
d) **120** e) **760** f) **910**

Q2 579 → 600
780 → 800
445 → 400
950 → 1000

Q3 **70**

Q4 a) **80** b) **40**

Activity:
E.g. 420 g rounds to 400 g to the nearest 100. It remains 420 g when rounded to the nearest 10.

Page 39 — Rounding, Sheet 3

Q1 a) **2000** b) **4000**
c) **6000** d) **6000**

Q2 a) **5700** b) **2700**
c) **5800** d) **6800**

Q3 5327 → 5330
5372 → 5370
5355 → 5360
5318 → 5320

Q4

Height	Nearest 1000 m	Nearest 100 m
8611 m	**9000 m**	**8600 m**
8091 m	**8000 m**	**8100 m**
1085 m	**1000 m**	**1100 m**
4810 m	**5000 m**	**4800 m**

Activity:
Any numbers between 2500 and 3499 inclusive will round to 3000 to the nearest 1000.
Any numbers between 2995 and 3004 inclusive will round to 3000 to the nearest 10.

Page 40 — Rounding, Sheet 4

Q1 a) **300** b) **8500**
c) **3900**

Q2

Number	to 1 decimal place	to the nearest whole number
14.71	**14.7**	**15**
7.29	**7.3**	**7**
21.98	**22.0**	**22**

Q3

surfboard	to the nearest pound	to the nearest 10p
£23.99	**£24**	**£24.00**
£31.50	**£32**	**£31.50**
£50.25	**£50**	**£50.30**

Activity:
E.g.
Protein: 8.8 g ⇒ **9.0 g**
Carbohydrate: 12.1 g ⇒ **12.0 g**
Fat: 1.2 g ⇒ **1.0 g**
Fibre: 3.8 g ⇒ **4.0 g**

Page 41 — Adding and Subtracting, Sheet 3

Q1 a) **53** b) **19**
c) **83** d) **67**
e) **89** f) **27**

Q2 a) **20 cm**
b) **32 cm**
c) **48 cm**

Q3 a) **70 and 80**
b) **90 and 50**, **80 and 40**, **50 and 10**, or **70 and 30**
c) **90 and 20**, **80 and 30** or **70 and 40**

Activity:
E.g. a 3 and a 4 thrown could be read as 34 or 43.
34 + 66 = 100
43 + 57 = 100

Page 42 — Adding and Subtracting, Sheet 4

Q1 a) **4000**
b) **2800**
c) **790**

Q2 a) **£5.50**
b) **£9.10**
c) **£1.60**

Q3 a) **330**
b) **5090**
c) **930**
d) **210**

Q4 **250 — 170**
640 — 560
950 — 1030
1020 — 940

Answers

Activity:
Any map can be drawn with roads of different lengths marking different landmarks or buildings.
Route lengths can then be calculated, as shown in the example on the sheet.

Page 43 — Adding and Subtracting, Sheet 5

Q1 a) **3.9** b) **8.7**
c) **0.2** d) **0.7**

Q2 a) **6.4 cm** b) **4.2 cm**
c) **1.7 cm**

Q3 From left to right:
10.2, 4.6, 6.1, 1.7, 2.2

Q4 **12.7 and 14.3**

Q5 **6.3 and 9.9**

Activity:
E.g. 3 = 0.1 + 2.9
0.2 + 2.8
0.3 + 2.7
0.4 + 2.6 and so on...

Page 44 — Checking Calculations, Sheet 2

Q1 a) **12**
b) **6, 4** or **4, 6**
c) **53 – 31 = 22**
or **53 – 22 = 31**

Q2 a) **8, 4** b) **30, 6**
c) **80, 8**

Q3 **30**

Q4 **8**

Activity:
E.g. 15 × 3 = 45, 45 ÷ 3 = 15

Page 45 — Checking Calculations, Sheet 3

Q1 9 × **9** = **81**

Q2 a) **£3**
b) **£7**
c) **£5**

Q3 **80**

Q4 **200**

Q5 a) The same number must be used in each box. Any number can be used.
A subtraction sign should go in the circle.
E.g. 9 + **2** – **2** = 9
b) The same number must be used in each box. Any number can be used.
A division sign should go in the circle.
E.g. 7 × **2** ÷ **2** = 7

Activity:
To get from 30 to 5 using the inverses, you must do –5, ×2, ÷10.
To get from 2 to 15 you could do ×10, +3, –8.
The inverses to get from 15 back to 2 would be +8, –3, ÷10.

Page 46 — Checking Calculations, Sheet 4

Q1 **5, 10, 10, 5**

Q2 Paul: **£5.94**
Amy: **£13.88**

Q3 a) **200 ÷ 50 = 4**
Jim's statement seems about right.
b) **52 × 4 = 208**
Jim is wrong. There aren't enough seats.

Activity:

E.g.	£1.39	⇒ £1	
	£2.99	⇒ £3	
	£0.95	⇒ £1	
	£4.29	⇒ £4	
Total:	£9.62	Estimate:	£9

Page 47 — Checking Calculations, Sheet 5

Q1 For a) and b) two of any of the following answers:
14 + 13 = 27
27 – 14 = 13
27 – 13 = 14

Q2 a) **2** b) **9**
c) **42** d) **15**

Q3 **583 – 318**

Q4 a) 8 **×** 4 = 32
b) 32 = 4 **×** 8
c) 32 **÷** 8 = 4

Q5 **1700 – 900 = 800**

Activity:
For example, the distances might be:
15.7 miles, 6.3 miles, 10.2 miles, 0.6 miles and 2.9 miles.
An estimated total might be:
36 miles

Page 48 — Doubling and Halving, Sheet 2

Q1 a) 14 doubled is 28, then halved is 14.
Other answers for b), c) and d) might include:
7 doubled is 14, then halved is 7.
18 doubled is 36, then halved is 18.
23 doubled is 46, then halved is 23.

Q2 a) **17** b) **2**

Q3 Day 1: 1, day 2: **2**, day 3: **4**, day 4: **8**, day 5: **16**, day 6: **32**.
In reverse:
Day 6: **32**, day 5: **16**, day 4: **8**, day 3: **4**, day 2: **2**, day 1: 1.

Activity:
For example, a shoe size might be: 11
Doubled it would be 22, halving it to check should result in 11.

Page 49 — Doubling and Halving, Sheet 3

Q1 a) **52** b) **220**
c) **31** d) **180**

Q2 a) Either:
190 + 190 = 380p or
190 × 2 = 380p
b) Either:
150 + 150 = 300p or
150 × 2 = 300p
c) **18 ÷ 2 = 9p**
9 × 10 = 90p
d) **26 ÷ 2 = 13p**
13 × 10 = 130p

Answers

Q3 a) 240 + 240 = **480** or
240 × 2 = **480**
b) 240 ÷ 2 = **120**

Activity:
For example, there might be 554 students in a school.
Doubling that would make **1108**.
Halving it would make **277**.

Page 50 — Doubling and Halving, Sheet 4

Q1 a) **7.6** b) **7.2**
c) **8.4** d) **8.2**
e) **0.6** f) **7.8**

Q2 a) **37** b) **3.7**

Q3 a) **48** b) **4.8**

Q4 a) **3.4** b) **4.1**
c) **0.1** d) **7.2**

Q5 a) **7.6** b) **9.6**
c) **19.4** d) **1.0**

Activity:
For example, the spare change might come to £13.72
Double this would be **£27.44**
Half of this would be **£6.86**

Page 51 — Fraction Pairs, Sheet 1

Q1 $\mathbf{\frac{2}{3}+\frac{1}{3}}$ $\mathbf{\frac{3}{4}+\frac{1}{4}}$ $\mathbf{\frac{8}{10}+\frac{2}{10}}$

Q2 a) $\mathbf{\frac{1}{2}+\frac{1}{2}}$ b) $\mathbf{\frac{2}{3}+\frac{1}{3}}$
c) $\mathbf{\frac{2}{5}+\frac{3}{5}}$

Q3 a) $\frac{4}{6}+\mathbf{\frac{2}{6}}=1$ b) $\frac{3}{8}+\frac{5}{8}=\mathbf{1}$
c) $\mathbf{\frac{8}{12}}+\frac{4}{12}=\mathbf{1}$

Activity:
Many possible answers, for example:
There are 10 pens.
4 pens are blue, 3 are red and 3 are green.

$\mathbf{\frac{4}{10}}$ are blue, $\mathbf{\frac{6}{10}}$ are not blue.

$\mathbf{\frac{4}{10}}+\mathbf{\frac{6}{10}}=\mathbf{1}$

Page 52 — Fraction Pairs, Sheet 2

Q1 a) $\frac{3}{4}+\frac{1}{4}=\mathbf{1}$

b) $1\frac{1}{2}+2\frac{1}{2}=\mathbf{4}$

c) $2\frac{2}{3}+\frac{1}{3}=\mathbf{3}$

Q2 a) $\frac{2}{8}+\mathbf{\frac{6}{8}}=1$

b) $\frac{1}{3}+\frac{2}{\mathbf{3}}=1$

c) $1\frac{3}{4}+1\frac{1}{\mathbf{4}}=3$

d) $3\frac{7}{10}+\mathbf{\frac{3}{10}}=4$

Q3 $\mathbf{\frac{5}{20}}$ or $\mathbf{\frac{1}{4}}$
of the marbles fell out.

$\mathbf{\frac{15}{20}}$ or $\mathbf{\frac{3}{4}}$ were left in the bag.

$\mathbf{\frac{5}{20}}+\mathbf{\frac{15}{20}}$ (or $\mathbf{\frac{1}{4}}+\mathbf{\frac{3}{4}}$) $=\mathbf{1}$

Activity:
Many possible answers, for example:
3 big books, 5 smallbooks.

$\frac{3}{8}$ are big books.

$\frac{5}{8}$ are small books.

$\mathbf{\frac{3}{8}}+\mathbf{\frac{5}{8}}=\mathbf{1}$

Page 53 — Fraction Pairs, Sheet 3

Q1 $\mathbf{\frac{1}{3}}$

Q2 $\mathbf{\frac{1}{4}}$

Q3 **Quarters - for 4 people**

Q4 $\mathbf{\frac{7}{12}}$

Q5 a) $\mathbf{\frac{1}{2}}$ b) $\mathbf{\frac{1}{4}}$ c) $\mathbf{\frac{1}{8}}$ d) $\mathbf{\frac{1}{16}}$

Activity:
Many possible answers, for example:
Darren Hayman:
4 vowels, 8 consonants.

$\mathbf{\frac{4}{12}}=\mathbf{\frac{1}{3}}$ are vowels.

$\mathbf{\frac{8}{12}}=\mathbf{\frac{2}{3}}$ are consonants.

$\mathbf{\frac{1}{3}}+\mathbf{\frac{2}{3}}=\mathbf{1}$

Page 54 — Multiplication and Division, Sheet 4

Q1 Circle **236**, **900**, **404**, **788**, **634**

Underline **900**, **865**

Q2 a) **6** b) **20**
c) **6**

Q3 a) 30 ÷ 5 = **6**
b) 20 **÷ 4** = **5**
c) **9** × 3 = **27**
d) **8 × 3** = 24, 24 + **2** = **26**

Activity:
For each of the 10 multiplications, there should be 2 divisions.
E.g. 6 × 1 = 6 gives...
6 ÷ 6 = 1 and 6 ÷ 1 = 6,
6 × 2 = 12 gives...
12 ÷ 6 = 2 and 12 ÷ 2 = 6. Etc.

Page 55 — Multiplication and Division, Sheet 5

Q1

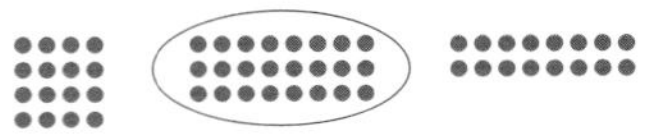

Q2 a)

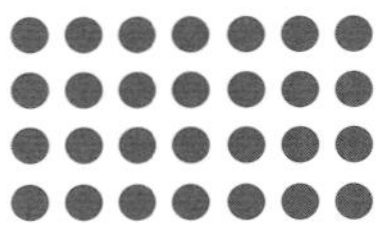

b)

Q3 a) 5 × 8 = **40**, 10 × 4 = **40**,
5 × 4 = **20**
b) 40 ÷ 8 = **5**, 40 ÷ 10 = **4**,
40 ÷ **8** = 5

Q4 a) **56** b) **49**
c) **32**

Answers

Activity:
False. 18 ends in 8 but isn't a multiple of 4.

Page 56 — Multiplication and Division, Sheet 6

Q1 **32, 40, 64, 72, 80**

Q2 a) **24**
b) **24**
c) **6**

Q3 E.g. 7: **14, 21, 35, 70**
8: **16, 32, 40, 64**
9: **18, 27, 63, 81**

Q4 **3 and 9**

Q5 8 × 9 = 72
72 + 4 = **76**

Activity:
Boris: 40 ÷ 8 = 5
Doris: 40 ÷ 4 = 10
Noris: 40 ÷ 2 = 20

E.g. 16 steps could be climbed in 8 steps of 2, or 4 steps of 4.

Page 57 — Multiplication and Division, Sheet 7

Q1 a) **7** b) **54** c) **8**
d) **9** e) **8** f) **8**

Q2 a) 21 – 1 = 20
20 ÷ 5 = **4**
b) 4 × 6 = 24
24 + 3 = **27**
c) 6 × 6 = 36
36 ÷ 4 = **9**

Q3 a) **24** b) **2**

Activity:
1, 2, 3, 5, 7, 11, 13, 17, 19

Page 58 — Multiplication and Division, Sheet 8

Q1 a) 24 ÷ 6 = **4**
4 × 6 = 24
b) 63 ÷ 7 = **9**
9 × 7 = 63
c) 32 ÷ 8 = **4**
4 × **8** = 32 or **8** × **4** = 32

Q2 a) **80** b) **800**
c) **180** d) **1800**

Q3 a) **30** b) **70**
c) **5** d) **4**

Q4 Multiples of 20 = **60, 120, 160, 200, 240**
Multiples of 30 = **60, 120, 150, 240**
Multiples of 40 = **120, 160, 200, 240**
Multiples of 50 = **150, 200**

Activity:
E.g. 6 × 6 = 36, 5 × 7 = 35, 70 ÷ 2 = 35, 96 ÷ 3 = 32.

Page 59 — Calculators, Sheet 1

Q1 a) **3564** b) **24**
c) **748** d) **185**

Q2 a) £3.32 × 5 = **£16.60**
b) £16.60 – (5 × 9p) = **£16.15**
or (£3.32 – 9p) × 5 = £16.15

Q3 75p + £1.12 + 9p + £1.00 + 3p + 76p + £3.45 = £7.20
£20 – £7.20 = **£12.80**

Q4 a) **–156** b) **–105**
c) **–79** d) **–624**

Q5 a) £3.72 ÷ 12 = **31p**
b) 31p × 25 = **£7.75**

Activity:
Many possible answers. For example: 11 × 3 + 12 + 5 = 50

Page 60 — Calculators, Sheet 2

Q1 a) **46,292** b) **143**
c) **25,346** d) **920**
e) **697** f) **–4145**

Q2 £14 ÷ 5 = **£2.80**

Q3 a) **£1.22** b) **£1.22**
c) **79p** d) **£84.08**
e) **£1.99** f) **£157.20**

Q4 a) **–142** b) **–9**
c) **79** d) **15**

Q5 £10.92 ÷ 13 = 84
84 ÷ 7 = **12 weeks**

Activity:
Many possible answers depending on your chosen adverts.

Page 61 — Calculators, Sheet 3

Q1 a) **1.69** b) **31.25**
c) **6.25** d) **5.45**

Q2 a) **68** b) **204**
c) **79** d) **237**
e) **22** f) **110**
g) **21** h) **147**

Q3 a) **9 metres and 90 cm (or 990 cm)**
b) **10 cm**

Q4 a) **187.2 cm or 1.872 m**
b) **1.3 m**
c) **11.722 km**
d) **28.61 m**
e) **10.868 m**
f) **1.212 m or 121.2 cm**

Activity:
Many possible answers depending on the length of your stride. For example if your stride is 60 cm, you would walk 1.2 km in 2000 steps and 1.8 km in 3000 steps.

Page 62 — Mental Maths, Sheet 3

Q1 a) **10** b) **66**
c) **83** d) **5**

Q2 a) 53 + 27 =
50 + 20 + 3 + 7 =
80
b) 38 + 25 =
30 + 20 + 8 + 5 =
63
c) 27 – 12 =
27 – 10 – 2 =
15

Q3 a) **4 °C**
b) **Tuesday**
c) **Friday**

Activity:
30 + 40 = 70
10 + 1 = 11
70 – 11 = 59
Or, 30 + 40 – 10 – 1 = 59
And 40 + 10 + 1 – 30 = 21

Answers

Page 63 — Mental Maths, Sheet 4

Q1 a) **12** b) **64**
c) **28** d) **35**
e) **12** f) **39**

Q2 **41 and 29**, **25 and 37**

Q3 a) 19 + 35 =
20 + 35 – 1 = **54**
b) 31 + 17 =
30 + 17 + 1 = **48**
c) 78 + 20 =
80 + 20 – 2 = **98**

Q4 a) **7p** b) **57**

Activity:
E.g. some of the phone numbers might be:

555 729
555 646
555 984
555 812

Adding the last two digits the closest to 100 they could get without going over would be:
84 + 12 = **96**

Page 64 — Mental Maths, Sheet 5

Q1 b) 20 × 3 = **60**
(double 10 × 3)
c) 50 × 5 = **250**
(5 × 5 × 10)

Q2 a) 5030 – 2997 =
5030 – 3000 + 3 =
2033
b) 2003 – 900 =
2000 – 900 + 3 =
1103

Q3 a) 15 × 5 = **75p**
b) 68 ÷ 4 = **17p**
c) 24 × 4 = **96p**

Q4 a) 11 × 25 =
10 × 25 + 25 =
275
b) 2834 + 2999 =
2834 + 3000 – 1 =
5833

c) 14 × 4 =
10 × 4 + 4 × 4 = **56**
(A different method can be used as long as they arrive at the same answer.)

Activity:
53, 54, 55

Page 65 — Multiply by 10, 100 and 1000, Sheet 2

Q1 **× 10**
3 × 10 = 30
7 × 10 = **70**
39 × 10 = **390**
59 × 10 = 590

× 100
17 × 100 = **1700**
46 × 100 = 4600
2 × 100 = **200**
11 × 100 = 1100

Q2 10 × 21 = **210**

Q3 16 × 10p = £1.60
10 × 20p = £2.00
£2.00 + £1.60 = **£3.60**

Q4 **The 7 changes from being worth 7 tens to being worth 7 thousands.**

Activity:
For example, to make 800:
1 × 100 = 100
3 × 100 = 300
4 × 100 = 400
100 + 300 + 400 = 800
For example, to make 1000:
2 × 100 = 200
3 × 100 = 300
5 × 100 = 500
200 + 300 + 500 = 1000

Page 66 — Multiply by 10, 100 and 1000, Sheet 3

Q1 **84**

Q2 a) **100** b) **1570**
c) **23** d) **100**

Q3 a) **4500** b) **562**
c) **270** d) **86**

Q4 680 ÷ 10 = **68**

Activity:
Examples for 6 × 7 = 42:
6 × 70 = 420,
6 × 700 = 4200,
600 × 7 = 4200,
60 × 70 = 4200.
Examples for 3 × 8 = 24:
30 × 8 = 240
3 × 80 = 240
3 × 800 = 2400
300 × 8 = 2400
30 × 80 = 2400.

Page 67 — Multiply by 10, 100 and 1000, Sheet 4

Q1 a) **10** b) **10**
c) **100**

Q2 a) **250** b) **1000**
c) **4.2** d) **564**
e) **7360** f) **10**
g) **16**

Q3 2.5 cm × 100 = **250 cm** or **2.5 m**

Q4 61 × 10 = 610
610 × 100 = **61 000**

Activity:
For example, one cake needs 200 g butter, 150 g sugar and 100 g flour. 100 cakes would need 20 000 g or 20 kg butter, 15 000 g or 15 kg sugar and 10 000 g or 10 kg flour. To make a tenth of one cake, you would need 20 g butter, 15 g sugar and 10 g flour.

Page 68 — Using Fractions, Sheet 3

Q1 This is the completed table:

Runner	Fraction of 20 km race completed	Distance run
Ahmed	$\frac{1}{2}$	10 km
Alison	$\frac{1}{4}$	**5 km**
Jenny	$\frac{1}{5}$	**4 km**
Roland	$\frac{1}{10}$	**2 km**

Alison: 20 km ÷ 4 = **5 km**
Jenny: 20 km ÷ 5 = **4 km**
Roland: 20 km ÷ 10 = **2 km**

Answers

Q2 b) $\frac{1}{3}$ of **9** = 3

c) $\frac{1}{4}$ of **12** = 3

Q3 a) 15 litres ÷ 5 = **3 litres**.
b) 25 litres ÷ 5 = **5 litres**.
c) **35 litres** ÷ 5 = 7 litres.
d) 20 litres ÷ 5 = **4 litres**.

Activity:
There are **7** ways to complete the number sentence:

$\frac{1}{2}$ of **2** = **1**, $\frac{1}{2}$ of **4** = **2**, $\frac{1}{2}$ of **6** = **3**,
$\frac{1}{2}$ of **8** = **4**, $\frac{1}{2}$ of **10** = **5**,
$\frac{1}{2}$ of **12** = **6**, $\frac{1}{2}$ of **14** = **7**,

Page 69 — Using Fractions, Sheet 4

Q1 There are 30 ÷ 5 = **6 boys**.
So number of girls is
6 × 4 = **24 girls**.
(or 30 – 6 = 24)

Q2 a) 24 g ÷ 8 = 3 g
3 g × 3 = **9 g**
b) 21 cm ÷ 7 = 3 cm
3 cm × 2 = **6 cm**

Q3 Joanne: 32 ÷ 8 = 4
4 × 5 = **20 points**
Lee: 32 ÷ 8 = **4 points**.

Q4 Sweets: 50p ÷ 10 = **5p**
Pencil: 50p ÷ 5 = **10p**
Stickers: 50p ÷ 10 = 5p
5p × 3 = **15p**
Comic: 50p ÷ 5 = 10p
10p × 2 = **20p**

Activity:
Many possible answers. Make sure that the fraction sentences are sensible.

Page 70 — Using Fractions, Sheet 5

Q1 a) 120 ÷ 3 = 40
40 × 2 = **80**.
b) 120 ÷ 10 = 12
12 × 7 = **84**.

Q2 Using the hint,
5% is half of 10%.

10% of 60 = 60 ÷ 10 = 6
6 ÷ 2 = **3**
(the answer should be written in the triangle).

10% of 140 = 140 ÷ 10 = 14
14 ÷ 2 = **7**
(the answer should be written in the oval).

10% of 120 = 120 ÷ 10 = 12
12 ÷ 2 = **6**
(the answer should be written in the star).

Q3 First row:
20 m ÷ 5 = 4 m
4 m × 3 = **12 m**
40 kg ÷ 5 = 8 kg
8 kg × 3 = **24 kg**
80 mins ÷ 5 = 16 mins
16 m × 3 = **48 mins**

Second row:
25% is the same as $\frac{1}{4}$.
40 kg ÷ 4 = **10 kg**
80 mins ÷ 4 = **20 mins**
£1.20 = 120p.
120p ÷ 4 = **30p**

Activity:
One fifth of 35 = **7**
One fifth of 100 = **20**
One fifth of 75 = **15**
One fifth of 150 = **30**
One fifth of 60 = **12**

Any number in the **5 times table** that is **smaller than 75** will give whole number answers less than 15. Not including the numbers given above, these are:
5, **10**, **15**, **20**, **25**, **30**, **40**, **45**, **50**, **55**, **65** and **70**.
Choose any three of these numbers.

Page 71 — Written Adding and Subtracting, Sheet 2

Q1 a) **36** b) **78** c) **227**

Q2 Using number line and counting to hundreds:
difference = 47 + 200 + 9
= **256**

Q3 a) **63** b) **201** c) **46**

Q4 110 – 58 = **52**

Activity:
62 – 15 = **47**
Any five sets of two numbers with a difference of 47 e.g. **73 and 26**.

Page 72 — Written Adding and Subtracting, Sheet 3

Q1 a) **675** b) **839** c) **591**

Q2 845 – 386 = **459**

Q3 £2.25 + £0.12 + £1.95
= **£4.32**

Q4 a) 24**6** + 1**5**4 = 400
b) **9**42 – 23**7** = 705
c) 134 + 39**4** = 528
d) 7**8**7 – 1**2**6 = 661

Activity:
Largest difference
= 634 – 342 = **292**
Smallest total = 342 + 478 = **820**

Page 73 — Written Adding and Subtracting, Sheet 4

Q1 a) **394** b) **4.19** c) **372**
d) **143.9**

Q2 a) 1.07 + 2.85 = **3.92** b) 27.8 – 2.5 = **25.3**
c) 83.6 + 2.19 = **85.79**

Q3 £27.16 + £27.16 = **£54.32**

Q4 84 + 198 = 282
300 – 282 = **18 nails**

Activity:
E.g. **20** + **90** = 110
60 + **80** = 140
50 + **50** = 100

Answers

Page 74 — Written Multiplying and Dividing, Sheet 3

Q1 20 ÷ 3 = 6 r 2
28 ÷ 3 = 9 r 1
34 ÷ 4 = 8 r 2
44 ÷ 5 = 8 r 4
You should have circled 20 ÷ 3 and 34 ÷ 4.

Q2 a) 240 + 18 = **258**
b) 60 × 4 = **240**
2 × 4 = **8**
240 + 8 = **248**
c) 20 × 3 = **60**
8 × 3 = **24**
60 + 24 = **84**

Q3 78 ÷ 5 = 15 r 2.
He will need 16 5p coins to buy the toy.

Q4 110 ÷ 4 = 27 r 2.
She plants 27 seeds in each pot (but has 2 left over).

Activity:
The highest answer is **42 × 5 = 210.**
The lowest answer is **45 × 2 = 90.**

Page 75 — Written Multiplying and Dividing, Sheet 4

Q1 a) 20 × 4 = **80**
6 × 4 = **24**
80 + 24 = **104**
b) 70 × 5 = **350**
4 × 5 = **20**
350 + 20 = **370**
c) 50 × 3 = **150**
7 × 3 = **21**
150 + 21 = **171**

Q2 a) 50 ÷ 5 = **10**
29 ÷ 5 = **5 r 4**
10 + 5 r 4 = **15 r 4**
b) 60 ÷ 6 = **10**
21 ÷ 6 = **3 r 3**
10 + 3 r 3 = **13 r 3**

Q3 a) 96 = 60 + 36
60 ÷ 6 = 10
36 ÷ 6 = 6
10 + 6 = **16p**
b) 25 = 20 + 5
20 × 9 = 180
5 × 9 = 45
180 + 45 = **225 m**

Activity:
Possible question where answer is rounded down to 9:
"How many 8p sweets can you buy with 74p?"
Possible question where answer is rounded up to 10:
"A box can store 8 hats. How many boxes are needed for 74 hats?"

Page 76 — Written Multiplying and Dividing, Sheet 5

Q1 a) 300 × 8 = **2400**
40 × 8 = **320**
5 × 8 = **40**
2400 + 320 + 40 = **2760**
b) 10 × 26 = **260**
4 × 20 = **80**
4 × 6 = **24**
260 + 80 + 24 = **364**
c) 5 × 9 = **45**
0.3 × 9 = **2.7**
45 + 2.7 = **47.7**

Q2 a) $8\overline{)9\,{}^{1}2\,{}^{4}8}$ = 1 1 6 **r 0**
116 complete boxes can be made.
b) $4\overline{)7\,{}^{3}6\,6}$ = 1 9 1 **r 2**
They get £191 each and there is £2 left over.

Activity:
Many possible answers, including 5.4 × 6 = 32.4, 5.6 × 4 = 22.4, 6.4 × 5 = 32.

Page 77 — 2D Shapes, Sheet 2

Q1 a) **Circle**
b) **Square**
c) **Rectangle**
d) **Triangle**

Q2 No right angles:
Circle, kite, pentagon.
More than 3 sides:
Rectangle, kite, pentagon.

Activity:
Many different shapes can be made. Make as many as you can.

Page 78 — 2D Shapes, Sheet 3

Q1 There are:
4 rectangles
12 triangles
3 pentagons
3 circles

Q2 a) Square — **4 equal sides, 4 right angles.**
b) Equilateral triangle — **3 equal sides, no right angles.**
c) Regular pentagon — **5 equal sides, no right angles.**

Q3 Many possible answers. For example:

a) 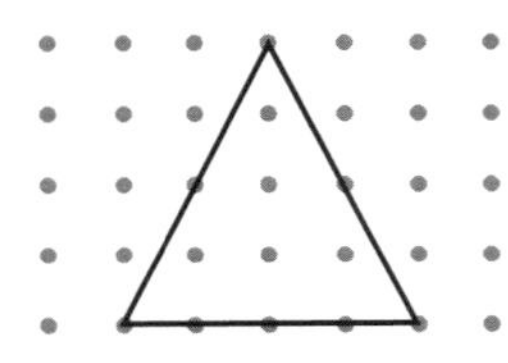

An isosceles triangle (2 equal sides)

b) 

A pentagon

c) 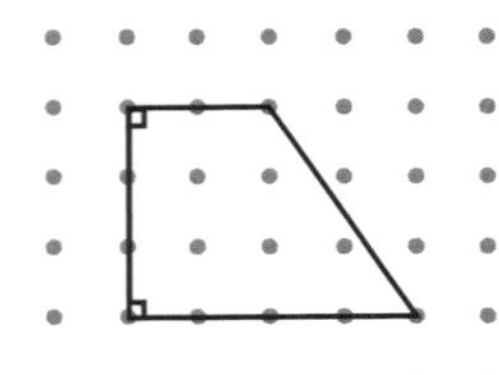

A 4 sided shape with only two right angles

Answers

Activity:
Many possible answers.
For example:

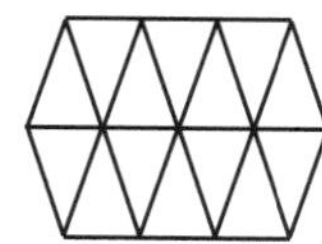

Page 79 — 2D Shapes, Sheet 4

Q1 a)

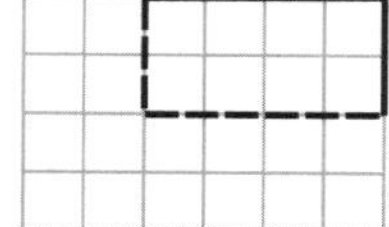

b)

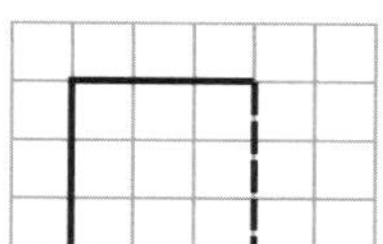

c) Many possible answers.
For example:

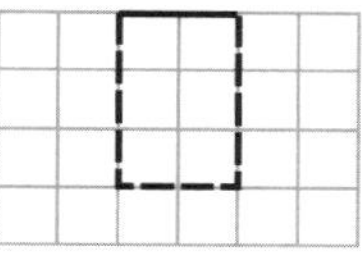

Q2 a) **Regular pentagon.**

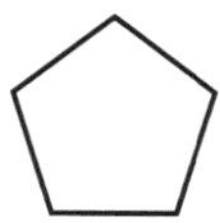

b) **Kite or parallelogram**

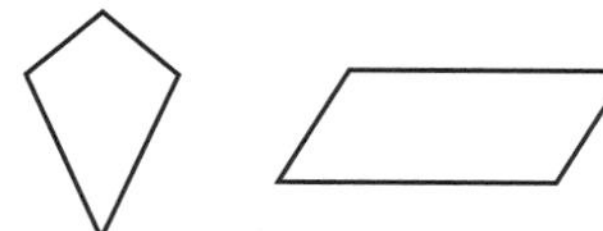

c) **Octagon**

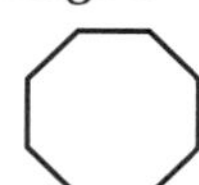

Q3 a) **Equilateral triangle**
b) **Right angled triangle**
c) **Isosceles triangle**
d) **Scalene triangle**

Activity:
Many possible answers. Make sure your triangles are labelled correctly. Use the descriptions on the worksheet to check.

Page 80 — 3D Shapes, Sheet 2

Q1 The correct numbers of faces are:

3 faces 1 face

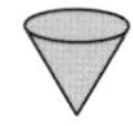

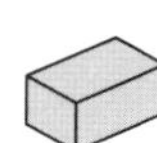

2 faces 6 faces

Q2 a) A cone has **2** faces and **1** curved edge.
b) A cube has 6 **faces** and 8 **vertices**.
c) A **triangular prism** has 6 vertices and 5 faces.

Q3 a) **Cuboid**

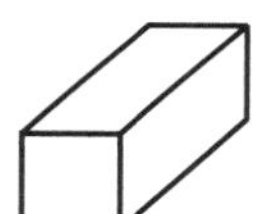

b) **Sphere**

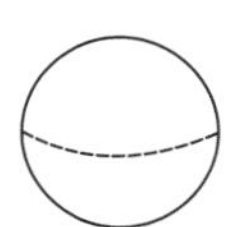

c) **Cylinder**

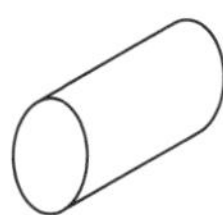

Activity:
Many possible answers. Find as many 3D shapes as you can.

Page 81 — 3D Shapes, Sheet 3

Q1 a) **Square-based pyramid**
b) **Cylinder**
c) **Triangular prism**

Q2 The picture should be coloured like this:

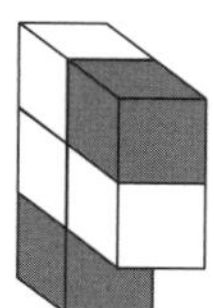

Q3 **Net a)** and **net b)** should be circled.

Activity
To make your own cube, you could use net b) from Q3 and put on tabs like this:

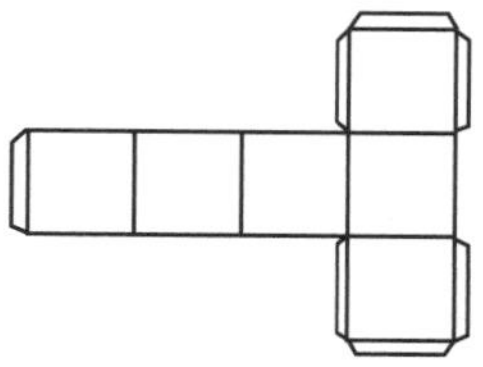

Each side of the cube should measure 5 cm.

Page 82 — 3D Shapes, Sheet 4

Q1 Diagrams **a)** and **d)** are nets of cuboids. They should be circled.

Q2 a) **Triangle-based pyramid**
Net:

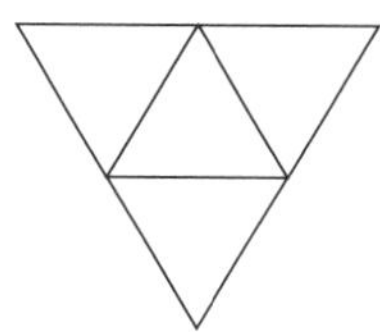

b) **Triangular prism**
Net:

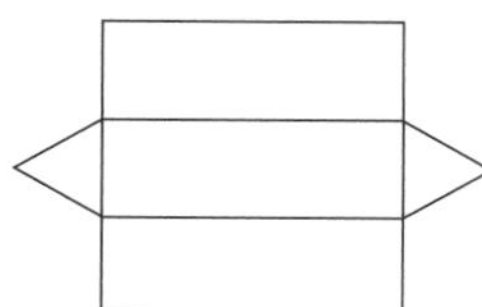

Q3 Faces: **8**
Edges: **12**
Vertices: **6**

Answers

Activity:
There are many possible ways to make a net for this triangular prism.
For example:

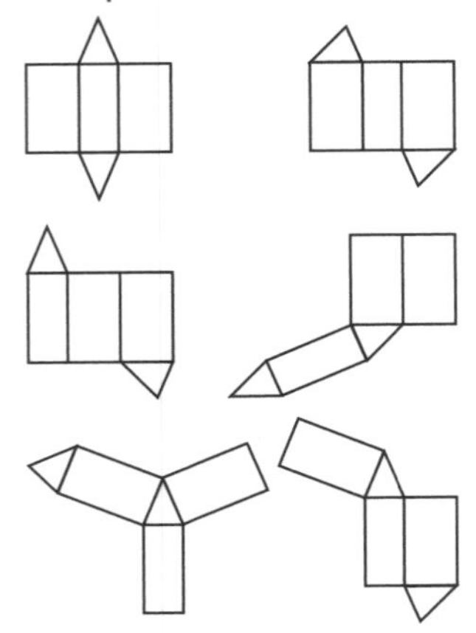

Page 83 — Angles, Sheet 2

Q1 A = **less than a right angle**
B = **right angle**
C = **more than a right angle**
D = **less than a right angle**

Q2

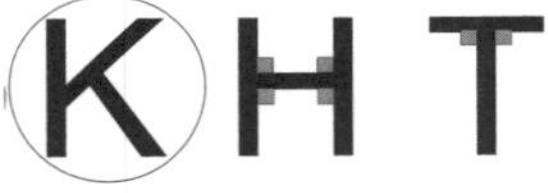

Q3

Activity:
Many possible answers.
For example:

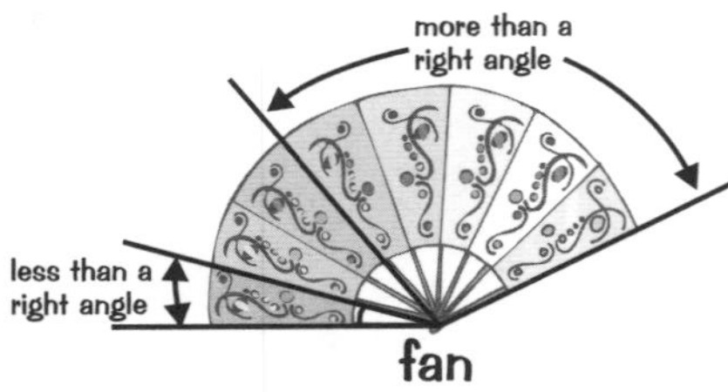

Page 84 — Angles, Sheet 3

Q1 a) **370°**

b) **360°**

c) **325°**

a) and **c)** are wrong.
The angles don't add up to 360°

Q2 a)

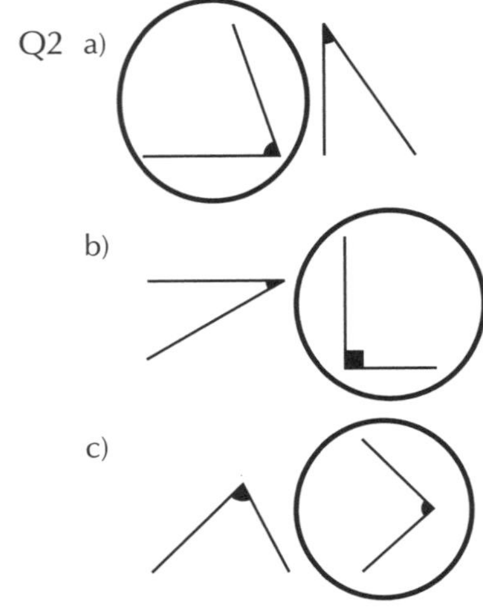

Q3 **B A D C E**

Q4

Activity:
Many possible answers.
For example:

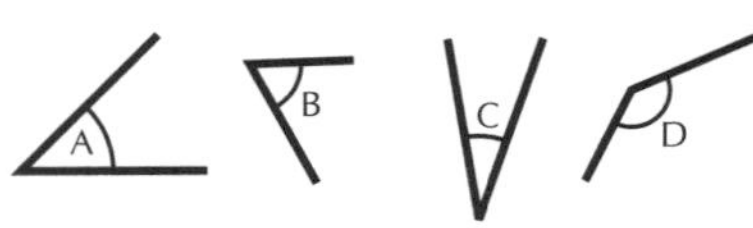

Smallest to largest: **C A B D**

Page 85 — Angles, Sheet 4

Q1 a) 55° (Accept **50°** or **60°**)
b) 88° (Accept **90°**)
c) 123°
(Accept **110°**,**120°** or **130°**)

Q2 (Accept answers 2° either way:)
a) **52°** and **90°**
b) **130°** and **35°**
c) **112°** and **168°**

Q3

Activity:
For example:
a) I drew this for 90°:

with a protractor it measures 92°, so I was 2° out.

Page 86 — Coordinates, Sheet 2

Q1 a) **north**
b) **south**
c) **west**

Q2 a)

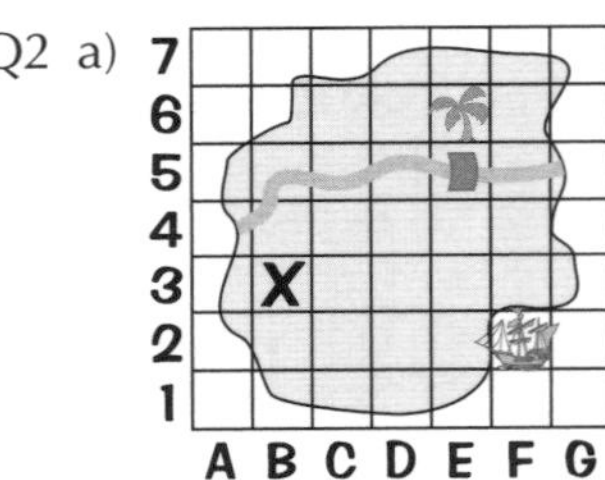

b) **B3**
c) Go **east 4** squares. Go **south 1** square.

Activity:
E.g.

To get from the elephant to the tree, go west 1 square and north 2 squares.
To get from the giant hat to the lighthouse, go north 1 square and east 3 squares.

Answers

Page 87 — Coordinates, Sheet 3

Q1 **south-west**

Q2 a), b), c)

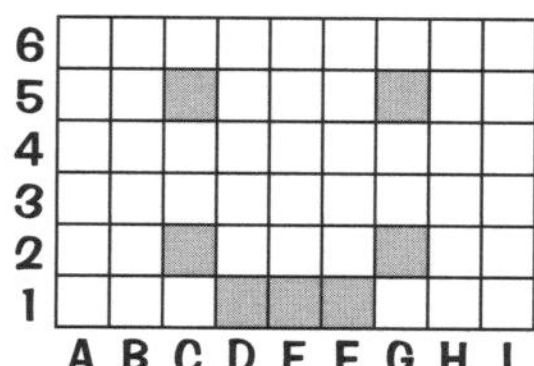

Q3 a) **north-west**
b) **north-east**
c) Go **4** squares in a **south-west** direction.

Activity:
E.g. the map could be based on a holiday.

Page 88 — Coordinates, Sheet 4

Q1 a) **(2,5)**
b) **(7,4)**
c) **(10,5)**
d) **(5,1)**

Q2 a) (1,7) (5,7) (1,2) (5,2)

b) **rectangle**

Q3 right-angled triangle

Activity:
E.g. (2,1), (3,7) and (5,4) are the vertices of a scalene triangle. (2,2), (6,2) and (4,7) are the vertices of an isosceles triangle.

Page 89 — Drawing Shapes, Sheet 2

Q1

Q2 e.g.

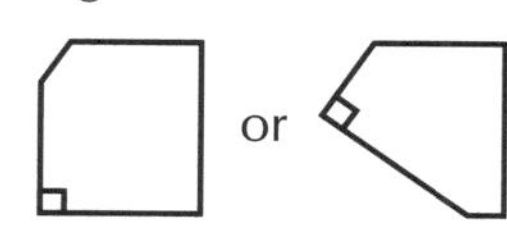

Q3 There are **5** right-angles.

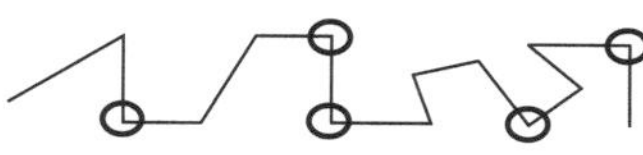

Activity:
E.g. corners of rooms, large windows and old furniture are unlikely to be exact right-angles.

Page 90 — Drawing Shapes, Sheet 3

Q1 a) Horizontal lines go **across** the page.
b) Vertical lines go **up / down** the page.

Q2

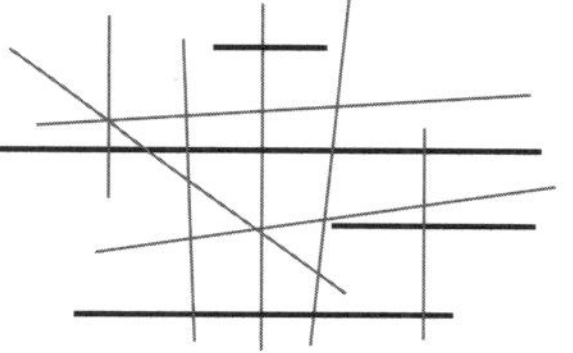

There are **4** horizontal lines.

Q3

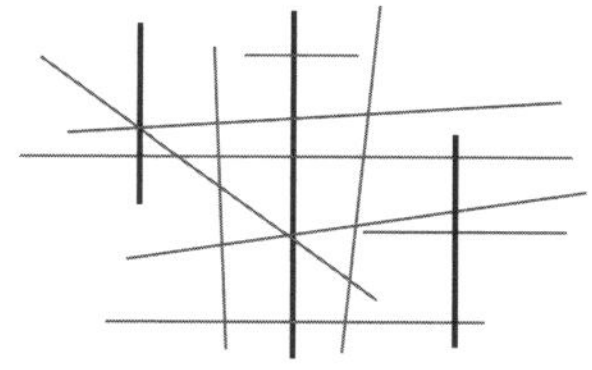

There are **3** vertical lines.

Activity:
The letters used should only be made up of horizontal and vertical lines.

Page 91 — Drawing Shapes, Sheet 4

Q1 Sets of lines **a)** and **e)** are parallel.

Q2 **C** and **E**

Q3

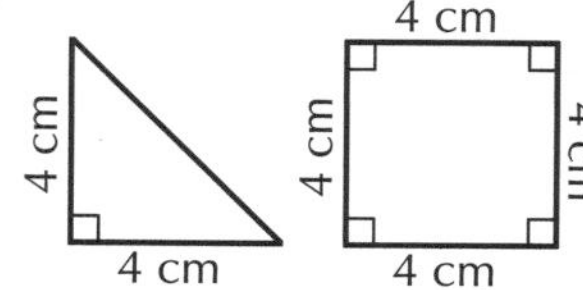

Measure the lengths of the sides and the angles in the drawings. Each side length should be correct to the nearest mm and each angle correct to the nearest degree.

Activity:
Make a plumb line and hang it next to things you think are vertical, if they are parallel to the string, they are vertical.

Page 92 — Symmetry, Sheet 2

Q1

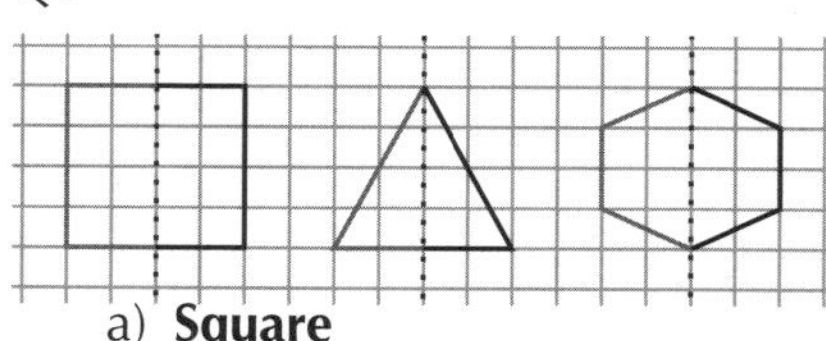

a) **Square**
b) **Triangle**
c) **Hexagon**

Q2 Word: **DOT**

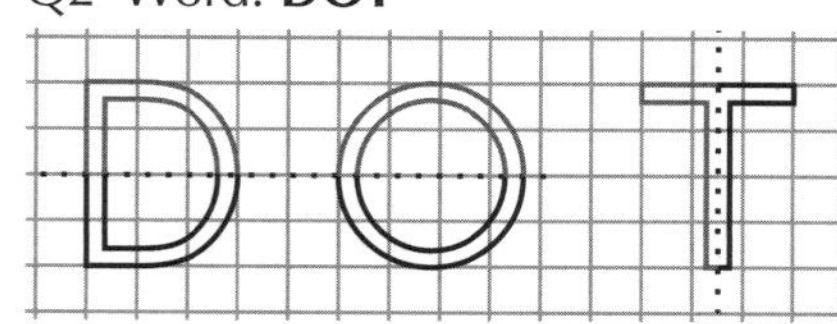

Q3

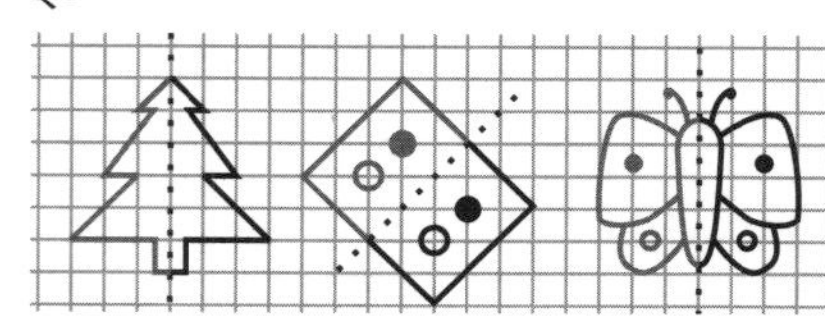

Activity:
These letters are all symmetrical and make a symmetrical word along the line of symmetry:

Answers

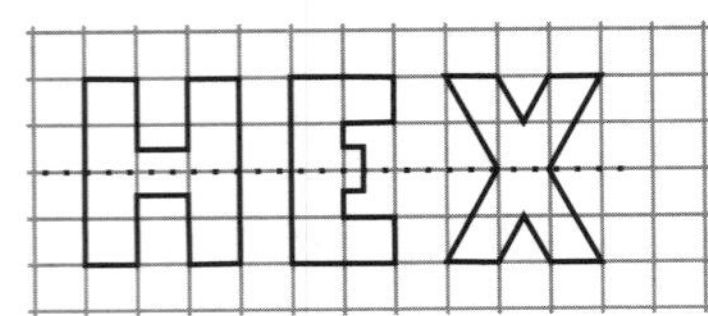

Page 93 — Symmetry, Sheet 3

Q1 Any 2 lines drawn through the circle are acceptable, and any 2 of the 5 lines of symmetry on the star are acceptable.

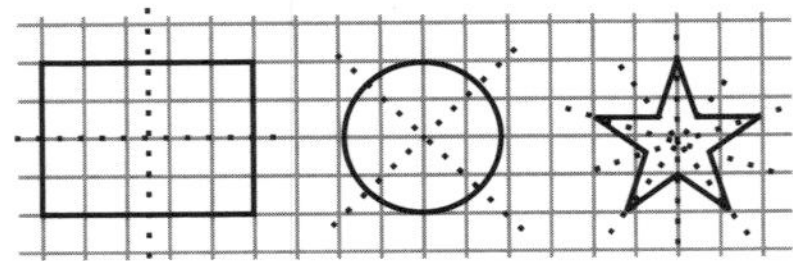

Q2

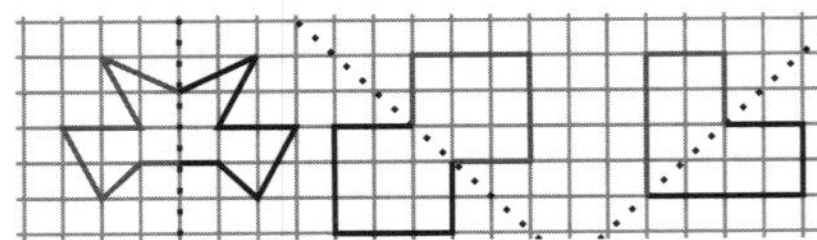

Q3

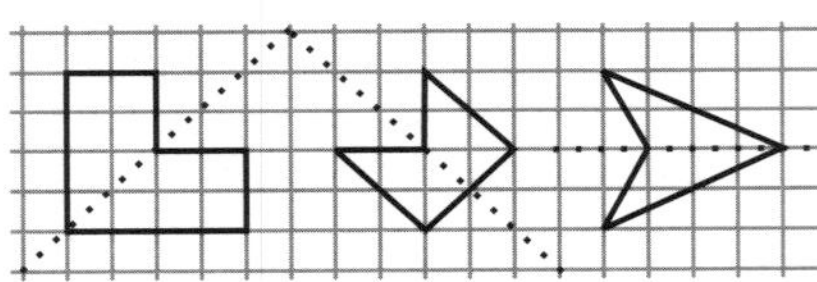

Activity:
For example:

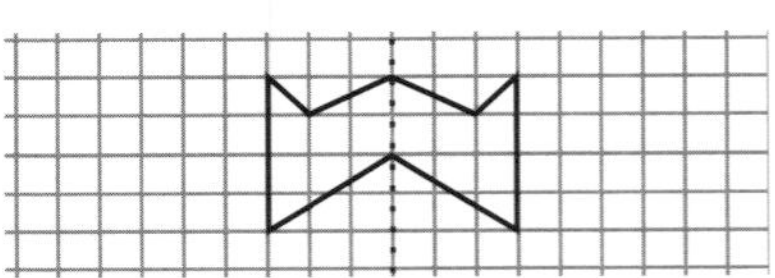

Page 94 — Symmetry, Sheet 4

Q1 Any 2 of these lines of symmetry:

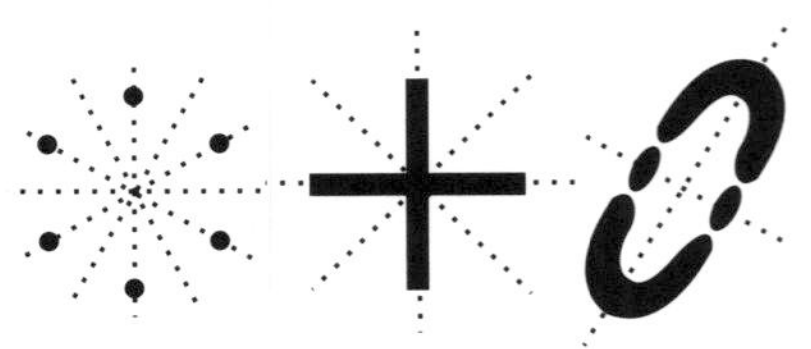

Q2

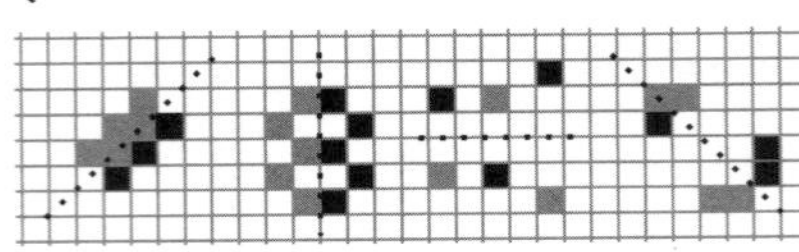

Q3

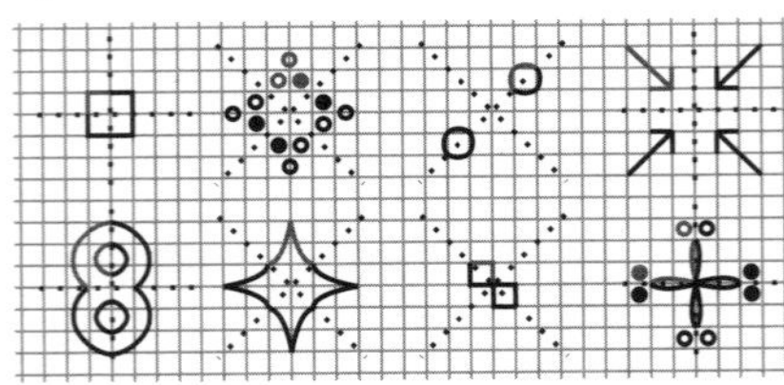

Activity:
For example, another pattern might be:

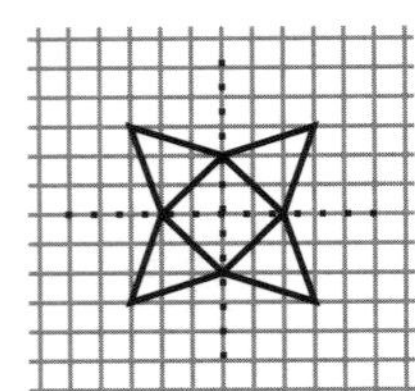

Page 95 — Calculating Perimeters and Areas, Sheet 1

Q1 3 + 2 + 3 + 2 = **10 cm**
4 + 3 + 4 + 3 = **14 cm**
5 + 4 + 5 + 4 = **18 cm**

Q2

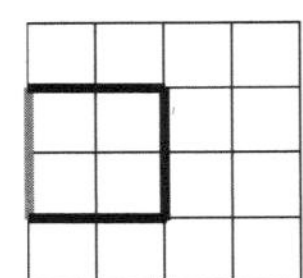

Q3 **6 cm²**
6 cm²
6 cm²
12 cm²

Activity:
Many possible answers, e.g.:

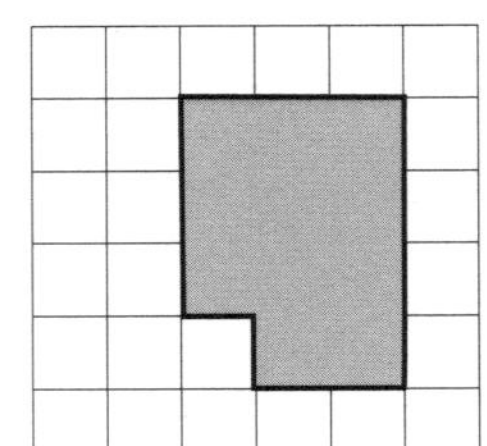

Page 96 — Calculating Perimeters and Areas, Sheet 2

Q1 a) Several possible answers, e.g.

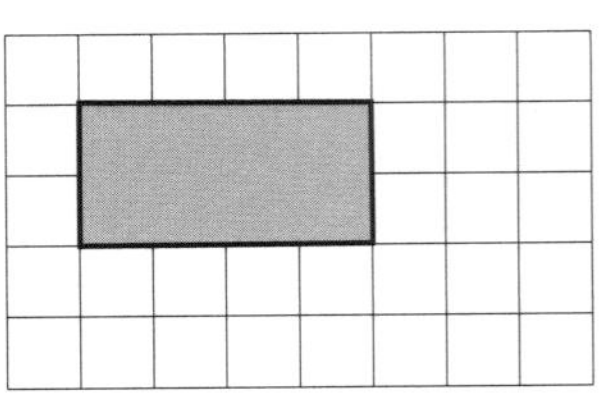

b) Several possible answers, e.g.

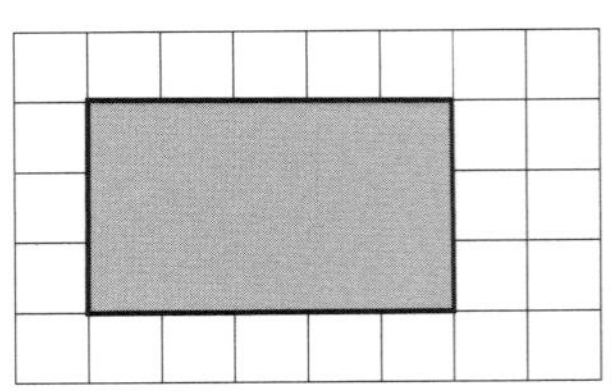

Q2 a) 30 + 40 + 30 + 40 = **140 cm**
b) 90 + 50 + 90 + 50 = **280 cm**

Q3 a) **8 cm²**
b) **10 cm²**
c) **7 cm²**
d) **11 cm²**

Activity:
Answer can be any three shapes as long as they have the same area.

Page 97 — Calculating Perimeters and Areas, Sheet 3

Q1 a) **10 cm**
b) **12 cm**
c) **12 cm**
d) **14 cm**

Q2 a) **9 cm**
b) **24 cm**
c) **50 cm**
d) **14 cm**

Q3 a) 4 cm × 3 cm = **12 cm²**
b) 5 cm × 8 cm = **40 cm²**
c) 9 cm × 7 cm = **63 cm²**
d) 2 cm × 4 cm = **8 cm²**

Answers

Activity:
Many possible rectangles, e.g. length 4 cm, width 6 cm, or length 2 cm, width 8 cm.
The area will be different for each rectangle (unless any are congruent).

Page 98 — Drawing and Measuring, Sheet 3

Q1 a) **10 g**
b) **25 g**
c) **45 g**

Q2 a) **4.5 cm**
b) **3 cm**
c) **3.5 cm**
d) **2.5 cm**

Q3 a) This mast should measure **3 cm**
b) This mast should measure **1.5 cm**
c) This mast should measure **2 cm**
d) This mast should measure **1 cm** (no extra line should be added)

Activity
Many possible answers.

Page 99 — Drawing and Measuring, Sheet 4

Q1 a) A 3 cm × 2 cm rectangle should be drawn.
Its perimeter is **10 cm.**
b) A 4 cm × 2 cm rectangle should be drawn.
Its perimeter is **12 cm.**
c) A 5 cm × 3 cm rectangle should be drawn.
Its perimeter is **16 cm.**

Q2 For each part, check that the rectangles have been drawn with the correct width and height.
The perimeters are:
a) **15 cm**
b) **17 cm**
c) **13 cm**

Activity
If the length and width of a rectangle add up to 10 cm, its perimeter will be 20 cm.
The possible rectangles are:

Length	**Width**
0.5 cm	9.5 cm
1 cm	9 cm
1.5 cm	8.5 cm
2 cm	8 cm
2.5 cm	7.5 cm
3 cm	7 cm
3.5 cm	6.5 cm
4 cm	6 cm
4.5 cm	5.5 cm
5 cm	5 cm

You can also swap the length and width of any of these rectangles.

Page 100 — Drawing and Measuring, Sheet 5

Q1 a) **44 mm**
b) Width = **38 mm**
Length = **22 mm**
c) **32 mm**

Q2 For parts a) – f), check that the lines have been drawn with the correct length.

Q3 A rectangle of **width 30 mm** and **height 9 mm** should be drawn. The gap between each box should measure **4 mm.**

Activity
Many possible answers.

Page 101 — Reading Scales, Sheet 3

Q1 Patsy = **6** mins
Sam = **17** mins
Amy = **11** mins
Paul = **9** mins

Q2 **30, 55, 65**

Q3
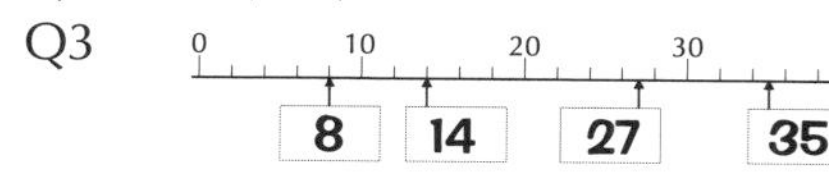

Q4 a) **150 kg**
b) **125 kg**

Activity:
E.g.
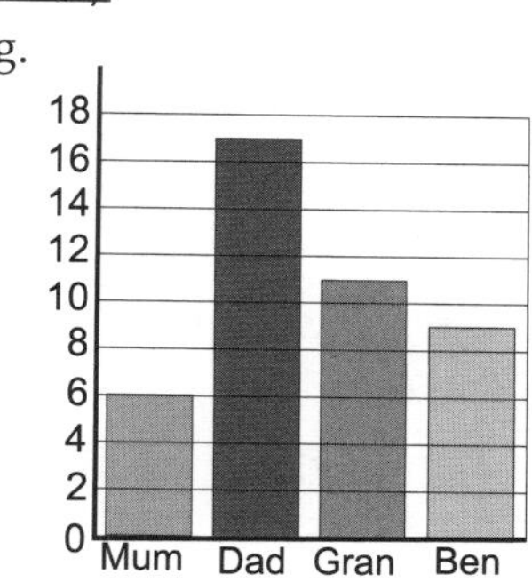

The bar chart could also be horizontal like the one on the sheet.

Page 102 — Reading Scales, Sheet 4

Q1 a) b)
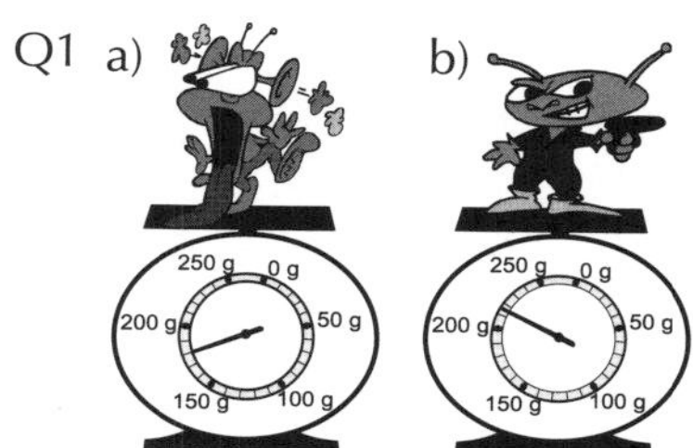

c) d)
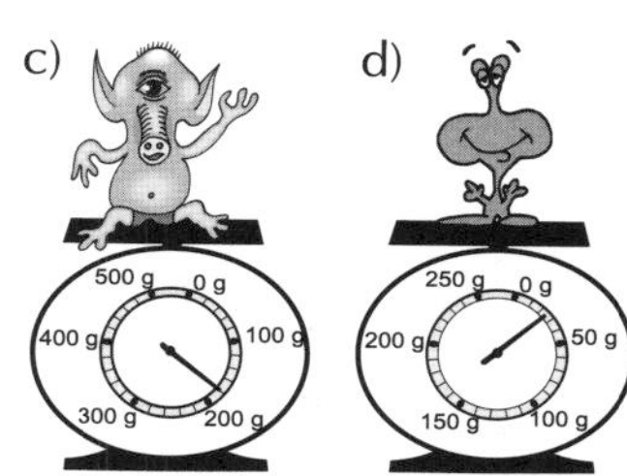

Q2 0.1, **1.3, 2.5, 3.8**

Q3
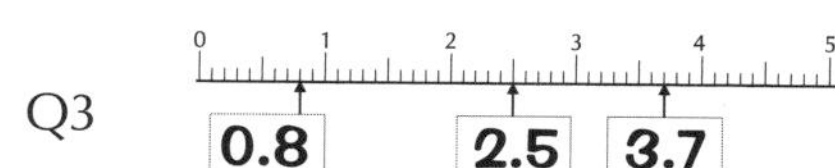

Q4 a) **36.8 °C**
b) **38.2 °C**

Activity:
E.g. pencil = 10.3 cm, rubber = 4.8 cm.

Page 103 — Reading Scales, Sheet 5

Q1 a) **36.4 °C**
b) **21.7 °C**
c) **23.6 °C**
d) **37.2 °C**

Answers

Q2 a) **250 ml**
b) **425 ml**
c) **3.5 litres**
d) **1.4 litres**

Q3 a) 70 – 55 = **15 kg**
b) 95 – 25 = **70 kg**

Activity:
The exact capacity readings will depend on the sizes of the yoghurt pots and other containers used.

Page 104 — Reading Scales, Sheet 6

Q1 a) **200, 450, 700**
b) **780, 805, 830**
c) **150, 250, 375**
d) **140, 180, 230**
e) **0.4, 1.8, 2.5, 3.6, 4.9**
f) **0.75, 2.5, 5.25**
g) **0.4, 1.2, 1.9, 2.7**

Q2 a) **600 ml**
b) **150 ml**
c) **7.5 litres**
d) **2.8 litres**

Activity:
A tape measure should be used to measure height, a set of scales to measure mass and a ruler (or tape measure) to measure handspan.

Page 105 — Time, Sheet 2

Q1 a) **11:05**
b) **5:45**
c) **7:25**
d) **8:35**
e) **12:15**

Q2 a) **30 minutes**
b) **135 minutes**
c) **11:00**
d) **4:45**

Activity:
For example, the timetable might look like:

8.50 Registration
9.00 English
10.00 Maths
11.00 Break
11.30 PE
1.00 Lunch
2.00 Art
3.30 After school tennis club
4.30 Home

Page 106 — Time, Sheet 3

Q1 b)

c)

d) **7:42 (accept 7:41-7:43)**

Q2 a) **12:10 pm**
b) **12:35 am**
c) **7:00 pm**

Q3 a) **27 days**
b) **54 seconds**

Q4 a) **2 hours 23 minutes** or **143 minutes**.
b) **45 minutes**

Activity:
For example, the places might be Sheffield and Birmingham.

If a train left Sheffield at 1:13 and got into Birmingham New Street at 2:26, the length of time the journey takes would be **1 hour 13 minutes** or **73 minutes**.

Page 107 — Time, Sheet 4

Q1 a) **16:45** b) **18:15**

Q2 a) **11:50 pm** b) **5:31 pm**
c) **12.11 am**

Q3 a) **7:00 until 9:30** and **12:00 until 17:30**.
b) **8 hours**
c) **19:01. He will be late.**

Activity:
For example, a film might start at **20:00**, last for **1 hour 45 minutes** and finish at **21:45**.

Page 108 — Units and Measures, Sheet 3

Q1 a)

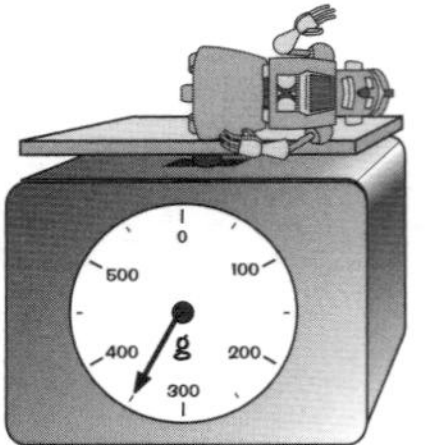

b)

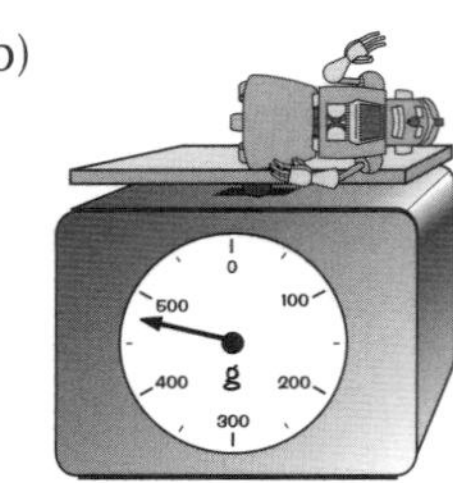

c)

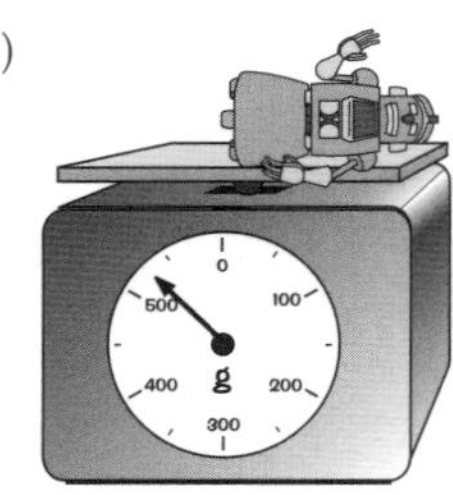

Q2 a) **1000 g**
b) **1500 g**
c) **2000 g**
d) **10 000 g**

Q3 a) **grams**
b) **millilitres**
c) **metres**

Q4 a) **3 cm**
b) **200 cm**

Activity:
E.g. an estimate of the distance to school might be **5500 m** or **5.5 km**. The best unit to use for this distance would be **kilometres**.

Page 109 — Units and Measures, Sheet 4

Q1 a) **1.2 kg** b) **2.3 kg**
c) **3.575 kg** d) **1.609 kg**

Q2 **300 ml**

Q3 **Pete is just over 1 metre tall.**

Answers

Amy's chocolate bar weighs 40 grams.

Q4 **40 kg**

Activity:
E.g. 600 g, 250 g, 530 g.
The order would be: **250 g, 530 g, 600 g**

Page 110 — Units and Measures, Sheet 5

Q1 metres: **3500**
centimetres: **350 000**

Q2 a) **240 km**
b) **140 g**
c) **2.5 l**
d) **250 cm**

Q3 **20 cm, 2 m, 250 cm, 2.6 m, 200 m, 2 km**

Q4 a) Length = **4.5 cm**
b) Length = **7 cm**

Activity:
E.g. 9.6 cm would round to **9.5 cm**.

Page 111 — Units and Measures, Sheet 6

Q1 8.7 cm = **9 cm**

Q2 **Scale 3** should be ticked.

Q3 The vase can hold 2.8 ÷ 2 = 1.4 litres.
It contains 1.4 ÷ 2 = 0.7 litres = **700 ml**

Activity:
E.g. if one apple weighs 90 g and the bag contains 8 apples, you could estimate that the bag of apples weighs **720 g**. It might actually weigh **750 g**. The estimate would be **30 g** different from the actual weight.

Page 112 — Data, Sheet 2

Q1 a) E.g. **Anne**, **Claire**, **Tim**, **Ashley**, **Rebecca**, **Chris**, **Laura**, **Alice**, **Victoria**, **Richard**

b) E.g.

Number of letters	3	4	5	6	7	8
Tally	I	I	III	II	II	I
Frequency	1	1	3	2	2	1

c) E.g.

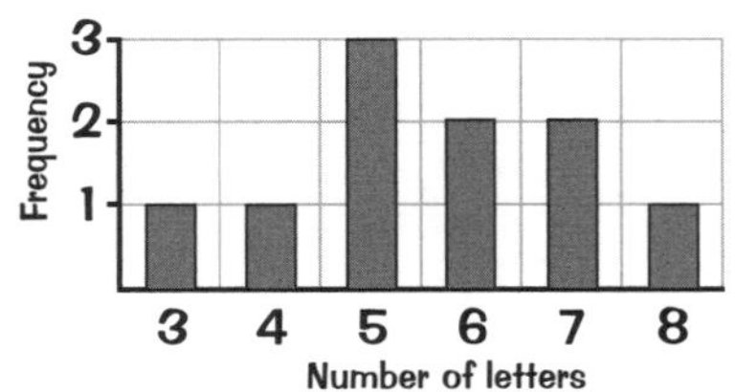

d) E.g. **5**

Activity:
E.g.

goals	0	1	2	3	4	5	6
tally	𝍸 II	𝍸 𝍸 III	𝍸 I	IIII	𝍸	II	I
frequency	7	13	6	4	5	2	1

Page 113 — Data, Sheet 3

Q1 a) E.g. **What are your two favourite colours?**

b) E.g.

game	musical chairs	pass the parcel	Simon says	musical statues	blind man s buff
tally					
frequency					

c) E.g.
Choose your favourite drink: cola, lemonade, juice
Choose your favourite sandwich: cheese, ham, egg
Choose your favourite sweet: ice-cream, jelly, cake

Activity:
E.g.

word	a	the	in	is	to	of
tally	III	𝍸 I	II	III	II	III

"**the**" is the most common word.

Page 114 — Data, Sheet 4

Q1 a)

Size	8	9	10	11	12	13	14
Tally	𝍸 II	𝍸 I	𝍸	II	II	III	IIII
Frequency	7	6	5	2	2	3	4

b) **8**

Q2 E.g.
Record the colour of all the cars passing along a busy street for 10 minutes.
You could repeat the survey for a different street.

Activity:
E.g.

Score	1	2	3	4	5	6
Tally	𝍸 IIII	𝍸 III	𝍸 𝍸	𝍸 IIII	𝍸 II	𝍸 II
Frequency	9	8	10	9	7	7

Each number comes up a similar number of times. (You can expect quite a bit of variation though.)

Page 115 — Tables and Charts, Sheet 2

Q1 a) **11**
b)

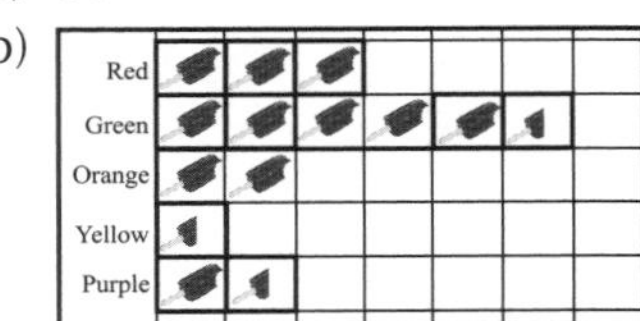

Q2

Vowel	Tally
a	𝍸
e	𝍸 𝍸 I
i	I
o	III
u	II

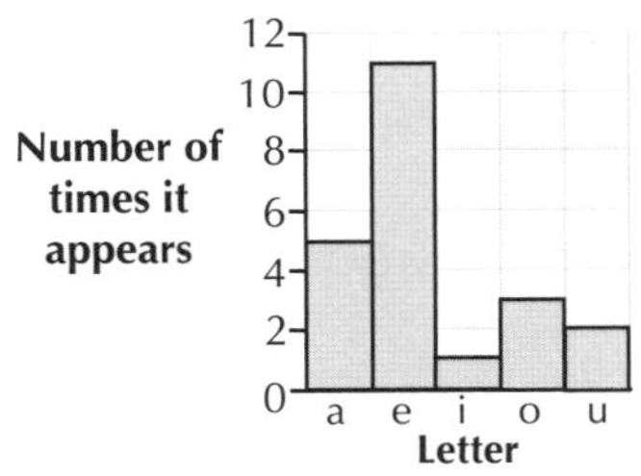

Activity:
A possible answer might look like this:

Number on Dice	Tally
1	𝍸 II
2	IIII
3	𝍸 III
4	III
5	𝍸 I
6	𝍸 II

Answers

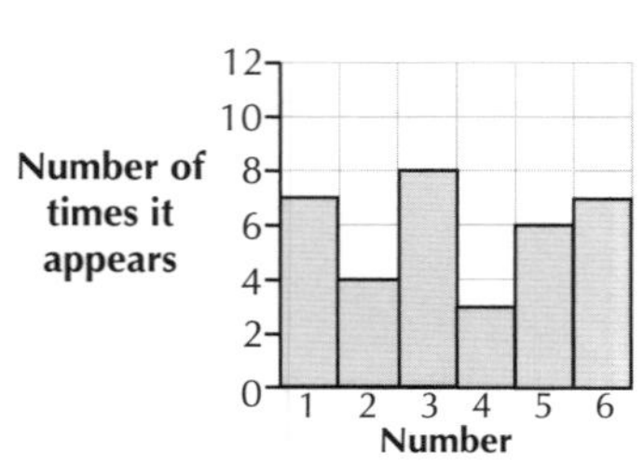

Page 116 — Tables and Charts, Sheet 3

Q1 a)

Time	Tally	Total
9 am-10 am	~~||||~~ ~~||||~~ ~~||||~~ ||	17
10 am-11 am	~~||||~~ |||	8
11 am - 12 noon	||	2
12 noon - 1 pm	~~||||~~ ~~||||~~ ~~||||~~ ~~||||~~ |||	**23**
1 pm - 2 pm	~~||||~~ ~~||||~~ ||||	14
2 pm - 3 pm	~~||||~~ ~~||||~~ ~~||||~~	**15**
3 pm - 4 pm	~~||||~~	5

b) **25** c) **afternoon**

d)

9 am -10 am	
10 am -11 am	
11 am - 12 noon	
12 noon - 1 pm	
1 pm - 2 pm	
2 pm - 3 pm	
3 pm - 4 pm	

Q2 a) From bottom to top — **5, 10, 15, 20, 25, 30**

b) **A**

Activity:
A possible answer is:

Hearts	7
Clubs	10
Diamonds	7
Spades	6

Page 117 — Tables and Charts, Sheet 4

Q1 a) **7**

b) **36**

c)

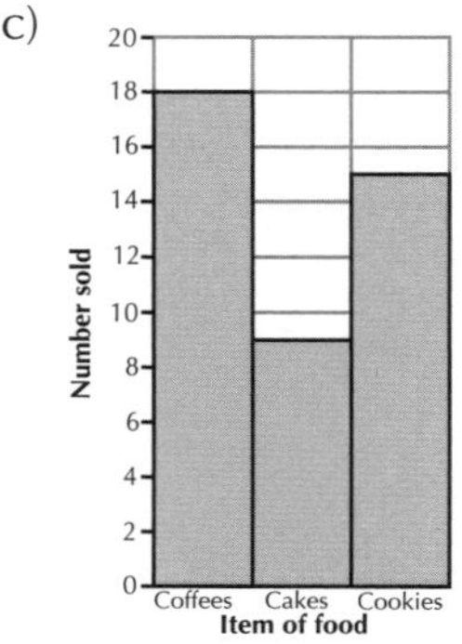

Q2 a) **10**

b) **105**

c)

Mon	5
Tue	15
Wed	10
Thurs	25
Fri	20
Sat	30

Activity:
A possible answer is:

Cups	9
Plates	5
Bowls	6
Pans	6

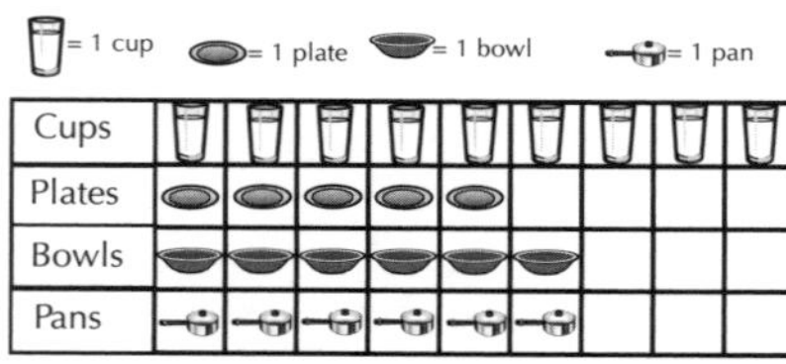

How many pans are there?
How many more bowls are there than plates?
Which item is there most of?

Name: .... Date: ....

 Name: .... Date: ....